What's Your Sun Sign

What's Your Sun Sign

CHETAN D. NARAIN

Fun Way to Understand People
Strike Great Conversations &
Build Joyful Relationships
Minus the Astrology Jargon!

First published 2010

ISBN 978-81-8328-180-5

Published by
Wisdom Tree,
4779/23, Ansari Road,
Darya Ganj, New Delhi-2
Ph.: 23247966/67/68
wisdomtreebooks@gmail.com

Printed in India at Print Perfect

Contents

Acknowledgements

With blessings and encouragement from my parents—Devendra and Anita Narain; love and support from my wife Parul and son Abir, I managed to put the book together with the help of Kanishka Ramchandani who sat through long question-answer sessions with me for each of the twenty-four write ups.

I would like to thank Prerna Pandarwani for assisting me with the initial editing, Sachin Gurav for the creative cover design, Neelam Singh and Urvi Vora for assisting me with technology related things and the website for the book.

Sincere appreciation to Shobit Arya, my publisher for believing in me and the content of this book and guiding me right. A big thank you to the Wisdom Tree team.

Preface

God made man and woman and she/he made them equal. This is a politically correct statement appropriate to our times. But does equality necessarily mean similarity? Of course not!

Each of us is born unique and different. This is something we all like to believe. Every one of us wants to stand out in the crowd. But if we are so unique and different what are we doing in the crowd anyways? That's simply because we need the crowd to define ourselves; to know there are others like us and to confirm that yet we are different. Haven't you asked your friends their sun sign and felt pleased if it was the same as yours? That's the underlying theme of human behaviour...the need to connect, be one with the world. After all, we are humans not snowflakes.

How can one live with such a contradiction? In fact it is this contradiction that makes one meet other people, befriend them, perhaps fall in love with them and get into a relationship. When we meet someone, we look at their outward appearance but at a subconscious level we analyse their behaviour. Ever wondered why we get along so well with a certain person, whereas we can't stand the sight of another? Where does the problem lie...with us or with the person in question? Actually there is no problem at all. We are like pieces of a jigsaw puzzle...some fit in while others don't. Our behavioural patterns are detrimental in deciding what kind of 'piece' we are.

However, culture, upbringing and social status play an important role in moulding human behaviour. These aspects can either aggravate or tone down certain personality traits in an individual. Sun signs and the attributes under each sign are like blueprints of human psyche—they are present in every individual of that particular zodiac. However, this does not imply that every Libran or Taurean is the same or that we can tag millions of people of any one sun sign as 'same'.

If you probe human psychology, we all follow a few set patterns. Someone asked me how one can classify people in twelve zodiac signs only. But what we do not realise is that under each zodiac there is 'Man' and 'Woman' and further each of them is either 'Aggressive' or 'Passive' which brings the total to forty-eight.

This book will help you explore and find out which of these forty-eight behavioural patterns represent your friends and you the best. The observations and writing is based on human psychology and behaviours alone and not on planetary movements and/or astrology. It is amazing how we can touch hearts, break ice and find quicker proximity to people when we speak to them about them.

— Chetan D. Narain
www.chetannarain.com

Capricorn
22 December-19 January

Capricorn man

Remember the most attractive girl in class, the one who wooed your best friend? And then one fine day, she got tired of him simply because he spoke only about himself. But our dear charmer wasn't even a bit upset about it. In fact it gave him an opening to seek out the next pretty face the very next day. Ladies and gentlemen…meet the quintessential Capricorn man!

A typical Capricornian male will be charming and ebullient yet intense to the core and often sombre. And then there's his incorrigible habit of covering-up all his feelings. He will continuously make and break your impressions of him. Let's go figure him out!

How can you identify a Capricorn man in a crowd?

Loud, flamboyant, centre of attraction, with oodles of charm…that's the briefest description of any conventional Capricorn man. This helps you identify him too. He moves in flashy cars, stands surrounded by people (usually women) and is the chief talker in a group. While his words will be directed at one, his eyes will be making out with another (maybe a woman).

Although a womaniser, he is a light-hearted one and a gentleman at that. He will delight women (and men too) with his suaveness and charm rather than force. If you observe closely, you will find him talking mostly about himself with topics ranging from his latest car to his last girlfriend.

Generally, Capricorn men are aggressive in their attitude with the exception of a mere 20-25 per cent.

What are the key features of his personality?

The most noticeable thing about a Capricorn man, according to me, is his attention-seeking nature. No matter where he is, with a small group of friends or at a large party, he likes to be noticed. He makes sure when he arrives at a social event that 'he has arrived'.

There is also much of a brag in a Capricorn male. He likes to talk explicitly about his achievements and successes. Don't mistake this for low self-esteem. This man has confidence by the ton but bragging is his way of playing the power game.

But whatever he talks about and however much he may brag a Capricorn man has the quality of attracting admirers and listeners by the hordes. He is great at entertaining people (but as all the fun comes at a cost, you should be prepared to bear his mood swings). When friendly, he will be one of the most charming beings and the funniest of men. A prankster at heart, his friends are often subject to leg pulling and practical jokes. But when in a black mood, he can kill with his sarcasm and slay with his anger. He has the most sarcastic wit amongst all zodiac signs. He can get zany with his humour, which can slice you like a razor at the drop of a hat.

Although he is confident and egoistic, he lacks inner strength. He is an easy prey to superstition, beliefs and rituals. At times a Capricorn man will take devious paths to pacify his fallacies.

There is something a Capricorn guy shares with his female counterpart. Very unlikely as the comparison may sound, there is a similarity between these two goats: both have a beauty that grows on them. They are serious and often sombre in their appearance in their youth, but with age they blossom...making the term 'ageing gracefully' fit them like a glove.

How is he on the following aspects?

Appearance: I have observed six out of every ten Capricorn men to have an oval face. They are usually very formally dressed in jackets and suits, replete with hats. They are the ones who can walk down a beach in a suit and still look extremely charming and never out of place.

Ambition: The Capricorn man is overambitious and will end up setting unachievable targets and goals for himself. The aggressive kind of Capricorns are also very competitive and will stoop to any level to attain success. Being extremely persuasive, he uses his charm to great advantage. His personal ego makes him see a battle in every situation, one that has to be won at any cost.

Ego/Self-respect: The Capricorn male has tremendous ego, something that surpasses his already high level of self-respect, but you may or may not be able to spot it. If he is doing something, he will make it clear 'he is doing it for you', while actually he would be doing it for himself. He often uses his girlfriend or wife or family members as an excuse to get what he wants. His ego doesn't let him take criticism well either. When criticised he is likely to fight and argue to prove his point or simply give excuses to cover-up his mistakes.

Responsibility: A Capricorn man is extremely responsible and dependable by nature, but sometimes his over ambitiousness comes in way of fulfilling his responsibilities. But still you will never come across a Capricorn man who forgets or shirks his duty.

His sense of duty is heightened by his love for his family. He takes the welfare of his entire family, and sometimes the extended family as well, as his business. More often than not, he prefers a life partner who is ready to share this sense of responsibility with him.

Etiquettes: Given his inherent charm and love for fine dressing, our man likes to put on his best face in any social setting. You will find him maintaining high standards in etiquettes.

He expects the same standards from others too. Social decorum is high priority on his list and his wife and children are foremost in the line of people he wishes to train. Don't expect him to tolerate shabby clothes or runny noses. And if you are planning to go non trendy or casual to his formal party...better keep yourself locked away. He will prefer your absence to a conspicuous you in a shoddy avatar...that too at *his* social gathering.

What is his approach towards life?

Hmmm...it would be incorrect to say everything. This man has desires that go beyond everything. The word 'enough' does not exist in his lexicon. Be it success, material comforts, love or happiness...he wants all and more of it. He *must* have the best of everything life has to offer and he will stop at nothing to achieve it. His ambition drives him from one milestone to the next.

I don't want to make him sound callous and he isn't either. His ambition is his own thing and he will never deliberately hurt anyone in his uphill climb. He also has immense patience. He knows he has to take one step at a time and that every step takes him closer to his goal. No matter how much hard work or sacrifice is required a Capricorn guy will do everything possible to achieve success in life. And what next? Will he rest? Not likely. He would have set another goal for himself by then and he will be on his way again.

How does he score on the following points?

Cynicism: He is one of the most cynical men of all zodiac signs, but beneath this cynicism lies a romantic heart. A Capricorn man is likely to hide his emotions behind a mask of cynicism, but if you look deeper you will find him as steeped in romance as a Shakespearean hero. Once drawn out of his shell (which can just be shyness or reserve), he will open up to show a tender heart full of dreams. And like all dreams his dreams too close with 'happy endings'.

Suspicion/Jealousy: He is also extremely suspicious by nature and very protective of his family. But when it comes to jealousy, though quite jealous himself, he abhors the idea and so playing tricks to make him jealous, is a sure shot way of losing him.

Dishonesty/Infidelity: If there is a man who knows his way with women, it's him. A hardcore womaniser, you cannot be in a relationship with him and not feel insecure. He is a natural charmer and women get easily attracted to him (in such situations, matters of honesty and loyalty are definitely not top priority for him) but once committed he will stay committed.

Hardships: Not as charming as he is in other matters, a Capricorn man cannot take hardships well. But being an achiever, he will make sincere efforts towards overcoming the obstacles to change his situation or fulfil his responsibilities.

Success and Failure: With success he is loud and flamboyant. He will make sure everyone he knows hears about his success story. Don't be surprised if the party he throws is not in proportion with what he has achieved. But, Capricorn men are poor losers. They cannot accept defeat, gracefully or otherwise. A Capricorn man's failure will be accompanied with a long list of explanations and excuses.

Host: Added to the inherent charm of a Capricorn man are his self-bred qualities like grace and meticulousness. All these together make him a very good host, one who is detailed in his organising and pays special attention towards the comfort of his guests. The laid-back kind or the passive kind of Capricorn men, however, are a little more casual and less detailed.

Guest: As a guest, the Capricorn man believes he is the end all and be all. He will make sure his entry at any event, big or small, is dramatic. He wants people to not just sit-up and take notice but also appreciate his presence. Since he is a real foodie, he would try all kinds of cuisines from five star gourmets to roadside delicacies. The best way to keep him happy at your party is to offer him a delectable meal and of course good company.

How does he handle difficult situations?

Being extremely emotional and sensitive, a Capricorn man gets deeply affected by quarrels or disagreements. He enjoys keeping everyone around him happy. Having said that, I would like to add that he is not averse to the idea of creating scenes, so if angry or upset, someone is sure to meet the rough side of his tongue if not his elbow. He totally believes in keeping his accounts straight...an eye for an eye, a tooth for a tooth. That usually is the unforgiving Capricorn man for you!

What is his characteristic weakness?

A Capricorn guy is a complete control freak. He likes to control everything around him...especially his loved ones. He wants to know what is happening in their lives and minds and will be seriously hurt if someone he loves takes a major decision without informing him, so much so that he can get childish about it. His controlling nature at times borders on being dictatorial.

He is also distrustful of people. His aloofness becomes all the more forceful if he finds himself with people he cannot trust. He cannot believe that goodness exists and that people can be humane. He is always looking for ulterior motives and this affects his trust in people to a great extent.

Blessed with good looks and pleasant appearance Capricorn men can get rather conceited. The importance with which they treat themselves tends to make them vain and arrogant.

They can also turn obstinate and short-tempered if rubbed the wrong way. Their patience is selective—it works in their favour only when it comes to achieving goals, otherwise it can run out rather fast.

Is there more to his persona?

It isn't easy to get up close and personal with this guy. He likes being sociable, will behave in a gentlemanly way and will also show a degree of chivalry, but when it comes to looking into his eyes right up to his heart, he reserves the privilege for a select few.

He can turn into a turtle and get into the hardest of shells to shun the world.

He lives in a cocoon to which very few people have access. And I find this to be his most peculiar trait. Lest I am blamed for being contradictory, let me explain. A Capricorn guy is funny, charming and likes to talk and connect with people. At the same time he isn't someone whom you can describe as a people's person. There is a thin yet rather strong veil between him and those around him...a veil which he wants to keep so that his true self remains hidden. And in this trait lies the Capricorn man's real fear. He is scared of getting emotionally hurt or his feelings being ridiculed and so he prefers keeping his own counsel.

Here is a man who loves to be praised. He likes nothing better than a conversation with a decent amount of compliments (for him!) thrown in. But that doesn't mean you can have your way with him through flattery. No sir! He wants genuine admiration and loads of it. This includes everything from the smartness to his looks to his bikes, cars and yes... even girlfriends.

Given his ambitiousness, he is an early starter and at a young age will start dreaming big. With time as he achieves the innumerous milestones he has set for himself, he is likely to become more relaxed and lively. With every success his energy level gets a boost.

When I said he is overambitious, I don't mean that his ambitions are rampant. No way! He is on the contrary very organised and particular about the goals he sets for himself. He knows how to take each day as it comes and how to achieve one goal at a time with determination and dedication. With a sharp eye he knows how to get the best and most of every opportunity (and this is what makes Capricorns good entrepreneurs) and because of this you will rarely come across a Capricorn man who is not successful. But however serious he is about his ambitions, he takes life easy every now and then, giving himself room to enjoy and have some 'serious' fun.

How should one deal effectively with him?

To deal effectively with a Capricorn man, be his 'yes man'. He likes people who agree with him and hates those who don't. Since he is incapable of handling criticism it is best to avoid it as you will be met with lot of explanations and excuses. He cannot accept his mistakes or defeat easily either and so it is better not to look down upon his failures. The best way to be in a peaceful relationship with a Capricorn man is to be submissive and supportive, give in to his charms and accept all his excuses as genuine.

As a wife, you must realise early on that his family means a lot to him. He will want you to be good at every role you play within his family circle. Since he is a food lover, make sure you attend your cookery classes regularly as he might want you to cook every delicacy under the sun or at least be aware of his likes and dislikes if you plan to get a cook or chef.

A Capricorn man is also very decisive about matters of the heart. If things don't work out, he will walk out of a relationship (even marriage) and close that chapter of his life forever. The term 'second chance' doesn't exist for this man!

How does he handle money matters?

A Capricorn man is very careful with his money. But he is compassionate and not one to shy away from charities and donations. If you have borrowed money from him, he will be extremely patient with you. But his patience comes with an expiry date. He knows how to get his money out, if need be. But interestingly if the amount he has given is negligible compared to his wealth, he would generously write-off his debts (of course, not before letting the borrower expresses his deep gratitude for the same).

A Capricorn male is one person who knows the power of money. For him, money is a tool that allows him to be independent. He craves for the power that comes by virtue of being wealthy rather than the actual monetary aspect.

How is he on the professional front?

Given his leadership qualities, a Capricorn man makes for a good entrepreneur, (however, the non-entrepreneur types tend to be rather laid-back). He also likes to lead by example, so trust him to create milestones for others to follow. He can take his followers along with him as he scales new heights of success.

He is also extremely competitive and hard-working. He will never fall short of effort and the only thing that might deter him from achieving his ambitions is 'destiny'.

It is important to know that a Capricorn guy can be extremely down to earth. He has a steady connect with reality and all his desires are therefore practical. You won't find him setting impossible targets or giving empty talks about his plans. When he has decided on achieving something, be sure he has planned everything in his mind...from a very pragmatic angle.

How is he in various relationship roles?

Capricorn men are generally mama's boys and have healthy relations with their family members. As a spouse, this man is practical and approachable. Of course you will have to put-up with his flirtatiousness and inevitable charm. But that shouldn't be a problem for a woman with the right attitude. He would expect you to do a tight rope walk. He expects his wife to be charming and presentable, an excellent cook (if possible) and a good homemaker. His wife should be a dutiful daughter-in-law and a perfect mother to his children. And in return he will be a responsible husband who will provide for the entire family. And with all this, his love for you will strengthen.

He is loving and caring towards his children, although he may not be too devoted or doting. As a father, a Capricorn man can be a disciplinarian. He likes to show his kids how strong the rod is every now and then, but he will also put his children's needs above his own.

As a girlfriend, it takes a lot to keep him enticed in love as his attention span is generally short. That doesn't mean he will not commit himself but he needs more space for himself. He likes challenges, so the more 'unconquerable' you are, the more forcefully he will pursue you.

Overall, a Capricorn male is demanding in every relationship. He won't play second fiddle to anybody, hates being ignored and has to be at the centre of everything. As long as he is able to control people around him, he is totally committed and dedicated. People get sucked into the whirlpool of his charms and they tend to overlook his shortcomings. But a relationship with a Capricorn man can go sour if you disagree with him or oppose him and if you have displeased him, he is not likely to forget it for a long time.

How is he when alone?

The cynic that some are, the Capricorn male is prone to bouts of irritability and will withdraw deeper into his shell, becoming completely unapproachable. Words of advice...when he wants to be alone—LEAVE HIM ALONE—unless, of course, you like being derided and at the receiving end of a barrage of sarcastic criticism.

The lone Capri man is like the Sphinx—once he's fixed something in his rigid mind, he is just as immovable, unwilling to express or share any of his locked-up thoughts. When alone, he would brood and cook-up even more negative thoughts (another side effect of his being a cynic) and continue with them during the course of the day, even after getting back to his normal routine. His periods of 'get out of my face and leave me alone' can be quite long, some time lasting even a few days. But given time, he'll come around, behaving totally normal, exhibiting no regret or explanation for his hibernation.

How is he when in love?

A Capricorn guy is a romantic. There, now I have gone and trapped myself by making such a statement. It's true he is a romantic but his definition of 'romance' is slightly different from the rest of us. And that's why I said I have trapped myself because now I will have to delve into what makes him a romantic, albeit a different one.

You will hardly ever notice a Capricorn man in love. Not because he can't be in love, but because he won't show it. He will not shout from rooftops or pour his story into eager ears. On the contrary he will be very subtle and even shy in displaying his love (but on the inside he is steaming with untold fantasies and bursting with energy).

If a Capricorn guy is in love with you, you might find the usual romantic stuff missing only to be replaced with gentle concern. He may forget your birthday, but he will never forget to kiss you good-night. He may criticise your culinary skills but he will lap-up everything that's served. A shawl draped over you as you doze on a chilly afternoon, a phone call in the middle of the day to inquire if your cold is better, and many such small yet significant gestures will be his way of telling you he loves you. Although he is not a possessive lover, he will be protective of you. He may not recite poetry or write love letters but he will hold you in his strong arms when you are down and out. And as he grows his love will grow too. And you are sure to have an admirer in your husband even when you are sixty.

Once in a relationship with him, you will realise his love is not to be measured with the number of times he says 'I love you' or the price tags on his gifts. But his love shows in the way he tucks his credit card in your purse when you go shopping or when he shushes and rocks the baby to sleep without waking you up.

What does he look for in his partner?

This is one man who wants it all...a perfect home to come to at the end of the day, well fed and clean, well behaved children, and a perfectly dressed wife with a welcoming smile, who's got a delightful spread for him. The 'I'm worth it all' outlook of the egocentric Capricorn man calls for a liaison with someone who can accept his chronic mood swings while still being the perfect woman. Capricorn men like to be 'in charge' of everything that happens in their domain and appreciate the company of ladies who can hold their own in the outside world but gladly accept who the real boss is! No! I don't want them to come across as some kind of tyrant. Your efforts won't go unnoticed or unappreciated. A woman who gives him what he wants will have a very pleased and appreciative man by her side...for life.

While dating him, you should...

...never forget his definition of romance. It saves a lot of trouble in the long run. He will take you to the best restaurants, buy you gifts, whisper sweet nothings and be very funny and amiable. But it is likely that this behaviour won't continue beyond the courtship period. I am not implying that this guy is a fake. He's not! He means every word and every gesture but he is too practical to continue this mushy love once he gets into a steady relationship. It is for you to understand how things change as a relationship progresses and accept the transformation. He won't actually give you any cause to complain as he will be a good companion to you, with his feet firmly rooted. Remember, his constant reality checks!

Here is a man who knows how to treat a girl like a lady and it is for you to behave as much ladylike as you can. Be presentable on your dates (manicured fingers et al)...in fact it would be better if you treat every date with him as your first one. He likes and appreciates pleasant appearances and proper manners.

Your Capricorn date might seem shy and reserved in the first few meetings. Don't form a negative impression of him based on that. Like I said before he prefers sitting composedly in his shell and needs a gentle tug to get him out. You will have to believe in him and his dreams if you wish to have a long-term relationship with him. Once he is on a certain comfort level with you, he will floor you with amusing anecdotes and interesting conversation.

Like mentioned before, he will also indulge in lighthearted flirting with other (good-looking) women. Although this is no reason to doubt his loyalty towards you, you can't remain complacent either. Remember this guy is a slow starter. He will think a hundred times before committing himself and prefers keeping his options open. It is one thing to have him in love with you and quite a task to keep him in love.

Compatibility quotient

Compatibility is a much used term in behavioural study. A Capricorn male is undoubtedly popular for his flamboyant style and persona. But does that make him compatible in a long-term relationship? Find out for yourself.

Capricorn man and…

Aries woman: 8/10. A workable combination but both will have to work a lot to make it a happy one. Expect lots of sparks. The Capricorn guy needs to be more expressive to meet up the vivacity of the Aries woman, or at least be able to put-up with it. And she will have to make do with his usual reserved way of life.

Taurus woman: 8/10. An excellent match for both! The Taurus girl knows how to trust and love a man, while the Capricorn guy knows how to make a woman feel secure and comfortable. She also has the ability to make him relax in her company with her good humour.

Gemini woman: 5/10. Both will have to walk a long way to be on the same plane. It is impossible to rein-in the free spirit of a Gemini and the Capricorn guy will find this disconcerting.

Cancer woman: 7/10. Once the Capricorn guy is able to match the Cancer girl's emotional quotient to some extent, this relationship can work out to be simply perfect. He needs to be more expressive of his feelings and more understanding of hers.

Leo woman: 8/10. A Leo woman has qualities that the Capricorn guy hates; for instance excessive socialising. While he is way too predictable to suit her fancy, I have given them an eight...he will love her for her determination and she will appreciate his dependability.

Virgo woman: 9/10. A great match for both! These two are quite compatible as they understand each other implicitly. Each can act as an anchor and a source of support for the other.

Libra woman: 5/10. Again a midway deal! While both love the nicer things in life, the level of extravagance in a Libra girl can be a little too much for the Capricorn guy to digest. Moreover, she is likely to get bored of his sombre nature sooner than later. But with compromises, this can be a workable relationship.

Scorpio woman: 9/10. The Scorpio girl is the Capricorn guy's real dream girl. She has the right amount of vivacity to make him comfortable and she can win him over easily with her devotion and loyalty. He in turn will give her a strong shoulder to lean on.

Sagittarius woman: 4/10. Trouble is likely to brew between the two, after the courtship period. The essential differences in their personalities will make them take offence at the drop of a hat. Overall, a difficult relationship!

Capricorn woman: 7/10. This relationship can go a long way. Both are intense and dependable by nature, with the right amount of humour. But he will have to rein his hovering eye, while she will have to be a little less possessive. The only thing that can make this relationship work is effective communication.

Aquarius woman: 4/10. Both would require putting in extra efforts to make this alliance work. A Capricorn man may find the Aquarian free spirit and feminism a bit too much to take to.

Pisces woman: 9/10. Whoa! Now we're talking! This is a woman the Capricorn guy will love since she will never try to dominate him. She can be completely feminine and dependant on him and he is capable of taking care of her fragile self (a role she enjoys playing even if that's not her true self in some cases). This relationship would be ideal.

Famous Capricorn men personalities:

Dhirubhai Ambani
Hrithik Roshan
Tiger Woods
Elvis Presley
Salman Khan

Capricorn woman

A Capricorn woman is someone who'll instantly strike you as 'nice'. There is a certain warmth and friendliness in her smile and when she talks (oh so softly!) she will envelope you with tenderness that is too cushiony to resist. Not one to stand out flamboyantly, she will still make her presence felt through her quiet charm and disarming diffidence.

Now come a little closer and you will notice a certain aura of melancholy about her. She has an intense, serious and 'lost-in-thought' kind of personality, but thanks to her lively humour, it is well balanced.

Don't ever make the mistake of thinking of her as a pushover; she's not that at all. Beneath the soft, gentle nature, lies a strong-willed heart. She is a steady and sure climber. She will reach your heart before you even realise it...and win it over too!

How can you identify a Capricorn woman in a crowd?

See that lively and sparkling woman gliding across gracefully, with a warm smile for everyone? This one's got to be a Capricorn female. These women have a natural aptitude of standing out in a crowd because of their liveliness and good humour, without being over the top.

A Capricorn woman is always subtle, be it in her words or behaviour. When deep in conversation, she will be totally absorbed and attentive towards the subject and will hardly notice the presence of a stranger in the crowd. But if she catches you staring at her, she is very likely to blush with self-consciousness...a blush that easily melts into a smile as she is artlessly friendly and approachable.

While at a social do, a Capricorn woman can either be friendly and chatty or icy and aloof. When in an affable mood, her femininity will strike you instantly and you will yearn to be part of that one group that is warming up with her radiance. Otherwise she will seem distant and formal. However, in spite of being generally approachable, you might find it difficult to approach her not because she is repulsive in any way (on the contrary she is quite charming) but there's something in her that will tell you to keep away if you are in any way not presentable enough or your intentions not honourable enough.

What are the key features of her personality?

A heart-winning quality that all Capricorn women possess is simplicity. Beneath all kinds of outer façades lies a simple and non-materialistic heart. However, lack of materialism does not necessarily make this woman devoid of desires; in fact, she aspires for all things good and wants the best for herself and her loved ones. She is also a 'quality' over 'quantity' woman, so don't be surprised if the Capricorn woman in your life prefers having a single pair of branded shoes rather than six non-tagged or average quality ones.

Capricorn women are high on emotions and can get high with emotions, but the strong practical front of their personality evens out the towering emotional quotient. Their practical nature helps them to strike a balance and not go overboard with emotions.

But even the most pragmatic Capricorn woman can often be found engaged in thinking out the hows and whys of life's many mysteries.

Restless and impatient, she is constantly looking at newer things to do and cannot wait to do them. If it is her birthday, she is impatient to know what surprise is planned for her or if she is reading a book, she'll be up all night to find out how it ends. But as everyone else when a Capricorn woman discovers her true self, she realises that she has a vast reservoir of patience within her and this generally comes with maturity and as she moves from girlhood into womanhood.

Although she can be quite egoistic at times, a Capricorn woman prefers to live life without stressing on the quintessential 'I'. As her maturity increases she is able to grasp better the meaning of life's important things and to understand what to let go of.

She is also impulsive and often takes off at the spur of a moment. Decisions are made and activities taken up on impulse, which often make her adventurous and a risk-taker. But at the same time she is submissive and flexible and can also get easily influenced. And this does not always work in her favour.

A Capricorn girl is a silent and steady worker. She will keep moving towards her goal, sometimes at lightning speed and sometimes like a snail. But she will eventually make it. Since she believes implicitly in her dreams and is sure about achieving them, she only needs that firm push to propel her ahead. A right partner can do wonders to her self-confidence and she can be a success at her workplace or business.

How is she on the following aspects?

Appearance: At the first go you may find a dull and distant look in a Capricorn woman's eyes. Her complexion too (50 per cent of them) is slightly pale and her demeanour cold. But that's just the surface...a moment of familiarity and she will award you with the warmest of smiles, and a glow in her eyes that sparkles and speaks to you in the friendliest manner.

A Capricorn woman is very impulsive in her dressing. She believes in creating her own fashion statement rather than blindly following trends and she usually succeeds in doing so! But she belongs to that category of women who don't require getting dolled up to get noticed. The warmth of her usual self is enough to attract people towards her.

Ambition: A Capricorn female is as ambitious as one could be. She wants to achieve her set goals in life and has a wish list to fulfil as well. But sometimes being too adjusting can bring a change in her ambitions. She is known to change her course of things to suit that of her dear ones. For instance, while doing well in a comfortable job, a Capricorn girl is likely to give it up, relocate, look for another job and start a career in a totally different field just to suit the lifestyle of her boyfriend, partner or husband. That's how compromising she can get!

Another thing that impinges on her progress is her laziness. She can be extremely languid in matters concerning her personal development. So although she has the ability, sometimes she lacks the desire or shall I say 'the go-getting' attitude required to achieve goals (unless pushed or challenged).

Ego/Self-respect: She is high on self-respect. She believes in maintaining her self-esteem in any given situation. This may arise from her innate lack of confidence or her overly submissive nature. But that is not to say she doesn't have an ego. It's just that she is rather careful of displaying it and often camouflages it by her show of self-respect. But no matter how much she hides it, it manages to butt in. Usually in situations like quarrels and disagreements, she finds it difficult to patch up or apologise (especially as she has already put her foot in her mouth).

Responsibility: She is great at taking up responsibilities. Be it any relationship, she would plunge into the scheme of things with a fully responsible stance. She takes charge of siblings when the mother is away, monitor classmates at school when the teacher is away and the like (but while being responsible, she maintains grace and fun for all around her, including herself). This makes her extremely reliable and dependable. And this also makes her intolerant of irresponsible behaviour in others.

Etiquettes: This is one of the most unique qualities I have observed in Capricorn women. No matter where they are born and how they are brought up, their sense of etiquettes is unmatched.

What is her approach towards life?

She wants everything...and the best at that! If this short and precise answer has shocked you, let me elaborate. Although I have described her as level-headed, emotional and intense (and she *is* all that) I would like to repeat myself here, that she is not desire-less. She has her own wish list, which can be short or long, depending upon her situation in life, but you will usually not find her discussing her desires publicly. She will appear content with what she has, but in her own quiet way she wants to have the best of everything and the right amount of adventure in her life.

How does she score on the following points?

Cynicism: The word cynicism brings an interesting twist to the nature of Capricorn women. I have often observed that a Capricorn female's mind works like a detective in a work of fiction, a la Miss Marple. She is constantly looking at the nuances of life, be it emotion, action or the metaphysical. Details and various shades of life interest her a lot. And from this complicated thought process, arises her cynicism. But most of this stays within the confines of her mind. In life she is a lot more uncomplicated and realistic in her approach.

Suspicion/Jealousy: In spite of what I just said about her cynicism, she is low on suspicion. Following the diktats of her nature she trusts people easily. But where she lacks on suspicion she makes up with intelligence. So don't think you can get away with occasional falsehood with your Capricorn partner...she is shrewd enough to catch you. So beware!

As far as jealousy goes, she is moderate (as with everything else in life). She usually dismisses her own jealousy pangs as mere annoyance and silliness. Be it relationship or professionalism, she is more on the path of improving herself, than going green over what others have.

Dishonesty/Infidelity: Both dishonesty and infidelity are taboos for her. A Capricorn woman will never accept or forgive either of the two faux pas, with the one exception of her getting bowled over in love. Love makes this woman blind, literally.

Hardships: A Capricorn woman knows how to maintain 'grace under fire'. She is capable of facing hardships herself and stopping them from affecting those she loves. Trying times get the best out of her and she will strive endlessly to overcome hardships.

Success and failure: With success she is as subtle as ever. She believes in enjoying the fruits of her success with her family rather than being loud and displaying it to the whole world. But when it comes to losing, she is rather poor at it. Even her usual maturity fails here, but with time and age, she learns to accept her failures and you will undoubtedly find her working doubly hard to overcome them.

Host: As a host, a Capricorn woman will walk that extra mile to make her party the very best. Detailed to the core, you will find her being particular about everything from the first course to desserts and from caterers to entertainers; she will be involved in every aspect of planning and execution and will leave nothing to others or to chance.

Guest: Usually she is high on expectations as a guest. As she has lofty standards of hospitality and an eye for detail she is hard to please, but you will never find her complaining. Even if she is disappointed, she will be gracious enough not to show it to the hosts. But at a gathering organised by family or friends she may react differently.

How does she handle difficult situations?

The Capricorn woman is usually undaunted if in the midst of conflict. Not one to easily own up her mistakes, she can often be found trying to reason out by giving excuses for her shortcomings. That said, she would usually avoid a head-on with anyone, since she knows she can go overboard once she loses her cool.

When challenged or faced with trying situations, the resilient lady would assess the situation in great detail, the way her zodiac symbol, the goat screens a mountain face before deciding which path to choose for her upward climb. She understands the importance of planning in advance and knows that fore knowledge would come to her aid in such tough situations.

What is her characteristic weakness?

It has got to be her lack of confidence. If you see her conversing with easy grace with a good number of people or watch her conducting herself with assurance in a difficult situation, you will never be able to suspect the diffidence she suffers from, but there it is lurking just beneath the surface. It arises from her fear of failure and of doing the wrong thing. However, she knows how to handle her weakness effectively without letting people around her notice it.

Another limitation in her nature is that she can't take criticism well. Under criticism, she usually offers excuses in her defense and is not likely to accept her faults.

But her Achilles' heel is undoubtedly her knack of putting her foot in her mouth. Like I had mentioned before she likes to hold on to her emotions and frustrations and can let go of them at an instant. This creates unpleasantness for those around her. And during such times she is on a non-stop verbal tirade. And the finishing touch is when she says something that is totally uncalled for...and what I have termed as her 'foot in the mouth punch line'.

Is there more to this easy-going lady's persona?

She has a low battery life; her energy store is rather limited. She is too lazy to help herself but when it comes to others she will use the last ounce of her energy to help them, especially family and loved ones.

Capricorn women are known to grow younger with age. That is because the child in them that is hiding just below the surface, is playful and ever ready to spring into action. This childlike quality makes them as appealing to a three-year-old as to a sixty-year-old. Being warm and friendly towards people of all age groups comes naturally to them.

A Capricorn woman prefers to be by herself as she is basically satisfied with herself. She is artistically inclined and often dabbles in hobbies like pottery, designing and painting. Her art too reflects simplicity as she knows how to make things simple using her creative talents.

Although hesitant by nature, all she needs is a gentle push and support to take the road less travelled. Be it work, home or a business venture, with proper calculation and support, a Capricorn woman is likely to succeed as she has the right mix of determination, grit and will-power. Moreover, she can be quite adventurous, even crazy, in trying out new things. She is a staunch believer in doing everything at least once...even if it's something as wild as bungee jumping.

A Capricorn woman has great inner strength; she is resilient and determined in her actions. At the same time she is not entirely emotionally independent. And this is one of her dark secrets. In spite of her pragmatism and belief in independence, she needs the support of a man. She always gives her spouse or the man in her life ample space. And although she likes to believe that she too requires this space, she actually wants her man to protect her always. She needs a strong shoulder to lean on and a protective cocoon to live in.

How should one deal effectively with her?

I have discovered that the most effective way of dealing with a Capricorn woman is to be like her—simple, straightforward and direct—and yes, graceful too, almost as much as she is! Also remember that she has high standards about social etiquettes, behaviour and principles and if you can't match up to those, you won't make any inroads into her good books.

Another important aspect when dealing with this lady is to believe in her. She dislikes Doubting Thomases, especially when her capability, emotions or sincerity are at stake. She doesn't go around asking for advice or prying into other's secrets, people come to her on their own with their queries and if anyone dares to show any disbelief, he is likely to get a cool stare from the usually warm Capricorn lady...a stare that says 'why ask me if you don't trust me'. And that would be the end of all conversation too.

How does she handle money matters?

A Capricorn woman is a 'materialistic' female. Shocked! I did intend to shock you with this statement. But I mean materialistic in a totally different sense. She will put practical considerations above sentimental stuff when it comes to handling money. She believes in financial security and will rather improve her bank account than spend recklessly on romantic outings.

When it does come to spending money, Capricorn woman is strictly a no-risk-taker. Conservative in thought and action, she believes in savings and likes to have something tucked away for a rainy day (she knows that this will get her financial freedom too).

A Capricorn female will never put her money in any dubious or questionable business. She needs to be absolutely sure about the financial returns and ethical status of any organisation before she trusts her money to someone.

How is she on the professional front?

A Capricorn woman believes in giving whatever she does her best. You'll seldom find a Capri woman cribbing about being stuck in a profession that she doesn't like. Prone to spending hours on pre-planning everything, she would have her career mapped out, right down to intricate details one usually doesn't even think of.

Resolute and determined to achieve what she sets her heart on, a Capri woman would gladly slave away at work, as long as she knows she's heading closer to that much desirable post or whatever target she has set for herself. She will not shy from using her knack of bonding with people across all groups to her advantage on the job front. A climber, she often befriends her seniors to smoothen her upward climb in the organisation.

Ethics rule the mind of the Capricorn woman and she would never give up her ideals for making money on the sly or for other personal gains. She makes for an ardent worker, whom most find easy to work with, making her a great team worker.

How is she in various relationship roles?

Family is the centre of a Capricorn woman's life. She is dedicated towards her family members and treasures her relationships. In spite of ambition and drive, she would prefer being with her family members. Even while at work, her heart and mind are at home. This makes her an excellent homemaker. Her dedication also makes her submissive to those she loves. While others might get a taste of her fighting spirit at times, she generally lets her loved ones have their way with her. She avoids creating scenes and you will find her gliding diplomatically and gracefully through difficult filial situations. Being responsible and proactive, you will find her taking the lead in making any relationship a success.

As a girlfriend, you will not find her very demanding. While she will look forward to your surprise gifts, she will surely reprimand you if she sees the price tag. Nor is she dominating. Once she is convinced of your love, she will remain committed to you however, in return she will demand absolute loyalty from you.

A Capricorn girl will carry on the devotion she shows as a girlfriend even after she becomes a wife. She will take great pains in being a good wife and a dutiful daughter-in-law. She will take your siblings under her wing and will gracefully assume all responsibilities of running your household.

As a mother, she is both loving and doting but she is also a disciplinarian. She wants her kids to be well behaved and presentable (read 'well dressed'). She looks after the needs of her children from end to end...from breakfast to lullabies she'll be there on her toes to be a good mother.

I would like to add a funny observation about Capricorn women in relationship roles. A Capricorn woman is good at observation and at taking notes for future use. This makes her excel in her latter roles as a mother and mother-in-law too. She learns from the mistakes of her mother and husband's mother and takes care not to repeat those when she dons these titles.

How is she when alone?

Content with what she has in life, the Capricorn woman sometimes is laid-back in her approach towards life. Not one to get flustered easily, she often likes to take a break from the routines of everyday life and spend time alone.

As I mentioned earlier, she has an avid interest in extra-curricular activities and when left to her musings, she would indulge in any form of entertainment, from art to music that interests her and allows her the liberty of taking time to be herself.

How is a Capricorn woman when in love?

Once a Capricorn woman falls in love, she does so blindly and can change drastically. For her love she will be ready to battle it out with her family—the very family that she adores. She will go to any lengths to attain her love. She is ready to plunge into a commitment without confirming if it is even worth it and if at all her instinct goes wrong, she has enough pride not to go back to her family or seek assistance from them.

In her own peculiar way, a Capricorn woman is a flirt at heart. She does not have the proverbial wandering eye, but it is more often than not her friendly ways that mislead people. Her 'extra niceness' makes her look like a flirt, and at times, act like one too.

This girl holds her heart in a crystal ball and prizes it above everything else as it is the source of all her emotions. Although her emotional nature is generally kept in check by her pragmatism, once in love her emotions can flow unchecked. It is up to you to respect her feelings when dating her. If you are in love, show her how much you care. All she needs is an assurance from you that you will shield her from all the worries and troubles of the world.

What does she look for in her partner?

It is strange yet true that the docile Capricorn woman gets turned on by aggressive and powerful men (in strength, attributes or attitude). I guess this is a case of opposite attracts!

She is often attracted towards tall muscular men (who exude power). This can be said to stem from her need to be protected. In a relationship, she desires protection and security. And brawn can easily represent all that. However, you don't always get what you see and she is well aware of that.

A Capricorn girl I know married a man similar to the one mentioned above, who had all the attributes of a macho man. He made her feel secure till the courtship period was on but after marriage things took a different turn. What she regarded as lot of space for herself was actually sheer negligence on her man's side. He was simply being uncaring and insensitive. She was able to decipher this quickly when she compared her inputs (usually a lot) to what she was getting back from the man.

A Capricorn woman desires love which is enveloping yet not overpowering. She wants her man to love and respect her...love that is exclusive and respect that is well-deserved. Loyalty in love is a must as a Capricorn woman is not looking for endless dating or one-night-stands. For her love is commitment and she will only approve of a man who has the guts to drop down on his knee to ask 'will you marry me?' But all this in good time...any kind of haste will send her back in her shell like a scared rabbit.

Scared she is and mostly of getting emotionally hurt. That's why she appears aloof and reluctant at first. And she is well pleased with any man who knows how to draw her out of her cocoon and infuse her with the confidence of his love. A man who can give her security—in love, family, home, children, emotions, finances and all the important aspects of life—is the man for her.

While dating her, you should...

...or rather you would fall in love. So if you aren't planning on being cupid's victim, stay away from a Capricorn girl. Her natural charm, simplicity and earthiness will evoke the fleeting emotion of love in you and she will slay you with a dart to the heart. On second thoughts, she won't date you at all if she fails to catch a glimpse of love on the horizon. She is cautious and will obviously gauge you from all perspectives before agreeing for a cup of coffee. Lunch, brunch or dinner will come after a considerable wait. And if you are the kind who likes to hurry, then forget about the night cap!

A Capricorn girl is romantic at heart and appreciates personalised gifts. She will graciously accept the bunch of expensive red roses you bought for her (the ones she sees everyday at the florist's shop!) but she will treasure the blue wildflower you picked for her on one of your cross country trips. While dating a Capricorn woman keep it simple and exclusive.

And most importantly don't brag. Let her talk first...let her open up and share her emotions, thoughts, dreams and aspirations with you and then she will gladly sit with you for hours listening to how your mom makes the best *aloo paranthas* in the world!

Take care while dressing up as well as deciding on the venue and time of your date. A Capricorn woman has high regard for etiquettes and will expect you to be as sophisticated and graceful as she is. Plan your date carefully and take her likes and dislikes into account.

Be moderate with your compliments but make sure they are sincere and heartfelt. Don't try your 'bachelor' jokes on her...she won't get them. And be constructive with your criticism—she likes a man who is honest as well as smart enough to know when not to be 'very honest'.

One last word of advice—while dating her don't, and I repeat, don't ever criticise her family, unless of course you can sugarcoat your words. She won't stand it at all. Period!

Compatibility quotient

A Capricorn woman is friendly and easy to be with but that doesn't make her compatible with all. When it comes to love and long-term relationship, one needs to understand the complete behavioural traits of two individuals. With a Capricorn woman on one side of the scales, let's see who has the capacity to 'weight' it out on the other.

Capricorn woman and...

Aries man: 9/10. The Aries man is the kind of guy who can sweep women off their feet; add to that his chivalrous nature and fondness for grandeur which the Capricorn secretly likes, and she'll gladly give in. Her being naturally submissive and patient can work in favour of this relationship. The Arien however will have to keep a check on his unruly temper and tongue. Other than that everything a Capricorn woman can dream of, from romance to passion, and what she wants her man to be or do is found in an Arien man. The Aries man would play the perfect Romeo to our Capricorn Juliet, with the fire burning bright throughout the course of this relationship.

Taurus man: 8/10. This relationship can be for keeps. Both are responsible and dependable and hence will be able to take care of each other. He is romantic and she is mature enough to effectively manage matters of the heart and home. Some Taurus men can be chauvinists and that could be a big no-no. But other than that love could blossom here.

Gemini man: 6/10. A difficult, yet not impossible match. He is too fond of his freedom to give her emotional need its due. He is also a lady charmer, which can leave her frustrated. She would need to accept his love for freedom and he would have to be patient with her to work this out. His diplomatic tricks are a turn-off for her as she looks for genuineness. Once he gives in and surrenders she can be cool about most things with him.

Cancer man: 6/10. Although it kick-starts as an intense affair, it is not likely to be fruitful in the long run. While each may find the other attractive, it is not necessarily a lasting impression. The major hitch here would be lack of communication. Also, a Cancerian man is a mix of conservative and liberal ideas which would leave her confused as she always seeks clarity and direction when making commitments.

Leo man: 6/10. Between a Capricorn girl and a Leo guy, understanding is the key. If they understand each other, their relationship will work. She may find his extravagance and attention hogging nature a little too much to take, while he may be impatient with her lack of expression.

Virgo man: 7/10. A Virgo man might be the answer to a Capricorn girl's need for security but that is if he knows how to share and also be graceful. While he will have to keep his flirting nature under strict check, her intense attitude will bring the best of his emotions to the forefront. However, he will have to make sure he gets his priorities in order and not take advantage of the cool Capricorn. She needs love and emotional security at all times!

Libra man: 7/10. This relationship can swing both ways. Both are too dissimilar for a long lasting relationship. He attracts too much female attention which she dislikes, and he is too disorganised which she can't stand. But perhaps both can tweak their natures to suit each other and make a relationship possible. If he turns out to be a guy who is not just a dreamer but also an achiever/provider, she could find solace.

Scorpio man: 8/10. A Scorpio man can bring a Capricorn woman's feelings out in the open, thanks to his vivacity, while she will make him feel secure with her devotion and loyalty. In a way, they complement each other wonderfully. On passion (not romance/love) front however the Capricorn woman will have to keep up with him for a lifetime which I am not very sure she is capable of.

Sagittarius man: 8/10. An amazing start and this relationship would be one helluva roller coaster ride. However, this duo can see a lot of problems once the initial courtship is over. A lot of compromises would be required to make this relationship a success. But his knowledge, philosophies and visionary nature do match her intellectual self.

Capricorn man: 7/10. Many of the stronger traits of both males and females under the Capricorn sign are common. That's why this relationship can work wonders. However, both should learn to emote and express themselves. Only when they are communicative will they be able to reach out to each other. Otherwise, it would be one boring, romance-less relationship.

Aquarius man: 8/10. A relationship between these two will blossom like friendship. The easy and outgoing nature of an Aquarian can gel well with the steady and cautious Capricorn girl.

Pisces man: 8/10. The Piscean is intense, dreamy and spiritual and this concoction is just right to suit the tastes of a Capricorn girl. She is reliable, trusting and loyal, which makes her appealing to him. She has the capacity to believe in his dreams and with such support he is quite sure of fulfilling them. However he must not lose her along the path while pursuing his dreams as she could find herself lost and disheartened.

Famous Capricorn women personalities:

Ava Gardner
Deepika Padukone
Divya Balan
Bipasha Basu
Gul Panag
Michelle Obama

Aquarius
20 January-19 February

Aquarius man

He's inquisitive, he's ambitious, he's energetic. He is a man who likes to know what's on your mind, but is not one to disclose what's on his. Secretive to the core, the Aquarian male is a strange combination of sociability and reserve.

He has a lazy charm about him. Casual and laid-back, he takes life one day at a time. But his casual attitude stops when it comes to ambition. Goal-oriented and focused, nothing will stop an Aquarian from realising his dreams.

And when it comes to dating Aquarian men, girls can be sure of having a ball. The water bearer will impress the babes with his capers and comic timing. Every time you meet an Aquarian guy, you are sure to have a good laugh. And the spectrum of emotions that he displays like flashes of lightening will keep you intrigued.

How to identify an Aquarian man in a crowd?

There are two distinct types of men under this zodiac sign. The Aquarian man falling under the first 40 per cent is cynical, opinionated and eccentric and shows strong traits of aggressiveness. He is loud and boisterous and likes to strut his stuff—showing off what he bought, where he went and the like. Most of this kind are usually full of 'me, myself and I' and rarely see beyond themselves.

The Aquarian man who falls under the balance 60 per cent is the passive type and exactly the opposite. He knows the power of underplay. Never loud or brash, he will not brag about his material gains even if it is a Ferrari he bought the previous day.

But Aquarian men, no matter what kind know how to make their presence felt. I strongly believe they can make very good contenders for political positions, thanks to their leadership qualities. The first type will lead the way with aggression and the passive will depend on their diplomacy and tact.

What are the key features of his personality?

Most Aquarian men I have met are full of energy. They are propelled into activities by an inner force. And this is true not withstanding their casual attitude.

I have also observed that most Aquarian men are likeable people. They mingle in a crowd and make friends easily. In fact, an Aquarian man is most happy in company. He can connect with people of any age, gender or background easily. Also, Aquarians have the unique trait of chatting up women and end up showing more interest in them in a social gathering. His inherent secrecy will make these traits hard to spot the first time, but if you follow the pattern over a few times, it may become obvious.

He is also rather inquisitive by nature. He likes to analyse human nature. He wants to know more about people around him, including their personal lives. He likes it when his friends share their lives, problems and successes with him. But when it comes to him doing the same, he recoils and shut out others.

It is this inquisitiveness that makes him a mystery lover. So much so that he looks for unlocking secrets and mysteries even where there's none. But one thing you can be sure of in your Aquarian man is that he is not selfish. You will never find him resorting to devious methods in order to gain his ends. He will always be considerate and kind towards the welfare of his fellow beings. And if there's one thing he hates...it is small mindedness.

Another very funny thing I have noticed about Aquarian men is their inability to lie. An Aquarian guy is a poor actor and can't keep a straight face while lying. He prefers confiding the truth however bad the consequences may be.

He is also very practical and spontaneous in his actions. You will hardly ever find an Aquarian on a wild goose chase. If he is after something, it will be with a specific purpose...even if it is only to satiate his curiosity.

How is an Aquarius man on the following aspects?

Appearance: An Aquarian man tends to have deep set eyes and rather blunt features. Most Aquarians have unconventional looks. He will either dress up in the most fashionable do or go for a totally eccentric style of dressing (that's because he dislikes being just another face in the crowd). He makes sure his clothes and appearance make a statement. Another pet peeve in Aquarian men is their comfort with colours and styles. They are likely to wear their favourite much too often; it could be a chequered shirt and blue jeans or the most complimented colours.

Ambition: For the conventional Aquarian, sky's the limit. His ambition knows no bounds. He might become overambitious and relentless in his drive to achieve and succeed.

The passive kind too is ambitious, but can strike a balance between his work and personal life and will devote as much time at achieving things as he would to himself and his family.

Ego/Self-respect: I find Aquarian men most interesting on this aspect. They either demand respect or command it. One way or the other they think it's their birthright. The passive kind may like to earn his respect; the conventional kind usually takes it for granted. However, both are terribly egoistic. Although the mellower Aquarian may show humility at times, his ego too is not far from the surface.

Responsibility: Here is a man who has the knack of over committing himself. This can be attributed to his over ambitiousness. He wants to achieve too many things in too short a time. A family oriented Aquarian considers himself responsible only towards his family; the rest of the world including friends and acquaintances are met with a casual attitude.

Etiquettes: Unless you come across an Aquarian male who holds a responsible and dominating position like that of a lawyer or CEO of a company, you will find him quite relaxed on finer details of etiquettes.

What is his approach towards life?

Undaunted and relentless, the conventional Aquarian will not rest till he has achieved what he set out for. And after that? He will have something else lined up for tomorrow. The passive Aquarian enjoys good living and manages to achieve a high-quality lifestyle for himself.

How does an Aquarius man score on the following points?

Cynicism: Overall all Aquarian men are cynical. While 50 per cent of them are possibly born hard core cynics, the other 50 per cent turn into cynics due to their stubbornness.

Suspicion/Jealousy: If there is one man who is constantly looking around with hooded, penetrating eyes, it is undoubtedly an Aquarian. Almost 90 per cent of them are suspicious by nature and this is not limited just to their girlfriends or spouses, but to everyone from colleagues at work to people generally around them.

Beware of this trait if you are dating an Aquarian. He will constantly stalk you with his presence, either through text messages or through phone calls. A part of his mind will forever be following your movements and marking any deviation in your behaviour. But once secure, as in a committed relationship, he will give as much space to his partner as he wants for himself.

But any display of jealousy from his girlfriend or wife will not be taken lightly. He hates when his partner gets jealous; for him it shows lack of faith in him and his love. Trust is an emotion he takes very seriously. If he has bestowed it on you, he expects you to do the same.

Dishonesty/Infidelity: I have observed that three out of every ten Aquarian men are sincere, loyal and dependable. Once they make long-term commitments, they try their best to remain faithful to that relationship. Since an Aquarian man appreciates open mindedness, he is not one to take dishonesty or infidelity lying down.

Hardships: Here again the difference between the coventional and passive kinds becomes starkly obvious. The coventional Aquarian male will take hardships in his stride. The passive Aquarian can't take hardships well. He will crib to the high heavens and is likely to fall into a long monologue titled 'Why is this happening to me?'

Success and failure: A conventional Aquarian is quite vocal about his success whereas the passive Aquarian is as subtle about his success as he is loud about his setbacks. The conventional Aquarian male is also capable of taking failure in good spirit and rise from it. But for the passive kind, failure can make quite a wimp of the man.

Host: The conventional Aquarian male prefers doing things in style and formality, which includes dinner accompanied by fine wine and concluding with cigars. Also, at his parties, he will make sure there is something in the 'works' to stun people. The passive Aquarian man is quite the contrary. Casual and informal, he would welcome you directly to his kitchen. And thereafter to help yourself!

Guest: As a guest, both kinds of Aquarian men will put on finer etiquettes only while dealing from a responsible position. Otherwise, they would prefer being casual and rather informal.

How does he handle a difficult situation?

This is a tricky one! Here the two categories of Aquarian men display characteristic differences and yet at the core of it, they remain similar. For instance, the conventional Aquarian will be like a blazing volcano in a difficult situation. He will be bubbling with lava, leaving no space for arguments or opinions. It is best to let him be in such a situation. Any inroads into his good books should be made only after he has cooled off his heels!

The passive Aquarian will come across as the most attentive listener in case you are pleading your case before him. He would listen and listen and then go ahead and do exactly what suits him. To put it briefly, he is just pretending to listen to you while actually strengthening his stubbornness within. Stuffed cotton, this man!

What is his characteristic weakness?

The Aquarian male's inability to commit easily often works against him. Be it in love relationships or professional liaisons, his hesitation to commit makes him come across as disinterested, and at times, even unreliable.

Unwilling to conform to common decorum just because he wants to be different can also cost him dearly. His eccentric ways make him lose out on many a friend who find his inert, guarded behaviour too much to handle.

Is there more to his persona?

Aquarian men, like their female counterparts, make great show of self-confidence. They like to go on a talking spree about things they know nothing about. They project the image of being 'master of all trades' while in reality they are neither masters nor jacks. They cover-up lack of knowledge and confidence by excessively exercising their tongues.

An Aquarian man hates to be tied down. Pushing him to do what he is not ready to do yet is a sure way of losing him. He dislikes being controlled and would do as he pleases, whatever the repercussions. He will take-up responsibilities only as and when they suit him. If duties are imposed on him, he will find a way to wriggle out of them or throw tantrums to show his disapproval. This trait makes him a difficult child too. No parent would know how to teach responsible behaviour to an Aquarian boy. So who can? Only life can be his teacher...and trust me he can't have a better one!

Both kinds of Aquarian men are extremely emotional and tend to be vocal about their emotions too. The passive kind is a backpacker and ever ready to go. This can be attributed to his need for constant change. He likes moving from one pasture to another, sometimes for no better reason than change in scenery. You will rarely find an Aquarian who likes to stay put for long or enjoy the composed state of things.

There is a peculiar trait that Aquarians display that I am at a loss for words to describe. An Aquarian takes mood swings to a totally different level. You will find him going from witty to whacko in a second. And the funny part is...this isn't exactly a mood swing! It is calculated change which springs from his incorrigible habit of trying to topple the boat. His purpose is to surprise you out of your wits. And he won't do this just to prove himself...he will also implicitly believe in what he is doing.

I am yet to meet an Aquarian who doesn't want to be the leader of the pack. Here is a man who wants to be first at everything...at work, in love, in social circles et al. If he is named the best employee in his office, he will be on cloud nine and if he happens to be your first boyfriend, lady, you couldn't have asked for a better Romeo.

How should one deal effectively with an Aquarius man?

Given his stubborn nature and ambitiousness, my observations tell me that the most effective way of dealing with a conventional Aquarian is with submissiveness and extreme patience. If you can win his heart with love and care, you will have a man who's a 'true blue' for life. And if you plan to marry him, remember he would prefer you to be a homemaker as he believes that's a role that's tailor made for women.

The best way to deal with the passive Aquarians is to be as casual as they are, or be one up on them. If you let them have the upper hand, the casualness is likely to go beyond limits. Overall, in relationships, Aquarian men have one motto—they should have their way.

While dealing with an Aquarian male for business, it is best to be clear about the terms and conditions at the outset as it can get difficult to make him shell out money later. He will drive a hard bargain too, so watch out for this one.

An Aquarian guy dislikes people who are pessimistic and 'wet blankets'. He prefers the company of those who are as happy-go-lucky and friendly as he is. And lastly, the one thing that impresses him more than anything else is 'brains'. Be it man or woman, an Aquarian will befriend anyone who is brainy and knows how to make intelligent conversation.

How does he handle money matters?

An Aquarian and his money are not easily parted. Period. The passive Aquarians are careful spenders and will be very selective in what they buy and where they put their money. Although semi-materialistic, the conventional Aquarian is flamboyant in his spending. But he knows his limits too. Both kinds also prefer partners who are not extravagant with money and are as understanding of money matters as with the matters of heart (one thing however hazardous with an Aquarian and his money is his fondness for gambling, so keep him away from casinos).

Having said that, I would like to share my experience with a unique Aquarian client cum friend who entrusted me with a makeover (interiors) of his property. Even after one year of completion he was not interested in the account of the expenses made. The amount ran into almost ₹3 million. He paid in full, every time on due date, and each time I prompted him to sit and run through the account, he was happy just not getting into it and totally trusted me. I guess these types of incidents and many others do prove that there are exceptions.

How is he on the professional front?

The innate inquisitiveness of an Aquarian man helps him establish rapport with people at work, as he comes across as someone who is a good listener (this also makes him an excellent candidate for jobs requiring investigative work). However, he does tend to go overboard at times, leading others to believe that he is more interested in hearing their story for his own personal interests. Most helpful and eager to share information, the Aquarian makes a great co-worker; dependable and fun to be with.

How is he in various relationship roles?

As a son, an Aquarian male will come across as relaxed and rather too easy-going. While he won't be irresponsible at home, he won't take-up responsibility unless forced to. An Aquarian son will prefer being out of home with friends or girlfriends and is quite independent and capable of looking after himself. Be rest assured that after his day long meanderings, he will come home knocking at dinner time.

An Aquarian male sibling can exhibit signs of competitiveness. But this is in a harmless sort of way as he is very sure of himself and feels no threat from his siblings.

As a husband, he is very demanding. Like I had mentioned before, he wants a spouse who is a good homemaker, a good wife and a good mother. That's because he wants her to be around him constantly. He is especially demanding of her attention, even at the expense of his children. But he makes for a loving and caring husband. He will remain devoted to his wife and family.

An Aquarian man's children will enjoy all the luxuries of a magic land. Not materialistically but imaginatively! He will encourage them to think beyond the senses of sight, sound and touch. Being a good listener, he makes for an attentive father and a good teacher.

But I think an Aquarian excels in the role of a friend. He attaches great value to friendship and treats it as a starting point for all relationships. But on second thoughts, his secret nature makes more acquaintances than friends. His actual friends are few.

An Aquarian likes to maintain cordial relations with everyone. So you will find him often overcoming his anger or ego to patch up quarrels at home or disagreements between friends.

How is he when alone?

Not one to indulge in solo projects, our Aquarian can often be found taking part in some whacky activity in the midst of a group of onlookers.

How is he when in love?

Very, very slow and calculative...that is not to say he is manipulative, but he likes to make his moves stealthily and with caution. Don't take this as shyness or quietness. This man is only analysing you before making his move.

As a lover, he is also full of surprises. He will woo you with the most unthinkable ideas and lure you into the most daring terrains. Be sure you fall in step with his ideas of honesty and commitment. Otherwise, his romance will take an instant U turn. Only if he is totally in love will he open up and lay bare his secrets. While in a relationship with him, you should have the tact to draw him out of his reserve and see the man he truly is...underneath his strong façade of friendliness.

Another quality he appreciates in his love interest is the ability to understand him and give him the warmth and care he requires. He looks for a friend in his partner, someone with whom he can share anything and everything.

If an Aquarian moves at a tortoise's speed when in love, he will turn into a snail when it comes to commitment. Usually Aquarians are prone to settling late in life. So stop admiring that solitaire ring in the jewellery window. Your Aquarian boyfriend will bolt at the first mention of a proposal. He will marry and have a family but in his own good time.

What does he look for in his partner?

Most importantly...an outlook to take things easy! He wants someone who gives him space, yet maintains enough charisma to hold his interest, so that he's encouraged to take the next step. Rush him...and you've lost him forever.

Being a very positive person, he abhors women who are whiney and instead appreciates women who are smart and bold. A woman who is feminine in every way but who is also independent minded is one that's perfect for an Aquarian man.

While dating him, you should...

...treat your date like a mystery novel. The more you intrigue him, the more he will be enticed. Nothing delights an Aquarian guy more than unravelling mysteries or unlocking deep secrets. He will probe into your innermost thoughts and desires making you feel like you are the one for him. But hold on...that's just his nature. He would do that to any other person. Whether the relation between you two would reach the next level depends on how long you are able to sustain his interest.

Another word of advice...this man is not a conventional lover. So what should be expected of him? Reciting poems? No! Expensive gifts? No! Romantic escapades, maybe? No! The answer is a good time. He can be funny, entertaining, romantic and protective in his own unique way. He can make you smile, laugh, blush and say yes to all his ideas...that's the power of his presence. You will be floored by the innovative ways he thinks of wooing you and the unconventional ideas he follows to prove his love.

When he comes to pick you up for a date, his heart is full of warm friendly feelings. He is looking for a long chat with you over a couple of drinks and dinner. And after he drops you off at your doorstep (and at this precise moment there would be some hesitation over the goodnight kiss) your Aquarian date will be planning another friendly chat with you for the next weekend. That's how he is programmed...to forge a friendship before falling in love.

Physical intimacy makes some Aquarian guys slightly uncomfortable. He is wary of taking the next step in dating. It's difficult to gauge whether he is scared of commitments or unsure of his own self. If you are truly interested in him, you will have to gently draw him out and talk about getting into a relationship. Otherwise your charming water bearer will keep smugly dressing up for another platonic date with you.

And now for the don'ts when dating an Aquarian guy. Don't bother to play any games. He hates deception and 'roundabout' way with words. Be as straightforward as you can and be steady on your words. He likes a woman who can hold her ground and yet be smart enough to know when to give in. He admires independence in a woman and appreciates intelligence. He won't stand on ceremony with you...so better get used to his whacky ways. If there is any pulling up of chairs or lugging shopping bags to be done, better do it yourself. I am not implying that he is ungentlemanly...it's just that he prefers women who know how to account for themselves.

Just in case things don't work out with him, here's his last rejoinder—can we at least be friends?

Compatibility quotient

The easy-going Aquarian is everybody's friend. He stresses a lot on building networks and being friendly with everyone, but when it comes to compatibility, one has to probe deeper into his psyche. What exactly does it mean for Aquarian men and women from other signs? Let's find out.

Aquarian man and...

Aries woman: 7/10. Between these two it is a wait and watch game. While each may admire the other's positive attributes, there would be small differences to contend with. But with a little bit of patience, they can hit a home run.

Taurus woman: 6/10. This relationship is somewhere in the middle. He can give her a lesson or two on how to have some fun and she can mellow down his bizarre nature. If they go slow on their innate obstinacy (both have plenty of it), theirs' can be a good combination.

Gemini woman: 8/10. Adventurous, spontaneous and non-conformist. Who am I talking about? Both. They share each other's prominent traits and therefore this relationship is likely to bring the house down!

Cancer woman: 3/10. A risky affair! Both are placed on opposite poles. He is too friendly and easy-going to fit into her intense and serious nature. And she is too emotionally dependant to meet his intellectual requirements.

Leo woman: 7/10. This relationship can be anything but boring. Filled with his unconventional behaviour and her powerful charm, their union can bring in a lot of crazy moments. But for a fruitful relationship, they would need to work hard on understanding each other.

Virgo woman: 6/10. Initial attraction and a lot of misunderstanding later—that's the briefest description of a Virgo-Aquarian combination. Things can work out between the two if they quit trying to improve the other.

Libra woman: 9/10. A match well made! There is an evenness of attributes in this case—his adventurous spirit is balanced by her practicality and her intellectual mind is balanced by his impulsiveness.

Scorpio woman: 7.5/10. A little hard work is required here. Their emotional disparity will madden them and 'might' make it difficult for them to tolerate each other. A long-term relationship may wear them thin and suck out all the charm from their stimulating conversations. If the Scorpio is or can be submissive and graceful throughout, this combo could really work well.

Sagittarius woman: 9.5/10. This one's the icing on the cake! Filled with passion, romance and limited emotions, this relationship will work wonders for both. The independent spirit in both will only bring them closer.

Capricorn woman: 7/10. A sustainable relationship that's more likely to succeed as friendship rather than a romantic affair. If these too are thrown in together over a long drawn affair, they are likely to get tired of each other.

Aquarius woman: 5/10. With his Aquarian counterpart, his relationship will be totally without ardour or depth. Since both live life on the surface, they will miss out on the deeper meaning of love and romance. Although their chemistry will be good, long-term compatibility is a question mark.

Pisces woman: 5/10. Both are too dissimilar to walk a common path. His love for adventure and fun-filled lifestyle will not go well with her serious and spiritual bent of mind. He in turn will find her too clingy and emotionally needy.

Famous Aquarian men personalities:

Abhishek Bachchan	Abraham Lincoln
Ashton Kutcher	Jackie Shroff

Aquarius woman

Isn't there something just so exquisite about the cheerful, silvery streams of champagne that pour out of a freshly uncorked bottle? There is something so alive, so vibrant about the act that it draws one's attention immediately. That's pretty much the same effect an Aquarian woman has on people when she enters a room. Full of life and bursting with energy, she infuses everyone around her with her electric presence.

She is peppy and full of laughter. One thing you can't help but notice is her incessant chatter. How this woman loves to talk! There's never a dull moment when she's around as she is constantly hopping from one topic to another, giving her opinions and passing judgments freely.

Aquarian women are by far the most forward looking tribe. They have a modern mindset and believe in living life with a meaningful purpose. The Aquarian girl has the ability to dream big and realise those dreams as well. It's game, set and match for this lady all the way!

How can you identify an Aquarius woman in a crowd?

An Aquarian woman is quite easy to spot. She is extremely chirpy and full of life. You will usually find her talking at the speed of lightening, involved in animated conversations or debates. A feminist to the core, she is a true original!

At times, an Aquarian female will come across as confused. That's because she lives in two worlds—the real world outside and the one within her head. But on the whole she possesses great personal charm.

What are the key features of her personality?

I have found Aquarian woman to be very unpredictable. She follows her own train of thoughts (when expecting her to come dressed to kill for your social do, she can throw you off balance by making an appearance in a pair of faded jeans and a worn out sweatshirt). Her active mind interweaves the past, present and future seamlessly. Possibly, these thoughts are responsible for her volatile nature as she mentally jumps from one idea to the next in split seconds or can change from practical to 'head in the clouds' in a snap.

An Aquarian female has her own set of rules, that she holds sacred. Not that she won't allow you to have your own too, but any infringement on her way of living will not be taken in good spirit. Her feminism and need for independence makes her crave for space more than any other woman.

She is highly opinionated and will hold her own no matter what. So if you are trying to impose your ideas on her, think again. She is not one to change her views under compulsion. She also hates to conform to rules, be it social norms or your personal peeves. She will always be one up on everybody.

The highlight of her nature remains her unflagging optimism. No matter whether she is mulling over the past or thinking about the future, she will be optimistic about everything.

An Aquarian female is a woman of purpose. You will see her championing social causes and lending support to the less privileged. But whatever she does is done with complete conviction and sincerity. She is idealistic to a great extent.

I have also observed that she is one of the few women who know exactly how to strike a balance between showing the right amount of authoritative and powerful nature with humility. She is also very mischievous and naughty, no matter what her age.

Flattery will help you to go a long way with her. She loves to hear herself being praised and will instantly forget all your mistakes if you give her the right compliments.

Most Aquarian women are also an incorrigible gossip mongers. These women can't hold a secret to save their life.

How is an Aquarius woman on the following aspects?

Appearance: Appearance wise Aquarian women fall into two categories: the first are those who sport a tomboyish look, from clothes to hairdos. This amounts to about 30-40 per cent of Aquarian women. The rest are very classy, detailed and extremely fashion conscious...a true emblem of femininity. But whatever the type, their dressing style is non-conventional and non-conformist in every sense. Their daring attitude is evident in the way they dress up and carry themselves.

Ambition: An Aquarian female is ambitious in two distinct ways—she is an achiever at heart and also craves for independence. So when she sets on scaling the ambition ladder, it is to reach the top position as well as attain complete freedom.

Ego/Self-respect: She has tremendous self-respect and ego. Depending on what age you meet her at, and her maturity level she will tactfully strike a balance with how much ego to show and how much to hide. Being extremely sensitive and touchy, she gets easily offended. When in such a mood, you are likely to get some crisp tit-for-tat answers from her.

Responsibility: She is responsible only to an extent and only where it is applicable. To her, responsibility is more towards her family than others. With friends and acquaintances, she needs to be in a certain comfort zone to do what's due on her part. But on the whole, she prefers to be footloose.

Etiquettes: With the tomboyish kind of Aquarian women, etiquettes hold little importance. For the more feminine kind, the sense of social etiquettes is strong and refined and they pay minute attention to grooming and manners.

What is her approach towards life?

Sub-standard living is not her cup of tea. She has keen interest in clothes, perfumes and all things nice. These comforts are necessary to make her life complete and comes from her feminine stance. Aquarian women are also less dependent on family/spouse and are capable of attaining the life they desire all by themselves.

How does an Aquarius woman score on the following aspects?

Cynicism: Usually Aquarian women get over their initial cynicism as they mature. With age they tend to grow more level headed and look at things with a much clearer perspective. Although there still would be moments of fits and tantrums, about things she must have or do and doesn't or isn't able to, the frequency goes down.

Suspicion/Jealousy: Extremely suspicious, an Aquarian woman is quite insecure at heart. She will question and cross question you till her suspicion abates, but that is no indication that she has entirely let go of her doubts.

Naturally the next step from suspicion is jealousy. Here again her insecurity clouds her perception. However, I have come across a beautiful exception here. Aquarian women who are good-looking and confident about themselves, are not easily bothered with such petty emotions.

Dishonesty/Infidelity: Dishonesty will not take her completely by surprise. Sometimes she almost senses it round the corner. However with infidelity it's a different ball game altogether. She takes this subject very seriously, given her strong feminist leanings. But very conveniently she reserves the right to have an occasional wandering eye for herself.

However, I would like to clarify one thing...an Aquarian girl will never indulge in acts of infidelity without strong reasons. And even if she lands up in a compromising situation like an extramarital affair, it won't last long. Majority of Aquarian women are highly principled and will not try anything that might bring them social disgrace.

Hardships: Used to enjoying the comforts of life, the Aquarian finds hardships rather cumbersome and annoying, and puts up with them only due to circumstances. But she is quite capable of overcoming hardships, working towards her dreams and achieving them without being dependent on others.

Success and failure: With success the picture turns rosy for the true Aquarian. The feminine kind of Aquarian woman will prefer showing off her success, rather loudly, while the rest of the water bearers will be subtle in displaying their success stories.

Like hardships, they can't handle failure well either. If met with failure, they end up blaming others. But failure cannot tie down a true Aquarian for long. She will strike back with a fresh wave of energy to prove herself. Since she is capable of emotionally detaching herself from a given situation (including break ups), she finds it easy to move on. This attitude coupled with her everlasting optimism, makes her a go-getter.

Host: I have found most Aquarian women to be graceful hosts. The feminine Aquarian will take more interest in décor than food while hosting a party. While her table will be set to perfection, the contents on it are likely to be outsourced. As a host, she is a great show off as well. The other category of tomboyish Aquarians may prefer cooking themselves but are not very elaborate as hosts.

Guest: When you have an Aquarian woman as a guest, she will run her eyes all over the place, take in the décor, table setting, food and general milieu. She is extremely formal as a guest and you will never find her arrive without gifts or a bottle of wine for the host. The catch however is...she expects the same from her guests.

How does she handle difficult situations?

Any difficult situation like a quarrel or disagreement will bring out the nag in her. She will crib endlessly and if need be will fight, moan and groan to make herself heard. In angry moments, her anger will be like a storm that lashes at everything in sight. But this storm is short-lived. With around 70 per cent of Aquarian women, this session lasts till they cool down. Once back in their element, they are able to kiss and make-up quickly. The other 30 per cent tend to hold grudges and find it difficult to let go of their egos and move on, but you will rarely find a vengeful Aquarian trying to get back at people who messed with her.

I would like to mention an interesting observation about Aquarian women and grudges. They are so devoid of resentment that they belong to the minority of people who remain on excellent terms with their ex-boyfriends and ex-husbands.

What is her characteristic weakness?

Her first characteristic weakness is that she thinks after she talks, and can land herself in trouble often.

The Aquarian woman possesses a fierce survival instinct that allows her to move on easily from a downslide in life. On the extreme side, this gives her personality a very cold and indifferent edge. Since she's not much affected by the events in other people's lives, as long as her interests are served, she does tend to be selfish more so if it means compromising on what she wants.

Though rare but when our Aquarian lady loses her cool, she can hurl spiteful remarks at her target, and be totally unrepentant of her act. With her ego in place, she would refuse to apologise, even when she knows she's in the wrong. Her false sense of ego would also not permit her to accept her ignorance and she would do whatever it takes to divert attention away from it. Only when in love she considers bending or apologising.

Is there more to this super confident woman's persona?

Her gift of gab that she possesses in abundance is actually a cover-up for lack of knowledge. She will spin instant yarns and talk nonsense with immense confidence to gloss over her ignorance.

Her need for independence also makes her self-centred. Her attitude takes an inward turn when it comes to proving her point or getting her way. I have often found Aquarian women making adjustments to suit their ambitions and not bother about those around them.

Another highlight of my observations about Aquarian women is their intuitiveness. Here is a woman who is constantly delving into the future and what it holds for her. This persistent attention is what likely sharpens her intuition.

Some Aquarian women I have met are rather low on passion. Although their commitment to their love, work or a cause would be intense, they lack the driving force. In case of love, one can conclude that passion is absent perhaps because of their feminist ideas. This may not be true for all, so you go explore your Aquarian.

An Aquarian's feminism seeps into everyday life too. For instance, she would prefer doing small things like pulling up a chair for herself at a restaurant or opening the door. This can also come from her low patience level that makes her do things herself rather than wait for someone else to do it for her.

Seven out of ten Aquarian women I know are into animal welfare. It could be looking after stray dogs and providing them with a home or helping injured or suffering animals. I love this compassionate quality in them and wish more people could think and do the same way.

How should one deal effectively with an Aquarius woman?

I believe that the most effective way of dealing with an Aquarian woman is giving her what she wants the most—space. She would appreciate your efforts at letting her be and will in return allow you to flourish in your personal space too. Show any signs of possessiveness or jealousy and you will end up talking to a wall. She abhors anyone doubting her commitment and would rather be alone than be with such a person. For the same reason, it is also advisable not to display emotions like suspicion and jealousy around this girl. She is wary of people who don't believe her or doubt her sincerity.

On the business front, an Aquarian woman cannot be trusted implicitly. She might keep you confused by agreeing to most of your ideas, but end up doing what she wants. So if you are in the midst of a business transaction with her, be on a lookout for ulterior motives.

How does she handle money matters?

Being extremely generous, she can be taken for a ride easily. A sob story from a family member or friend will quickly make her open her purse. She will take great pleasure in bailing out a friend in trouble and the loss of money will be the least of her concerns at the time. But when it comes to business, she is extremely shrewd in money matters. Only when she is thoroughly convinced will she invest in a new idea or experiment.

An Aquarian girl will always like to be known as a career woman, partly to be able to exercise her creative ability and partly for financial independence. Not one to share her bank account even with her husband, she will never ask for monetary favours from anyone. And if circumstances make her do that, be rest assured that she will spend sleepless nights till she has returned every penny she owes.

How is she on the professional front?

An Aquarius woman is responsible, responsive as well as competitive and has just the right amount of aggression to make her an achiever at work.

Given her penchant for speech and her undying curiosity, an Aquarian woman makes for a good journalist. She is an ace at Q&A's and interviews. She is also creative, which makes her do well in careers such as fashion designing and hair dressing. Also her need to be abreast with new things makes her excel in fields like advertising and public relations. Since she is a travelholic, the airline industry is another good option for her.

You may notice Aquarian women trying their hand at various professions. This stems from their need to prove themselves and also perhaps from their belief that they can do everything that a man can.

How is she in various relationship roles?

An Aquarian woman will be as friendly with you as a wife as she was as a girlfriend. Always remember she prizes friendship above all relations (she looks for the same even in her relationship with her husband or boyfriend). You will find her ready to laugh at your 'boy' jokes and accompany you on your beer bouts…just like the good ol' days of dating. And all this while she will take good care of your needs and look after your home too.

An Aquarian female makes a good wife and homemaker. She is loyal and faithful. Being full of energy, she makes for an interesting companion. There is rarely a dull moment with her around. But she will not be satisfied just within the realms of her home. Given her need for independence, she is likely to seek out a career for herself at the same time.

An Aquarian woman might find it difficult to devote her entire time and attention towards her children (just like while in love, she finds it complicated to give her time to one person only) but gradually she realises the benefits of being a responsible mother. Step-by-step she will start looking at motherhood as an extension of her femininity.

As a mother, she can be loving and caring, but she is not one to express herself by cuddling and petting her children all the time. She would prefer showing her love in more practical ways like sending them to a good school and providing for their future. She is a good teacher and a patient listener so kids find her comfortable to be around with.

But it is in the role of a friend where an Aquarian woman excels the most. She holds her select yet quirky friends very close to her heart. She is generous and free with them.

How is she when alone?

Super confident and fiercely independent, the Aquarian female enjoys her own company to the hilt. She enjoys her 'me time' and makes good use of it, taking time to relax and unwind. However, with her strong socialising nature, she mostly prefers being in the company of friends, lounging by the poolside or hosting a nice barbecue get together.

How is she when in love?

An Aquarian woman can be extremely emotional and sensitive. She is almost childish in her behaviour and can be unforgiving on silly issues. But flowers, chocolates, gifts and lot of flattery can undo everything at a speed you never could have imagined.

Although she is emotional, she is also a novice at expressing her emotions. If your love interest is an Aquarian woman, you may have to teach her to emote and show her love. Don't take her lack of expression as stiff necked pride; it's not that at all. She simply finds it difficult to put her heart out and express her love in words. She is the kind of person who will easily dismiss romantic ideas like holding hands and gazing into each other's eyes as silly, but at the same time she will walk the extra mile just to be with you...for instance cut short her meeting to keep her date with you. In spite of her confidence and independence, she is a 100 per cent woman within. She requires the warmth and comfort of a healthy relationship and the security of a dependable man.

When in love she means every word she says, and this remains true even when she falls out of love. So be prepared for her straightforwardness too. This girl doesn't believe in mincing words, if she walks up to you and says it's over, then it is 'over' and you have to behave intelligently about it.

An Aquarian woman appreciates intelligence and independence in her partner. If you are planning to propose your Aquarian girlfriend, make sure you have proved your mettle on these counts. Any hint of how much you have borrowed to buy the emerald ring in your pocket will send her flying down the road to 'Splitsville'. She also dislikes emotionally needy people. She can give you a shoulder to cry on once in a while, but don't make that a habit or she might instantly turn a cold shoulder on you.

And it is important to give her time. No Aquarian will rush into marriage. Commitment for her is for keeps and so she is likely to spend considerable time to arrive at a decision. And she won't advance a step further till you have assured her that you are her best friend. But after having committed herself, she will ensure she is the ideal wife for you. She will give as much time and effort to her relationship as possible but she finds it difficult to make her world revolve around one single being. She has a host of friends and myriad activities to fill her time. Don't be upset if your Aquarian girlfriend is not with you 24x7, for she will have you on her mind most of the time. And it will do your relationship a world of good if you respect her independence and devotion towards social causes as much.

While in a steady relationship with her (both pre-and post-marriage), don't give her any reason to doubt you. If she smells a rat it will be impossible to get her off your trail. Generally she will trust you implicitly (and that's because she has her hands full with too many activities to indulge in 'detective play' with you), but once she starts suspecting, there will be no end to her inquisitiveness.

Like the Aquarian man, the Aquarian girl too is clumsy and awkward during moments of physical intimacy. Her innate lack of emotional display is a big hurdle for her and the side-effects of this can be seen in her body language too. At such a time she needs the support of her man in terms of understanding, guidance and love.

While dating her, you should...

...never be mushy. An Aquarian girl dislikes overt display of emotions. So if you are the kind who wants to hear your girlfriend say 'I love you' everyday...steer away from an Aquarian. Like I explained before, she is emotional but isn't good at displaying her emotions. Similarly she would expect her date to be in control of his emotions too.

And don't get too possessive. Getting possessive will make her claustrophobic and she will run, far away from your presence. It is better to concentrate your energies in winning her heart rather than being her bodyguard.

If you think your first date will lead up to a 'movie on the couch at your place', you couldn't be more wrong. Like her male counterpart, an Aquarian girl likes to move at a slow and steady pace. She will examine you before dating you and completely deconstruct you in her mind before moving on to something important. If she feels you are not the one for her, you will be shown the door without much ado. She doesn't believe in wasting time, energy or emotions on something that is not likely to workout...and is also blatantly honest about it.

She is proud of her femininity but at the same time she has a strong desire to do everything herself. If you try to force down the fact that you are the one wearing the pants, she won't take it well at all. More likely she will give you a dose of 'if a man can, so can I' attitude of hers.

Also don't try to impress her with your flashy cars or Armani suits. Money is probably farthest from her mind when she is planning on dating someone. She will be suitably impressed with your display of wealth (even enjoy the associated benefits) but that is not enough to make her think of a long-term relationship. She will want more depth in her man.

The best way to getting in her good books is by being her friend—in the real sense of the term. Treat your date with her as a friendly encounter over a cappuccino and add her favourite cookies to the table. Garnish all this with interesting tête-à-tête and let her get comfortable with you. Just be yourself and love will follow in good time.

An Aquarian girl prefers a platonic relationship (at least initially) and you may feel that her passion quotient is slightly less, but she does not lack passion and it's up to you to draw her out. For her there is a thin line between love and friendship and you will have to guide her one way or the other to help her decide.

On an intellectual level, don't challenge her feminist views or argue with her over her involvement in social activities. She won't give up her true identity to be with you, and her individuality lies in her belief system, the people she befriends and the social causes she relates to.

A last word of caution—if you are serious about seeing her after your first date, you have to learn to appreciate her good qualities. She likes a man who knows the value of her as a woman. And you should be friendly enough with her to let her chatter on and man enough to know when to take matters in your hand.

Compatibility quotient

Compatibility with an Aquarian girl is more than just matching her zing factor. To be her partner, you have to understand her need for independence and her deep-rooted stand on feminism. However complicated she may appear, the mathematics of her life is quite simple...the man who wins her heart takes her home. Let's find out what is the compatibility quotient she shares with males of different signs in the zodiac.

Aquarius woman and...

Aries man: 8/10. For once the Aries man will have to let go of his position as the 'manager' of things. The Aquarius girl will know exactly how to deal with the fiery Arien. She would know how to manage his anger and ego, while he would be delighted to infuse passion in this relationship. Her independent streak is likely to floor him completely.

Taurus man: 6/10. This relationship is likely to start off well but soon after a 'war of wills' will be unavoidable. Add to that the disharmony between the conservative Taurean's view and the radical Aquarian's beliefs, and there will be constant discontent.

Gemini man: 9/10. An instant hit! The adventurous Gemini is a true match for the sociable Aquarian. Both value each other as friends and their relationship will grow from strength to strength...thanks to their love for freedom and good conversation.

Cancer man: 4/10. Long-term compatibility has slim chances of existing in this relationship. The Aquarian woman lacks the depth and heart-warming love that a Cancer man craves for.

Leo man: 5/10. A difficult yet not impossible match. Both will have to make sincere efforts to make this relationship work. In short, the Leo man will have to think a little less about himself and more about her, while the Aquarian woman will have to think a little less about the world and more about him.

Virgo man: 6/10. Once they know how to balance their outlook towards life, they can hit it off quite well. Since they have very little in common, they have to prepare a meeting ground for themselves. However, they do match up with each other on the ambition front.

Libra man: 9.5/10. A brilliant match! Their relationship will make a great start with good amounts of love and friendship. He is intellectual enough to appeal to her and she is spontaneous enough to suit him. This relationship is likely to be comfortable for both.

Scorpio man: 6/10. The Aquarian girl will find it difficult to take his bossy attitude and the Scorpio man will not find it easy to accept her outgoing ways. He is way too possessive for her comfort and this relationship is definitely not going to be an easy one for either of them.

Sagittarius man: 9/10. An excellent pair. The Sagittarian man and Aquarian woman share an unmatched understanding of each other. He is creative and she is intelligent and both are good at conversing.

Capricorn man: 7/10. This match will demand too many compromises on both ends. If he tries to dominate her too much, there may be a tug-of-war between them over authority and freedom.

Aquarius man: 8/10. Great chemistry! Since both share a lot in common, it is a match that can be an instant hit. But both will have to learn to curb their frivolous nature. Their independent outlook will help them forge a comfortable relationship.

Pisces man: 4/10. They have too many opposite traits to reach a common ground. He is too emotionally dependent, while she desires absolute freedom. He seeks a warm and understanding partner, while she is too involved with her social activities to be with him 24x7.

Famous Aquarian women personalities:

Jennifer Aniston
Paris Hilton
Shakira
Oprah Winfrey
Preity Zinta

Pisces

20 February-20 March

Pisces man

This zodiac has been assigned the sign of fish, but there is nothing 'fishy' about the Pisces man. Outgoing and easily approachable, he has all it takes to be a gentleman. The only characteristic he has akin to a fish is his love of swimming in deep waters; mystery, isolation and sympathy are dear to him.

When you meet a Pisces male recall the Piscean symbol—two fishes that are moving in opposite directions very much like the Piscean mind. This does not mean confusion; it is simply indicative of the depths to which he can go with his mysticism or the heights he can achieve with his dreams. For a Piscean male, there's nothing more real than dreams. A good listener, all in all, your Piscean friend is a wonderful companion. So with such a friend at your side, the only thing I say to you is 'happy fishing'!

How can you identify a Pisces man in a crowd?

That's a tricky one! Unless you are a part of a conversation involving a Piscean, it will be difficult to spot them in a crowd. Piscean men don't possess overt qualities that will set them apart from the milieu and if you are not keen in your observation, you are likely to miss identifying them.

When amongst people, a Pisces man can be identified from the limited hints that he drops, namely, over-friendliness and opinionated conduct. Certain emotional reactions or comments, unsolicited advice and an eagerness to comment are some of the other giveaways. But all these signs are quite subtle as he does not indulge aggressively in any of these traits. He is undoubtedly an extrovert but without being vociferous. One remarkable quality, though, that sets him apart would be his keenness to help, with advice or action, anyone and everyone around. While this doesn't make him a bad person, it can make him come across as interfering.

What are the key features of his personality?

'I dream, therefore I am.' Piscean men are a personification of Strindberg's (a Swedish playwright and writer) thoughts. Driven by ambition, the Piscean man believes in dreaming big. His being adventurous and impulsive by nature, only adds to his ambitiousness. Piscean men, with the achiever spirit, know how to welcome an opportunity when it comes knocking and how to make the most of it. Even his ambition finds roots in a desire to draw out the best from life, including materialistic pleasures. For the Piscean man, getting the much coveted home theatre system, or a fancy sports car is also a part of being successful in life.

And then there are the other kinds...the ones that simply go with the flow. What's wrong with that you might ask? Nothing! Except that if you want to realise your dreams you need to be realistic in your approach. And this type of Piscean men lack just that. Although they know how to dream, they don't know how to look beyond those dreams.

But a Piscean's ambitions do not arise out of nothing; on the contrary it's the work of a fertile mind. He is intelligent and sharp and whenever his efforts match his dreams, he is sure to pen his success story.

His easy-going and helpful nature makes it simple for him to connect with people. Additionally, he is totally non-judgmental and a good listener, qualities that are generally found to be endearing.

And if you're about to write him off as too sweet or even bland for your taste, think again, for our dear friend has a saucy side to him too. Imagine a Piscean man at an informal office party. While his colleagues are guffawing at the boss' joke, he will be merely smiling. While they are busy sneering at their competitor, he will be slurping his soup. While they are enticingly listening to the boss boasting about his foreign travels, he will be busy demolishing the food on his plate. By the end of the meal, he looks up and casually asks, 'Do you know that our company has discontinued holiday allowances? Sorry to interrupt you sir, now what was it that you saw at Athens?'

Aye, this man can sting! He looks on with a placid face as his colleagues hide their smiles behind their napkins and the boss turns a beet red. Sarcasm is not just a characteristic, but it is also a defence mechanism for the Piscean guy. He knows he won't be able to shout from rooftops and thus chooses to give it back with a few stinging remarks.

In a recent incident, a famous Hindi film actor was berated by another more popular actor in the media. Instead of calling a press conference to clarify himself, this actor simply chose to lash out with sarcasm as defence. And what did he do? He named his newly acquired dog after the popular actor. I won't divulge any names here but it didn't come as a surprise to me that this guy is a Piscean.

While a Piscean guy's humour can jump from casual to sophisticated and from simple to devilish, it is always laced with sarcasm and is very often scathing.

How is he on the following aspects?

Appearance: You will find him almost always lost in thought, with his forehead deeply creased in a frown. He dons formals only when the situation demands. Otherwise he prefers to be in casuals. Don't be surprised if you spot your Piscean colleague coming to work in jeans and tees rather too often.

Interestingly, about six out of every ten Piscean men have some sort of scars on their body. Pisceans are not usually aggressive but quite mellow, but there are around 30 per cent of them who are still mellower. Another point of distinction between these two categories would be their attitude—type A has an achiever spirit and is somewhat of a rebel, while type B likes to toe the line.

Ambition: Although he is low on aggression he ranks quite high on the ambition scale. After Capricorn males, Pisceans are the most ambitious men in the zodiac. For them it's all about pushing the limits! But there's a catch to their ambition. They are easily distracted by small events like helping a friend. A Piscean is also likely to forget or abandon his current activity if a more interesting enterprise presents itself. To achieve his goals, he needs to train himself in the art of being resolute else his ambition will remain merely wishful thinking.

Ego/Self-respect: A Piscean is not egocentric but that doesn't mean he has no ego at all. He sports selective ego—his ego is seen with certain people under certain circumstances only. He is extremely flexible in his attitude, which will largely depend on his achievements. If completely satisfied with himself, he will not feel the need to proclaim his manliness. For instance in a case where his partner earns more than him, he will not feel any complex,

A Piscean is also high on self-respect. He appreciates it when people around him realise his worth and respect him for that. Any lack of respect or insulting remarks can hurt him sorely, especially if they come from someone he loves.

Responsibility: His helpful nature makes a Piscean very dependable. His sense of responsibility, especially towards his family, makes him a good husband and father. But these very virtues tend to harm him too. He is often found making a fool of himself while trying to please everyone. And like I said before, his helpfulness sometimes is not taken in the right spirit by everyone and can land him in a soup. The flipside to his personality is his tendency to be selfish and uncaring of others (this is because his priorities in life are his ambitions and achievements).

Etiquettes: Since his attitude is very casual his manners follow suit. But that is not to say he is not well mannered. In fact a Piscean man is always courteous and polite. However, he is more comfortable in his own skin and dislikes pretensions and play-acting.

What is his approach towards life?

In two words, his mantra is ambition and adventure. For a Piscean man ambition takes precedence over all else. His ambition makes him aspire for all things good, including material pleasures. His nature is an odd mix of contradictions. Although you will find him generally satisfied with life, he will never be content with what he has achieved. For him each day comes with new challenges and aspirations. But it would be unfair to call him aggressively ambitious. Although he likes to climb the ladder of success, he is never deceitful or mean in his intentions. He would rather give up his ambition than hurt anyone deliberately. And remember the dreamer that he is! His dreams are founded on idealistic goals; that's why his ambitions are based on certain pre-defined ethics, but he is never aggressive about it either.

A Pisces male is also very adventurous at heart. There is something of a nomad in him, the unquenchable thirst of a wanderer. He is therefore given to impulsive travel plans...a knapsack, a map and our man is ready to go!

How does a Piscean score on the following points?

Cynicism: He is the least cynical of men. Unless driven by emotions or love you will find him practical and easy-going. He is also almost unbiased and tries his best to avoid passing judgment on others.

Suspicion/Jealousy: There is a thin line between suspicion and curiosity and the trouble with our Piscean male is that he seems to cross over rather too often. He is generally curious by nature and likes to know everything about everyone. This might lead to cross questioning and investigation. If he smells a rat, his curiosity may change into suspicion, otherwise he is totally trusting and does not doubt the motives or actions of others.

No man is bereft of the green ogre, the only difference being the degrees of jealousy that they feel and display. A Piscean man experiences jealousy albeit in a lesser measure. He actually rates himself above such petty emotions. But he is emotional as well as sensitive and is bound to feel jealous if his true emotions are at stake. But if he does end up feeling jealous, be sure that he will hide it well. He does not like to divulge details about himself, especially negative traits like jealousy.

Dishonesty/Infidelity: Since Piscean men are very sensitive, they find vices like infidelity intolerable. They are generally loyal and will not indulge in promiscuous relationships unless pushed beyond limits. If his partner has been licentious, the Piscean will be angry for a while and then extremely hurt.

Regarding dishonesty, Pisceans prefer to play underhand. A Piscean will tell a white lie now and then, predominantly to hide his true feelings. He doesn't like people getting privy to his life or thoughts. When in a sticky situation, to ward-off unnecessary attention, he will take the easy way out and lie about things. Also I have noticed that six out of ten Piscean men find it convenient to lie to be able get what they want from a relationship. I confronted a few I know, and asked them why they can't be forthright and honest? In their typical diplomatic style, they replied that while I am right, this route just seems more convenient.

Hardships: Difficult situations bring out the best in a Piscean. He likes challenges and has enough foresight and intuition to take hardships in his stride. His practicality teaches him that life is not a bed of roses and therefore he is prepared for every struggle. A go-getter and a hard worker, he believes in fighting till the finish.

Success and failure: When he tastes success he knows how to relish it. Although not one to publicise his success story, he is as excited as a toddler with a new plaything. He will prefer sharing his success only with his family and close friends.

When it comes to accepting defeat, the Piscean spirit takes a backseat. He finds it difficult to accept failure and you will see him cribbing about it endlessly.

Host: As a host he is graceful and detailed. You will find the Piscean personalised touch in whatever he does. For instance, he will remember which wine or cigar his friends like. Being a food critic and lover, he will take personal interest in everything related to food, from the menu to the service.

Guest: As much as he is easy-going as a host, he is also completely uncomplicated and unfussy as a guest. You will be delighted to have a Piscean as your guest as he makes himself at home and will not trouble you with unnecessary demands of attention (except maybe in case of the food or the menu).

How does he handle difficult situations?

Piscean males are hardly the quarrelsome kinds. You will rarely find them arguing aggressively or debating loudly. Given their passive nature, they make for good mediators and arbitrators. Their easy-going attitude also makes them vie for peace rather than partake in squabbles.

And if at all you manage to drag him into a quarrel, be rest assured he will be vociferous only to the point of making himself clear. After the initial outburst he will be his usual calm self again. A Piscean guy also finds it difficult to stay angry or upset for a long time. Not one to bear grudges, you will see him smiling back at you (even after the most intense of quarrels) and let me tell you...this guy knows how to smile his way into your heart.

What is his characteristic weakness?

The expression 'on one's toes' fits a Piscean male perfectly. He often finds himself overcommitted, entangled in the impossible task of pleasing everyone, running around multitasking and completing the endless number of jobs he has gotten himself. At the end of it all, he frequently ends up making a fool of himself.

What is worse, is that past mistakes can teach him nothing for he detests learning from them. In spite of his perspective nature and sixth sense, he can be easily fooled, especially with emotion steering stuff such as tears.

Don't take his casual attitude (which sometimes takes on a 'devil may care' stand) at face value; a Piscean is quite insecure at heart. This makes him easily suspicious and his possessiveness can turn his unfussy mindset into a jealous one.

Another irksome trait that a Piscean man possesses is his habit of giving evasive answers. Never will you find him giving a 'yes' or 'no' in reply to a direct question. His roundabout way of thinking leads him to evading straightforward replies. Add to it his sarcastic sense of humour, which brings up caustic punch lines, and he becomes quite a handful to deal with.

Is there more to his persona?

A Pisces male is artistic, creative and spiritual. He is highly intuitive and comes with a rather honed sixth sense, making it possible for him to see through people and it's not easy to fool him.

But he is also an emotional being and with a love for sob stories, he gets easily entrapped by tales of sorrow. He often gets misused also because of his eagerness to help people, by deed or money. This can hurt him sometimes. Given his sensitive nature, things like accusations, dishonesty, disloyalty and lack of faith don't go down well with him.

Once hurt, a Piscean needs space to make peace with matters. He uses his personal space and time to revitalise his energies and you will find him replete with enthusiasm and zeal once he is out of hibernation. He is also secretive, which is another reason for his want of space.

I have also noticed a peculiar trait in Pisces men. A Piscean has certain amount of duality in his nature but not in his personality. This duality can be interpreted as mood swings, (although it is much deeper than that). A Pisces male will be generous, sympathetic and kind most of the times, but depending on the situation he can turn selfish too. This aspect only heightens the aura of mystery that surrounds him.

How should one deal effectively with a Pisces man?

My observations have shown that there are two clearly distinct ways of dealing with Piscean men. The easy way is to take their friendliness and warmth at face value and treat them as good friends. The other and more complicated way is to first understand what they are and then deal with them accordingly.

I know I am repeating myself here, but it is necessary to reiterate that a Piscean is a man with depth. He is a reservoir of wisdom, intuition and spiritual knowledge and all this is innate. What he earns with maturity and experience, only adds to it. It is therefore important to take into account this aspect of his nature when dealing with him.

A Piscean guy loves mystery and ergo presents himself as one. He is a mystery you will have to unravel (don't worry as he will help you along) and the more you learn about him the more surprised you will be to discover his attributes. He is not an open book, so don't expect him to pour out his heart to you. The best way to know him is to befriend him and let him unveil his nature to you. Since he himself is a warm and friendly character, it is best to be the same when in his company. As suggested earlier, since he has a knack of seeing through people, it is best to avoid any pretense, especially if you are looking forward to a long lasting relationship with him. Also, keep in mind his sensitive and emotional nature when dealing with him—make use of tact and diplomacy, not to mention gentleness in manner. Any brash behaviour or loud-mouthed talks will send him scurrying for cover.

How does he handle money matters?

With utmost care! But that's just a euphemism; a Pisces male is actually quite a miser. He is extremely careful about spending money but if his emotional tide is full on, his stinginess will swing the other way. As I cited earlier, he is easily swayed by a sentimental account of events and you will see him shelling out money over a melodramatic tale.

Although he behaves like an emotional fool sometimes, he doesn't stay that way for long. Once his practicality is back, he will know exactly when and how to get his money out of you. Unless, of course, you are bankrupt!

If you want to teach a Piscean money management do it by way of example. Show him your good saving and investing skills and with time he will learn from you (the Piscean man has this incredible habit of picking-up lessons from people who touch his life). Being a fast learner, teaching him how to tackle money, is not difficult. On the flipside he takes his lessons too seriously. So if you teach him how to save for a rainy day, by the end of the year your Piscean friend may well be scraping and saving for all seasons.

How is he on the professional front?

Exactly as he is at home...dreamy, charming and easy to be with. He is hard-working but not laborious. At work, he likes to use his imagination (which he has aplenty) rather than muscles. You will find Pisceans generally involved in the entertainment industry. There is something of an actor in the Piscean guy, which when coupled with his innate creative sense, leads him into careers related to film-making.

Given his spiritual leaning and acute intuition, he tends to draw inner strength from the journeys of his mind. He is therefore likely to excel in fields that require strong intuitive powers like politics and mysticism.

But whatever career he chooses, the idealistic escapist in him will make him hunt for untroubled waters, serving his desire to live an unshackled life.

How is he in various relationship roles?

Because he wants to do everything at the same time, the male Piscean is usually overcommitted. So his relationships are rather like war zones, but that doesn't mean he knows not how to love or care.

As a son he can be independent minded and do what he wants or likes. But he is diplomatic enough to strike a balance and maintain good relations with his family. Being a team player he makes for a good sibling but only as long as his position is not threatened. If he feels insecure in any way, he will head for the nearest exit.

He is a loving and caring husband and father but here again for the shortage of time (with him) comes in the way. His commitments stop him from spending as much time with his wife and children as he wants. But he is an exceptional father (the best in fact amongst all zodiacs), who can give his children the best gift ever—imagination. His time with his children is fun-filled and although he is a good teacher, discipline is not his forte. With him around, there will never be a dearth of knowledge exchange, imaginative games and creative ideas. Since he is also a good listener, children naturally gravitate towards him with their secrets and end-of-the-day tales. With your Piscean husband around, you really don't have to bother about keeping a governess as you take your afternoon nap.

At work, a Pisces man is very easy to be with. He is authoritative only when required, and since he is easily approachable he makes for a good boss. He is also a good teacher (remember his zeal for unsolicited advice), so if your mentor at work is a Piscean, you are in for some impromptu schooling.

As a friend, he can be extremely devoted and a true blue. He will understand your struggles, be around to support you and will always have heartfelt compassion for you. And whenever help is needed, you won't have to ask twice!

How is he when alone?

He is a man who enjoys his company every now and then. I have discerned two distinct reasons behind this—ambition and compassion. On the one hand, his ambitious drive eggs him on to be alone for sometime and assess his situation. At such times, his practical mindset is at work, figuring things out and planning the next step. With compassion, he is often left drained out. Being attentive he is good listener and gets saddled with other peoples' woes and therefore needs to re-energise himself with some 'me time'. With his basic simplicity, his time alone will be spent in walking down the beach, exercising or merely having a drink with close friends.

His creative and often artistic bent of mind yearns for a personal space which is sacred to him. In that space he recreates himself and renews his steadfast hope in the goodness of life. Once his material targets are achieved, his intuitiveness will lead him towards spirituality.

How is he when in love?

If you are being pursued by a Pisces man, you will see the persuasive side of his nature in its full glory. The more you play hard to get, the more he will enjoy pursuing you. He will be all glib and slick in expressing his love and will say things a woman likes to hear.

But women who are in love with Pisces men should realise that their man has a goal-oriented mindset. Whatever his romantic dreams may be, his ambitions will always be his topmost priority (I sometimes wonder whether ambition is the right word to use for a Piscean but I am using it here for want of a better one). Actually this guy is an idealist and his dreams are his goals. He fights and works to achieve his dreams. But how well he does depends on how realistic his dreams are. If your partner is a Piscean, it will be up to you to back him in his plans. You need to be alert and clever enough to know if your man is actually stepping towards his aim or merely walking in a trance.

A Pisces man is compatible with only a select few. And if you are one of those, then you need to be emphatic or even aggressive in tone and manner to take things ahead. With his usual nonchalance and easy-going nature, he is likely to leave things hanging in the air. But once with you, and in love, he will be devoted to you. He will have a fair sense of his responsibilities towards you. He will also respect you for your intelligence and good humour. And in turn, he will expect you to respect him too. The touchy Piscean will be easily hurt if you show emotions like disrespect towards him.

Mostly, Pisces men are committed to their relationships, but men being men, some Pisceans are no different. They are quite capable of promiscuity although they will not be able to handle it if they're at the receiving end.

I recall having mentioned that he is not likely to become jealous easily, but that doesn't mean that he won't give you a reason to become jealous either. Since he has plenty of friends and given his warm and compassionate nature (as well as his curiosity) he takes special interest in them. This might give you a feel of jealousy pangs now and then, but don't doubt him unless you are very sure. Not only will you hurt him, but you will end up ruining a perfectly charming relationship.

Whilst he portrays that he is a man of the world, he is actually very conservative in thought. Hence he will look for compatibility with a woman who is a good homemaker. For him, a homemaker necessarily need not be a cook, but someone with an essence of creating a home from a house.

What does he look for in a partner?

Love is a lifetime commitment for a Piscean male. He seeks a partner who mirrors his ideals and complements his idealistic, romantic disposition, thus eliminating chances of conflict of temperament in the future.

With his dreams providing direction to his life, the Pisces man looks for a woman who not only understands and respects his aspirations in life, but also contributes towards his achieving them by being his firm emotional anchor.

To the Piscean lover, romance isn't all about physical pleasures. It's more about finding a soulmate for himself. His love transcends all levels of humanly pleasure and rests on building a special bond with his partner. He would thus, consciously and unconsciously, be attracted to women who are able to touch his soul and connect with him on a higher level.

While dating him, you should...

...be prepared to talk to a mask. For that's what a Piscean man is. He is a face with a mask; a smiling mask for sad moods, a pensive mask for playful moods and a nonchalant mask for intense moods, making him a funny mix of opposites. He will feel something and pretend to experience something else all the time. Don't think this to be confusion or lack of self-awareness; it is just his way of playing hide and seek with his emotions. He will constantly endeavour to hide them even if it means acting the exact opposite of how he feels on the inside.

Rather complicated isn't it? But once you know why he does so, it will be simple to start the dating game. A Piscean knows his sensitivity is his weakest bone and he completely avoids divulging his state of mind in order to shield himself from emotional harm. In the initial stages of dating him, you would need to get past his reserve to gauge what he really is.

But to get started, it's quite simple. A Piscean guy appreciates beauty and sophistication. Select a place that has both and get dressed in the most elegant outfit you can find in your wardrobe. He banks a lot on first impressions, so be sure you have created the right one.

The next step would be to let him know you have enough depth of character to sustain his interest. Remember he will be looking at you like a puzzle. If he is able to solve it in the first meeting, he won't be interested in having a next one. Keep him thinking, puzzled and hooked (no pun intended). He will indulge in a second date only if he thinks you are mysterious enough.

A Piscean likes intelligent conversation. He is a knowledgeable person with goodly amounts of spiritual awareness. If you too can combine these two ingredients, you can make fantastic conversation with this guy.

He is gentle and charming...and also curious. Clubbing these features together he will make all efforts to draw you out. He will ask you leading questions and probe deeper into things about you that make his interest peak. And you will talk...and how you will talk! It is impossible to be reserved with this guy. He knows exactly how to encourage someone with the right amount of persuasion.

And when you are talking about yourself, he will be all ears. He is a good listener (best of all the men on the zodiac put together) as he has immense patience and understanding and most importantly an earnest desire to hear you out. You will find him compassionate and sympathetic too.

But when it comes to talking about himself, it's a totally different ball game. Remember how secretive he is! He will rarely divulge details about himself. He will not even hesitate in telling a white lie to thwart any further investigation from you. You will never find him opening up, especially on first dates.

However, this doesn't mean he is not romantic or emotional. Rather he is spilling over with such emotions. You will have a ball of a time with him basking in the light of his romance, feeling the prick of tears in your eyes at the sight of his deep emotions and laughing your heart out at his wisecracks. Dating him will be as much fun as you can possibly imagine. But there will be a certain part of his personality that you will be unaware of...a part which he won't make evident unless he is doubly sure of your relationship with him.

Given his sensitive and emotional nature, a sensible woman can make a world of a difference to his love life. So if you are dating a Piscean, go ahead with it only if you are sure you can handle the responsibility of standing up for your man and believing in his dreams.

A word of caution here...while dating Pisceans, don't gossip about your romantic moments or after-date escapades with your girlfriends. If your Piscean boyfriend gets a whiff of it, he will be swishing his tail in displeasure. A Piscean male guards his romantic life a la Cerberus. Whatever happens between the two of you is too precious to him to be gossiped about.

Compatibility quotient

Relationships between people work on different levels. Compatibility cannot be measured and no alliance can be completely written-off. Given the exceptions and aggressive-passive ratio amongst people of different zodiac signs, I have made an attempt at summarising the compatibility quotient between Pisces men and women of various signs.

Pisces man and...

Aries woman: 3/10. The Aries woman is too self-absorbed to understand the needs of a Pisces man. Such a relationship can work out only if the Aries female shows patience, understanding and gentleness.

Taurus woman: 6/10. With a Taurean, the relationship will be harmonious as both are easy-going and dependable.

Gemini woman: 5/10. This combination might result in clashes as there is likely to be a battle between the Gemini's pragmatism and the Piscean wistfulness.

Cancer woman: 8/10. A relationship between a Piscean guy and a Cancer girl is likely to work out, given their emotional, sensitive and sympathetic nature, with a soft corner for filial ties.

Leo woman: 4/10. This is a case of opposites attract and both will need to make many adjustments to make this relationship work.

Virgo woman: 6/10. Again opposite forces are at work, but there are no conflicts involved.

Libra woman: 4/10. Although they share a lot in common, the essential nature of both the signs is quite paradoxical.

Scorpio woman: 8/10. Here there is a right balance between similarities and dissimilarities and therefore the compatibility amongst these two signs is strong.

Sagittarius woman: 4/10. The fundamental features of these two signs are quite different with Sagittarians being very straightforward and Pisceans being subtle, making it a difficult relationship that will need lots of efforts.

Capricorn woman: 7/10. There is a certain level of harmony between these signs as both are emotional, intuitive and introspective.

Aquarius woman: 4/10. The passive Piscean can never match the ardour of the exuberant Aquarian. Moreover, Aquarians are more practical than emotional, something that just doesn't gel with the Piscean nature.

Pisces woman: 9/10. One couldn't ask for a better match! The Pisces man and woman get along really well with each other, complementing each other's sensitivity.

Famous Pisces men personalities:

Aamir Khan
Edward Kennedy
Zakir Hussain
Bruce Willis
George Washington

Pisces woman

Ever met a woman who looks at you with eyes that search your very soul? And when she looks away, you can make out that she's glancing around the room, looking for Mr Perfect? She could well be a Pisces woman. Always on the look out for something, Piscean females constantly have a 'I'm looking for someone or something' gaze in their deep-pocket eyes. The zodiac has been assigned the sign of fishes. There is a 'possibility' that there is something fishy about one out of every three Piscean women.

A heart filled with desires and eyes that yearn for their fulfilment, a Pisces woman goes much deeper than her appearance. Although the term 'ulterior motive' has a negative edge to it, it fits her aptly. Her motive is not necessarily bad but she is always looking for its completion.

Piscean women can be equally divided into two camps. Firstly, the ones with hearts overflowing with materialistic desires and secondly, the ones who are soul searching or looking for soulmates.

How can you identify a Piscean woman in a crowd?

Ever seen those delicately designed crystal figures at display windows throwing a spectrum of light? That's how a Piscean will appear at first glance to an onlooker—as if she is made of glass. She will seem as fragile and brittle as crystal, not to mention as exclusive and expensive too.

In a social setting it is not difficult to spot her. If you are fairly observant, you will notice a Piscean woman to be totally feminine; she will laugh gracefully at the loudest of wisecracks, she will hold her drink with delicacy and eat with the propriety of British royalty.

And if you still can't make-up your mind if the girl next to you is a Piscean or not, just wait till you are invited to take your seat at the dinner table. If she waits for you to pull up her chair, be rest assured she is a Piscean. The true lady will always expect men around her to behave in the most gentlemanly way possible.

With conversations, she will let other members of the group (especially males) dominate the discussion. While she will not shy away from voicing her opinion, she will be more comfortable listening to others. But whether she is speaking her mind or lending an eager ear to others, she will do so with utmost elegance and grace.

What are the key features of her personality?

The materialistic kind of Piscean woman is aggressive albeit gracefully. She is caring and loving although a little sly. She is extremely impulsive, but her impulsiveness is governed by self-made standards. And she upholds these criteria with utmost tenacity. She is so focused on attaining her goals that she is likely to risk or entirely give up a relationship if someone more powerful, richer or charming comes along. To put it differently, she understands her materialistic desires and knows how to get her priorities right. She's not one to back a loser, no matter how much love is lost in the process.

The other kind of Piscean female is looking for compatibility rather than material comfort. Not to say that she is above material desires, but her ultimate aim is to be with someone whom she can call a soulmate. This kind is more emotional and submissive.

There's something Barbie-like about her, endearing, naughty yet elegant. She can carry off even a regular outfit like a pair of blue jeans and white tees with finesse. Given her passion for dressing up, she can be a big tease too. And this holds true for both kinds of Piscean women.

I have often found her an odd mix of modern and traditional. While she may be dressed in the latest fad doing the rounds of her college campus, she will appear extremely withdrawn when it comes to talking with strangers. There is a certain vulnerability about her, which makes her attractive as well as mysterious. If you are a protective and caring kind of a man, she's the woman for you.

Her mind at times works like the two fishes in her zodiac symbol. You can't make out at a glance which way she's headed. She can talk of the past and future in one breath and be equally emphatic about both. This is one reason why she is able to adjust herself with different people and situations.

How is she on the following aspects?

Appearance: Here's one woman who knows how to dress, nay, dares to dress as she likes. Both kinds of Piscean women are always well dressed in an utmost feminine manner. She'll be as comfortable in flowing dresses as in skimpy outfits and will have no qualms about a little cleavage display or wearing a bare back style top. In her private space, she is more likely to be in the flimsiest of lingerie. Some have a prominent jawline, while some have a fuller face (could be because of her obsession for chocolates and pastries).

Ambition: A good number of Piscean women are overly ambitious. This tendency may arise from their love for materialistic pleasures or an urge to create their mark. Their determination to achieve their ambition is not just steady but downright tenacious. A determined Piscean woman will work relentlessly towards her goal; she is not one to shy away from hard work. But such stubborn resolve can make her take alternative paths too…like marrying a rich man.

One way she takes to achieve this is by meeting the right people at the right time. She has no misgivings about 'using' people to forward her cause. But then again, all of them are not like this!

There are Piscean women who are not that ambitious. This is the emotional kind who is content with her life and falls beautifully in her role as a homemaker. Since she is also sensitive, she is likely to follow creative pursuits such as pottery and fashion designing, (but this is no comment on her ability to make a career for herself; she is competitive enough to be successful in professional circles).

Respect/Ego: Piscean women, both kinds, have an innate sense of pride. This will be reflected in her demeanour and her facial features (usually quite beautiful). Mostly you'll find her to be well groomed and well poised on all occasions. I have seen Piscean girls learning to carry themselves with grace from an early age and thereby commanding respect from others. But don't let her behaviour make you believe she has no ego. She can be full of it with people she wants to keep at bay. Since she is moody, her ego moves alongside her moods.

Responsibility: A Piscean woman scores low on this count to begin with, but as she grows, her sense of responsibility increases. But you cannot depend on this. Since she is impulsive and adventurous, she can conveniently let go of her duties as and when she pleases.

Etiquettes: A Piscean woman is a true lady. She effortlessly bags a nine on a scale of ten for etiquettes. Her social etiquettes are displayed at best when as a host, wherein she is both gracious and graceful. She is detailed in her planning and execution of every aspect of playing the perfect host.

What is her approach towards life?

The Piscean female is a blend of feelings and emotions ranging from being over sensitive to metamorphosing into a goal-crazed woman! Her attitude in life is driven by her state of heart and mind. Unwavering dedication and perseverance are critical to her cause and she works relentlessly towards achieving what she sets her heart on, sacrificing anything that she feels is redundant or a blockade of sorts.

Somewhat of a dreamer, the Piscean woman is successfully able to convert all her dreams into reality with the aid of her steadfast will power and cunning.

How does she score on the following points?

Cynicism: The majority of Piscean females are whacky and are governed by their current emotions. Whichever way her mood swings, her thoughts go. When not in her element, she can remain brooding over things for long. I may as well call this trait cynicism rather than sensitivity.

Suspicion/Jealousy: Her cynicism will take her to the next step, that of suspicion. Most Piscean women tend to be generally suspicious, while the rest can also be, if given appropriate reason. However, once she grows suspicious, the Piscean will go to the length of stalking or following her man to confirm her suspicions. Like with her ambition, she is relentless here too.

Jealousy too is an overpowering emotion with Piscean women. Almost all of them are prone to this emotion, but they know where to draw a line.

Dishonesty/Infidelity: Most Piscean women can take dishonesty or infidelity a little calmly. Their show of tolerance is not surprising as they themselves are not above fantasising about such digressions.

Hardships: Desiring prosperity, a Piscean woman, especially the materialistic kind, finds it difficult to face hard times. One reason could be that after overcoming her ordeals, even if she emerges a winner, she gets emotionally drained. In the long run, this will make her become more and more dependent on her husband/partner and family.

The emotional kind can carry herself off a bit more gracefully during trying times.

Success and failure: The worldly type of Piscean woman will do almost anything for success. She is relentless in her search for success, irrespective of what means she uses to achieve it. And by success I mean name, fame and money (and all the things money can buy!).

The passive kind knows how to deal with success and likes to share it with her family and close friends.

When it comes to failure, the Piscean lady ceases to be a lady in the real sense. She will rave and rant about it, blame everybody under the sun but herself and crib her heart out until she wins.

Guest: As she is extremely fond of good food, the first thing to ensure if you have a Piscean guest over is the menu. She likes appeasing her palate so you better have a multi-cuisine menu and a well-stocked bar when she's coming over.

Host: The Pisces woman is a gracious host. She is detailed and would take interest in knowing your likes and dislikes on cuisine before you arrive. She is extremely warm and affectionate as a host and makes every guest feel at home with her warm smile and hospitality.

How does she handle difficult situations?

If there is one thing that a Pisces woman dreads...it's conflict! Though she somehow often finds herself in sticky situations, Pisces women avoid confrontation of any kind. If pushed and shoved into messy circumstances, she will either try to work her way out through sweet talk or take on a belligerent, stubborn stance, (but only in the rarest of rare situations will you see her seething with rage or spewing expletives).

What is her characteristic weakness?

Surely her emotional nature. She is extremely touchy and could break into sobs at the slightest of insults or even prolonged jokes.

The Piscean woman is known for her sympathetic nature, an attribute that often burdens her by the worries plaguing others around her. Stressed out by unpleasant events, this sign is vulnerable to succumbing to addictions in an attempt to drown negative thoughts.

Is there more to this sensitive lady's persona?

If you admire femininity in women, this lady is the perfect example of it and a glamorous one at that. A Piscean woman has a charming personality. She knows how to entice her man. Mostly her charms are matched with her looks, which make her quite attractive. And her excellent dressing sense is nothing short of icing on the cake.

It's because of her ultra-feminine nature that she seeks a strong man, both in physical strength and mental abilities. She needs a man who can stand by her in difficult times and give her a shoulder to lean on when she feels like crying. Though not weak, the Piscean girl needs constant reassurances from a stronger personality.

There is absolutely nothing manlike about her and hence tomboyish Pisceans are a rarity. She is even tempered and good natured when at her best. However, like everyone else she has her black moods too. When angry she can be quite the nag and shower a series of acrid words on her offender. But whichever mood she is in...she is undeniably 'womanly' about it.

Piscean females mature at an early age. I have seen them show a strong sense of what they want, almost to the extent of keeping a wish list handy. However, both kinds of Pisceans, be it the materialistic minded or the spiritually inclined, are effectively subtle in their approach. They will take every step, every decision with a slow and steady mind. Whether it is love, money or work, they won't budge an inch till they are completely sure of themselves.

Another important feature of the Piscean nature is the ability to conceal emotions. Being emotional and hypersensitive, a Piscean instinctively knows how vulnerable she is. She is also scared of being ridiculed by others, who do not understand or value her emotions. To combat these fears, she dons a mask of inscrutability. She believes camouflaging her emotions is her only defence against the insensitive world. In a bid to hide her true feelings, she is likely to indulge in small harmless lies or evasiveness.

But I have to clarify that a Piscean woman is never consciously mean or bitter. She is always subtle and tactful, in fact with tact bordering on deception. Her deception however should not be taken in a negative way as with her it's only a mechanism for protecting her sensitivity. Her emotions lie very close to the surface and she is likely to cry at the drop of a hat!

And this is where you need to have your antennae up. If a Piscean woman can cry easily, she can also use her tears as a weapon. Her sensitivity is a double-edged sword and can swing either ways...in favour of or against her! Her psyche often works like a pendulum, swinging between the two extremes of materialism and mysticism. Because of this her mind tends to wander easily.

Although she is ambitious, some Pisceans lack the right amount of self-confidence. This too makes her dependent on others. Her self-belief is at times so low, you might have to fish her out of her diffidence. She needs someone around her to appreciate her qualities and talents.

A Piscean woman shares quite a few things with her male counterpart ...namely compassion, high emotional quotient and spirituality. Like a Pisces male, the female too feels deep compassion for others and hence is a good listener. If you are in trouble you can trust your Piscean friend to support you and help you look for solutions.

Since she is emotionally charged, she draws a lot of energy from her emotions. Like her counterpart she has oceans of energy within and all she needs to do is dive within to rejuvenate herself. Hence the essential 'my time' is close to her heart.

She is something of a spiritualist. Although she may get lost in the sea of 'real' life, she is sure to find her way out and discover mysticism within. Her compassion and spiritualism often lead her to perform acts of charity.

A Piscean woman's sixth sense is as sharp as a Piscean man's. If she listens carefully to her intuition, she can make for a good crystal ball reader. But unfortunately her sixth sense does not help her in choosing the correct life partner because she just focuses on tallying her needs versus what the guy is made of, and if all tallies she just goes for it.

How should one deal effectively with her?

If you are up against the overly and overtly ambitious kind, she will be filled with eagerness to know everything about you from which car you own to what kind of bank balance you have albeit in a subtle way. Her material streak will stop her from looking beyond the surface. The emotional Piscean would prefer less pretentious and straightforward people around her and will easily gel with people whom she finds hard-working and sincere.

If you are in love with a Piscean girl, make sure you hold her close to you. Not only does she need your emotional support but also needs a watchful eye overseeing her wandering heart.

Given her strong instincts and intuitive sense, a Piscean girl understands the art of wordless communication more than the verbal one. She prefers gestures, smiles, nods and a cuddly hug to verbose conversations. She's quite a master at understanding body language so when you are with her, keep your body movements in check. She will see through you much easily and much faster than you can imagine.

The best way to deal with her is to understand her emotional needs, take care of her sensitivity and give her ample personal time to rejuvenate herself.

How does she handle money matters?

I have seen both kinds of Piscean females to be extremely compassionate and hence they find it difficult to argue over money. Discussing or fighting for money isn't her strong point exactly. Being emotional she is likely to be submissive about money and give in easily to a more aggressive debater. She is also bad at saving money and will have to be convinced to do so.

She makes no qualms about spending on luxuries for herself since she is very aware of her own needs. She is also generous with her friends. This is another reason why she finds it difficult to think about the inevitable rainy day. But you will rarely find a Piscean woman who's broke as she has secret ways of sourcing money and keeping her head above water.

How is she on the professional front?

At work, she is extremely competitive, dedicated, sincere and goal-oriented. You will find her passionate about what she does and she will infuse her work with creativity and innovation. Her efficiency also makes her totally dependable.

As far as achieving her goals is concerned, some Piscean women will gladly trample over even a close confidante if it means inching closer to her final target.

How is she in various relationship roles?

A Piscean female can be an extremely devoted wife or girlfriend. But given her emotional temperament, she can get easily swayed and tempted into doing an occasional adventurous or crazy thing.

But she will make her man feel wanted and adored. You will never lack appreciation after marrying a Piscean girl. The best part about her is that although she is feminine she is not a feminist, at least not in terms of trying to 'wear the pants' at home. She will let her man be in charge, while she goes about creating a wonderful house for him and the family. And the best way to keep up her spirit is by being gallant towards her. Remember she married you because you are protective and caring and also gentlemanly. Don't disillusion her on this front, and you will have the most charming and docile wife.

She is an equally efficient mother who likes to pamper her children. So teaching discipline is something that's out of her range.

Friendship is a word she loves. A Piscean woman holds her friends very close to her heart. Being a good listener and a sympathetic person, she easily identifies with the deep emotions of her friends. But being a family person you are likely to find her best friends to her siblings or cousins.

How is she when alone?

Though she may end up spending a lot of alone time, the Piscean woman craves company, especially when in love. When in a relationship, she seeks out quality time with her partner, though she won't state it openly.

Left to herself, she would probably utilise her time reading books, indulging in some creative activity or just sitting and dreaming about what more she could accomplish and add that to her list.

How is a Piscean woman in love?

Having said everything about her desires for materialistic fulfilment, I would like to add that a Piscean woman is a romantic at heart. She wants a man who can love and cherish her and most importantly protect her. This is true of the emotional kind of Pisceans, who are generally afraid of being hurt by others.

She likes love to grow upon her…her idea of romance is a gradual progress of things. Make sure your courtship period is as per her standards or she will turn on her heel and disappear. Another reason for this is her innate shyness about love.

When you whisper sweet nothings into her ears, while wooing her for love, make sure you mean every word you say. Merely quoting Shakespeare really ain't going to help! A Piscean woman has the ability to see through deceit and fake charms.

Since she is totally feminine and emotionally dependent on her man, she makes him feel important (an ego uplift undoubtedly!). The warmth and dependability of her personality will ensure that she is at your side, through all times good and bad. But these traits are seen only in the sensitive kind of Pisceans. With the other kind, a relationship has to be a fine balance of love and material pleasure.

Don't be surprised if you see a change in her attitude post the transition from being a girlfriend to being a wife. Although she will retain her charm, she will show what a nag she is every now and then. When angry her words are laced with heavy sarcasm.

I would also like to add that she is not the kind to dominate her man. Nor does she like being dominated. The easiest way to deal with her is to reason with her with utmost subtlety. And be sure it will work like magic!

If you are truly in love with a Piscean girl, you may have to penetrate the few masks that she wears to cover her inner self. Especially in case of the materialistic kind, you will find her being a hard core feminist, independent and career-minded. However, she is not all that strong. That's just a façade to fool you and protect her vulnerability. Once she is convinced of you and your love, she will open up and show her femininity in its true colours. Just get this straight…a Piscean girl will hide from you her emotions, her sensitivity, her femininity and her vulnerability to avoid being ridiculed or hurt. Prove your love and understanding for her and she will blossom in your arms like a violet...tender yet endearing.

And always remember...a Piscean girl is first and foremost a romantic at heart. Everything else is just by the way.

What does she look for in her partner?

Being extremely sensitive herself, the Piscean woman seeks a partner who reciprocates in the same way...in a gentle manner, but with complete abandon. She yearns for a man who understands her emotional needs above all else and at the same time take care of all her material needs too.

Being aggressive achievers, most Piscean women would settle for men who are already well established and financially stable.

While dating her, you should...

...be extremely slow and steady and caring and understanding and sophisticated. And that's just for starters. A Piscean girl will expect the world from you while dating. Not only in terms of money spent, but the way you deal with her when it comes to dating will decide the fate of your relationship.

Let's begin with the first step. I am yet to meet a Piscean who agreed to date a man after the very first encounter with him. Love at first sight is not for her. Infatuation maybe but love...nah! She will take each day as it comes and will proceed in a gradual way towards love. Ever cautious and secretive, she will take you completely by surprise when she agrees to date you.

You will have to be at your elegant best to impress her on your date. Remember how fashion conscious she is about clothes and accessories? Add to that her penchant for gentlemanly behaviour. All these attributes have to clearly reflect in your behaviour while dating her. Piscean girls also appreciate good humour. They are ready for a good hearted laugh anytime.

You should also be considerate towards her feelings and show a deeper sense of understanding. Since a Piscean is fragile in her sensibilities, it is important to be attentive to her needs. Don't probe too much into her private life or inner thoughts. She dislikes unwanted intrusion upon her privacy. She will open up to you once she is totally convinced. But whatever you do, be subtle. She will enjoy all those rides in your flashy car but the first instance she hears you boasting of its price, she might be walking out on you.

Make a seamless transition from friendship to dating and from dating to courtship. She would enjoy being cajoled and courted. Dating has to be a gradual process...one in which you both could get to know each other. And she will cherish the intimacy that follows for her entire lifetime.

If you are planning on buying her gifts for a date, stick to the regular girlie stuff. She loves clothes, accessories, poetry books and music CDs. The fine print here is...the more expensive the gifts are, the more impressed she could be.

And while you are making all these adjustments to suit Miss Pisces, what should you expect from her? Loads! Lots of womanly charm, affection, warmth and above all...genuine friendship. Your Piscean date will be your best possible friend once you hit it off with her. She will also let you lead the way with everything...right from deciding what to order at a restaurant to your wedding preparations. She's a complete woman—one that every man dreams of.

Let me put 'what's in it for you?' in a nutshell...when a Piscean woman starts conversing, you will find yourself unwinding and relaxing under her gentle influence. Could you ask for more?

Compatibility quotient:

Here's a brief summary of the compatibility ratio between Pisces women and men of the other zodiac signs. Given the two kinds of Pisces women (as well as two kinds of men under the other signs), these observations are subjective. While there might be exceptions, the compatibility quotient mentioned here is by and large applicable to all.

Pisces woman and...

Aries man: 7/10. With Aries men and Pisces women it's rather hard to say which way the relationship will go. It all depends on the Arien's capacity to be subtle and give her space and the Piscean's ability to cope with his dominance. On the romance and passion front they may score a nine on ten as they are a perfect match. On general compatibility they can either be a good match or a disaster because of their egos.

Taurus man: 9/10. This combination can hit the bull's eye. The Piscean vulnerability and volatility will be balanced by the Taurean practicality and steadfastness. The Taurus man can be quite a charmer and a romantic and that can keep them glued forever.

Gemini man: 4/10. Both of them would need to be madly in love and eager to adjust in order to make this relationship work. The Gemini's penchant for change will keep the Piscean on edge, while his emotional fickleness can play havoc on her sensibility.

Cancer man: 9/10. A romantic alliance, the Cancer man will be able to fulfill the Piscean's need for ever lasting love. He has the capacity to shower her with care, attention and understanding, while the Piscean can be her true romantic self with a Cancer male. All in all, great chemistry!

Leo man: 8/10. The Piscean is the necessary feminine presence in the lion's life. She would give him a good home and he will be allowed to rule it as he pleases. If he's able to keep his anger and unruly tongue in check, this duo can go places.

Virgo man: 6/10. The barely-emotional and self-centred Virgo man is a complete mismatch for the sensitive Piscean. She will never be able to accept and cope up with his neglectful attitude and any relationship between these two is likely to result in a disaster unless the Virgo male is more grounded in terms of relationship management and also happens to be a romantic.

Libra man: 6/10. This may seem a great combination to begin with, but once the romance wears out the relationship will prove to be very demanding. Both of them would need to look beyond their selves to make their love long lasting.

Scorpio man: 9/10. Bring it on! A Scorpio man can strike an instant bond with a Piscean girl. Both are capable of meeting each other on the same emotional level. Of course the Scorpion will have to keep his possessiveness in check. Apart from that everything will be hunky dory in this relationship.

Sagittarius man: 5/10. Not easy, not comfortable, not possible! This is how either of them would react if the relationship is stretched too long. Although they may hit off on the first date, the chasm between dreamland (Pisces) and reality (Sagittarius) is too gaping to be ignored. But the, practical, easy-going and submissive Pisces woman might score higher (8/10).

Capricorn man: 9/10. Almost felt like giving a 10 here! This is a perfect recipe for a long lasting relationship. He is *the* man for her...strong, capable and caring, while she is *the* woman for him—one who lets him dominate. If he keeps his flirtatiousness under control, this relationship is for keeps.

Aquarius man: 5/10. Here again is a case of opposites. Although opposites attract, they seldom stick together for long. His thinking mind will find her an emotional muddle and her femininity will be crushed under his grossly liberal thinking.

Pisces man: 9/10. Since both the Pisces man and woman have so much in common, they make for a great match. Of course the catch here is that they will have to combat their weaknesses to make their relationship a success.

Famous Pisces women personalities:

Cindy Crawford
Elizabeth Taylor
Sharon Stone
Drew Barrymore
Eva Mendes

Aries

21 March-19 April

Aries Man

King James I once said, 'I can make a lord, but only God can make a gentleman.' Well thankfully, God did His bit in blessing us with the quintessential gentleman—the Aries man! Charming, attractive, energetic, humourous and above all chivalrous, the Arien male is the amalgamation of all things good.

A man of action, he makes his presence felt just by his very existence! At a party you can spot him behind the bar mixing drinks or at a night club he will be the one bullying the DJ to play his favourite tracks. But wherever he is, you can see people around naturally gravitating towards his charming persona.

Arien men can be categorised in two sets, broadly—the aggressive and the passive kinds. While the aggressive kinds have the majority stake, almost 80 per cent, the passive types are usually quiet, observant and speak only when spoken to, but if the topic interests them, they too make good conversationalists. And within the 80 per cent there are some who have a dark side to them. While they may show benevolent traits like compassion at times but they are mostly self-centred. I have encountered such Arien men and for the record, most of the above and what is written ahead does not hold true for them.

How can you identify an Aries man in a crowd?

Arien men are usually bursting at the seams with unbounded energy. This energy stems from their ever-flowing ideas and creativity. So that charming guy you spot having an animated conversation with someone or interacting with a group of people is possibly an Arien. And what will make him stand apart from others would be his sparkling demeanour.

A typical Arien will make himself comfortable in any surrounding. When in his true element, he can discuss even rocket science with easy grace. But when out of sorts, he is likely to recoil into a shell.

If he takes a fancy to you, an Arien man will be quick to take you under his wing and you will find yourself on a joyride with a dynamo. He is the one with quick actions and with a quicker mental process to match.

What are the key features of his personality?

The personality of an Arien can be defined in one word—passion. He is passionate about everything in life...from his first job to his golden jubilee wedding anniversary. You will never see him being lax about anything.

However he is rather low on patience. He cannot stand procrastination or half-baked jobs. So if you have to keep up with him, you better sprint. An Arien man is bold, confident and dead sure of himself and that includes his way with words.

But perhaps the most distinguishing characteristic of an Aries male is his dominating nature. Even the small percentage of passive Ariens is not completely bereft of this trait. For him dominance is a term that comprises absolute control, total mastery and often dictatorial attitude. There is something 'Herr Hitler-like' about his mindset, which coupled with cynicism makes a rather overpowering personality.

Obviously the next trait he has or rather what every Arien wishes to have is power. No man understands the importance of power more than the Arien male. He has the ability to use power effectively but has enough integrity not to abuse it either. However, there are exceptions too who prove that power corrupts and absolute power corrupts absolutely. Their inclination to be dictatorial often gives rise to superiority complex, arrogance and vanity.

'If you can't emote, you are probably a veggie.' This is an axiom Ariens implicitly believe in as they are highly emotional and expressive people. An Arien man does not shy away from showing his emotions. Any emotional drama is likely to have a cathartic effect on him and he believes that crying is a good outlet. So while watching a touching/emotional movie a box of tissues will come handy.

How is he on the following aspects?

Appearance: If you understand body language, then spotting an Arien will be easy for you. An Arien man sports a strong jawline and has fiery eyes. These features foretell his dominating and energetic nature. His egocentric attitude is also evident from his ramrod straight posture and confident gait.

The most striking thing about him though would be his stylish attire. Ariens are notorious for their fashion fervour. They are not afraid to experiment with different styles—be it their dress or looks. From goatees to clean cuts and from long tresses to going completely bald...they would try everything under the sun. This characteristic arises from their contempt for everyday things...they are always on a lookout for new stuff.

Ambition: Know anyone who is scaling the ambition ladder at breakneck speed? Check out his sun sign, it's probably an Arien. All Ariens are go-getters. Employee or entrepreneur, no matter what, he will show an extremely sharp mind that is bent on achieving success. With his natural leadership qualities, he finds it easy to take decisions and forge ahead of others.

He is also creative in his work. With his innate sense of daring, an Aries man is likely to choose the path less trodden and experiment with unheard of ideas. He will dive headlong into any challenge irrespective of gains. If not profits, his shrewd business sense will help him to strike a break even at least. This makes Arien men smart business people. I have also observed that in spite of successful jobs, most Arien men will steer towards entrepreneurship. Their ambition, astute business sense, leadership quality and daring nature are all conducive to entrepreneurial success. This maybe because he prefers his independence in decision-making and needs complete control and throttle.

Ego/Self-respect: Arien men are egoistic...but this blanket statement doesn't convey the real side of an Arien. More than being egoistic he is egocentric. He puts himself before everyone else. His self is his priority, everything else comes later. He is totally aware of himself and ensures that those around him also sit-up and take notice. Consciousness of his self makes him put his needs and wants above everybody else's, but at the same time he also possesses immense humility. He displays his ego only when rubbed the wrong way.

His egoistic outbursts are generally in reaction to an action, which to him makes logical sense.

Although he is self-centred, he is not selfish. You will find him generous and loving towards his dear ones, (but this is somewhat conditional). It follows only if he himself is properly looked after.

Responsibility: If you are a parent-to-be, an Arien boy is what you would wish for. His sense of responsibility at an early age is every parent's dream come true. For example, as a son he will be aware of the efforts put in by his father raising the family and his mother's struggles as a homemaker. With aptitude for independence and the constant hurry they prod themselves into, you will find most Arien men starting early when it comes to earning their living.

Etiquettes: To him, etiquettes top the list of social expectations. With his meticulous nature and eye for detail, he expects everyone around him to behave as gracefully as he does.

Given that he is a stickler for manners, he is also extremely chivalrous. He knows how to make women comfortable with his kindness (all real, nothing fake). He is also known to show utmost respect to elders and to those who are in the service industry, such as the waiters at a restaurant or staff at a hotel.

What is his approach towards life?

The Arien man is a born optimist. Failures and disappointments can never shake his belief in the goodness of life. He would treat his downfalls as stepping stones to learning the ways of the world and work on improving himself to give it another shot.

He is as ambitious as it gets and believes in fighting for what he rightly deserves. Not one to give up easily, you'll find him toiling away and putting in earnest efforts if it means providing a better and more comfortable life to his loved ones.

How does he score on the following points?

Cynicism: Ariens are born leaders, but their leadership comes with the rider of dictatorship and probably that's why his attitude takes a cynical turn. I believe cynicism is not necessarily a poor quality. After all it was only when Mahatma Gandhi got completely cynical about freedom that we got rid of the colonial rule. What would be unacceptable though is to go the Hitler way.

With an Arien, his cynicism makes him want to get things done completely his way. He is forging ahead at breakneck speed like a motorboat whizzing on the surf. Rafts and paddle boats better make way! He has no patience for drones. When he is in such a mood it is best to stay out of his way. If you wish to intervene, make it subtle. He is most likely to think over your point when in a calmer state of mind and if your idea or suggestion is good he will be sincere enough in accepting it and giving you the due credit.

Suspicion/Jealousy: Ariens are generally suspicious by nature. Although the Arien man tends to be very trusting his intuitive temperament makes him equally wary. He is always on his guard and prefers people who manage to win his trust rather than the ones who expect it of him. His suspicious nature is however wholly unmixed with curiosity. He likes to talk, but is not curious about things such as someone's personal life.

Let's move on to his next high strung emotion...jealousy. If there is a demon called jealousy, our man has swallowed it whole. On a scale of one to ten, I would give the Arien man a nine on jealousy. His jealousy stems from his extremely possessive nature. He allows no room for temptations. While dating an Aries man, his jealous disposition is a warning signal that will constantly keep you on a high alert.

But don't be afraid of this. It is just his additional way of saying he loves and cares. Jealousy is more often than not, a by-product of love. When in love the Aries man is totally involved. He loves the very idea of romance and will seek to make his affair for his lady love picture perfect. He will amaze you with his energy and drive, and you will enjoy every bit of his wooing. But all fun comes with a tag and in this case it is extreme possessiveness. If you are looking for space, you are with the wrong guy.

Dishonesty/Infidelity: Dishonesty and infidelity are touchy issues with an Arien man. He is capable of both and is also forgiving if he sees these vices around him...that is in someone other than his own partner. However, once he finds true love his attitude will have a roundabout change and he will never be dishonest or promiscuous; he will remain totally committed, unless of course the romance/passion dies and cannot be revived.

Hardships: Before delving further into this, I would like to repeat that an Arien is a go-getter. When bogged down by difficulties, he bounces back with vigour and sets out to get what he wants. He takes hardships in his stride and prefers learning from his mistakes.

Success and failure: Like failure he takes success too in a philosophical way. Because he is a mix of tremendous pride and humility, you will rarely find him discussing or publicising success. He would prefer getting a genuine compliment or simply an acknowledgment of his work instead of public adulation.

I believe no one takes failure as valiantly as an Aries man. He counts on failures as experiences. If something is not meant to be, he is capable of coming to terms with it. He is also able to make peace and be content and happy with what destiny has planned for him.

Host: If you are a demanding guest, an Arien's party is something not to be missed. He will go to great lengths to get things right—from crockery to cutlery and from serviettes to glasses, his detailed eye misses nothing. His involvement in everything ensures that his guests have no complaints, be it about food, service or ambience. However, his efforts don't lead to flamboyance; the end result is always upper crust and chic.

Guest: An Arien's meticulous nature can make him a host's nightmare too. He is so fond of getting things right that as a guest he expects finesse in everything. But that doesn't make him a bad guest. In fact in familiar surroundings he will blend in seamlessly and will rarely make the host feel the need to take care of him. However, if he is with people he is not obliged to be with, you may see his mood swing the other way making him critical and introverted.

How does he handle difficult situations?

Since both the passive and aggressive type of Arien men are short-tempered, a difficult situation with either of them can get rather tricky. You will mostly catch an Arien in the middle of a heated argument or debate, pushing his point not relenting till everyone is convinced he is right. The plus point is that he manages to stick to the subject (diverting from the topic will be of no help at all). His ability to reason and persuade is likely to floor the other person and make them shut up. Once the argument is closed, his temper cools off.

However, if provoked beyond limit, the quarrel may get stretched. But he rarely holds grudges as his memory for resentment is rather low. After cooling off, he has no qualms about apologising (sometimes even if he is not in the wrong). I have observed that one reason why he can do this more easily than others is because he always likes to move forward. But that should not make you lower your guard because if you mess with him big time but are unable to meet him on the same level of mending mistakes, then you are sure to get the cold shoulder from him.

What is his characteristic weakness?

The Aries male has major issues with taking orders. He often takes that as an insult to his intelligence and capability, exhibiting an aggressive side when expected to conform to subordination. With his bloated ego, he can at times create unpleasant situations at workplace, leading people to resent or shun him off completely.

Moved easily to jealousy, the Arien doesn't know where to draw a line and his casual questions to his partner might take on an ugly tone if he pushes it too far. His harsh tone could easily hurt the genuine emotions of an unsuspecting woman, who would want to break away from his 'controlling' environment, hating him for his distrust.

Is there more to his persona?

Very often with an Arien man it's a case of your own weapons turning on you. Cynicism in his nature often turns him into a self-critic. Also, it does not allow him to tolerate criticism from others. Cynical and short-tempered, an Arien man is usually found to have somewhat less self-control. To combat his cynicism, he takes to meditation, spirituality and philosophy. This gives him an insight, making him an interesting conversationalist.

Ariens are thinkers, dreamers and achievers. Their approach to life is realistic and practical. They are more emotional than sentimental but their realism helps in balancing their nature.

Being an achiever, an Arien sets goals and targets for himself; which need not be just monetary in nature. But true to his core temperament he will do things only his way else not do them at all. Frank Sinatra's song *My Way* sums up what I am trying to say.

With a strong innovative instinct, he will manage to carve a niche for himself in his career. You will rarely find an Arien living a regular, mundane life. He always aims for the best, yet the humility in him will make him content with whatever he has. An Arien man aspires for the best and is humble enough to accept the second best but his pride will not allow him to accept the third best. The man in question definitely has his priorities right!

How should one deal effectively with an Aries man?

Here lies the crux of the matter...how should one deal with an Aries man? Given his unbridled energy, pride, deep humility and emotional nature, dealing with him is no mean task. Grace and diplomacy are two golden qualities that can floor him instantly. He expects people around him, especially his partner, to be graceful and subtle in words and actions. His dominant and towering personality looks for an equal in submissive people.

The best way to deal with him is to let him have a field day. Give him space to exercise his own rules and be patient with him. But it is of utmost importance to curb his impulsiveness as he is likely to go overboard with it.

How does he handle money matters?

If anyone understands the true value of money, it's an Arien man. For him the dollar is another piece of printed paper. He is very casual with his money and understands that money is meant to be spent. Do you find these statements contradictory? Actually they are not. I am not implying that he does not value money. He knows its value and therefore understands that money is only a tool to work with, not the end. For him money is a by-product of sincere hard work, not the sole objective of life.

Ariens also possess the innate talent of making money one way or the other. Being extremely compassionate, they are often found giving generous tips and donations. They are also known for lending money to friends and family. But people can seldom take advantage of an Arien's generosity as he is very selective about who can approach him. As he matures in life he develops a distinct quality to keep favour seekers at bay.

How is he on the professional front?

On the work front, his dictatorial attitude prevents him from being a good team player. He prefers going solo especially when it comes to decision-making. Since he is a great motivator he makes for an excellent team leader. Because of his aggressive nature he likes to have 'yes sir' people around him, (but someone just saying 'yes sir' and not performing would be dealt with effectively). Since his tolerance levels are low, don't expect more than two chances or warnings. The third one is usually curt and full of fire rounds.

He is kind-hearted, compassionate and generous with money when it comes to his work mates and understands their needs. While he likes discipline he does not get impressed with number of hours or days put in and neither does he demands it. He prefers quality and end product to be delivered. So if your boss is an Arien, it's reason enough for you to rejoice!

How is he in various relationship roles?

Undoubtedly his responsible nature makes him an excellent son, although his streak of doing things his way can make him a parental nightmare as well. Extreme possessiveness and his love for romance makes him a good boyfriend/husband. But make no mistakes. He finds it difficult to forgive errors in love and his emotions are not to be trifled with.

As much as he can be a doting husband and father, he can be equally crude and rude when taken over by one of his moods. He wants his children to be well behaved and disciplined. He can be like a child with a child, wrestle with kids or cuddle them, but at the same time he is a tough father to deal with if you don't live by his rules.

At a party, you will often spot an Arien man talking to everybody. His ability to converse intelligently and take initiative in breaking the ice makes him do this naturally. Since he is capable of sharing his emotions because he trusts people easily, he has many friends. But this will not be before you have passed his qualifying rounds of trust. As a friend he is totally dependable. You can trust him with your secrets but then he expects the same of you.

How is he when alone?

You will rarely find an Arien alone. He needs people around him all the time and prefers company to being alone. His 'me time' generally lasts for two to three hours only, after which he gets restless. Prone to homesickness, he dislikes travelling. On a priority basis, he first wants his family to be with him and then friends unless the family is not supportive of his social plans.

How is he when in love?

An Aries man will never tire of experiencing love. If he fails the first time, he will gather the remains of his broken heart and begin again.

His love is full of passion, almost mounting to frenzy. He will wheel you round and round in the roller coaster of his emotions until you are puffing with excitement. No half-baked love! He will court you in style and woo you till you are dizzy with his attention. He will never hide his love or emotions. It will be a jolly ride all the way.

But of course there would be bumps and potholes aplenty. An Aries man, especially the aggressive kind, will be as much a control freak when in love as otherwise. He would want to know everything about you. Don't bother (or should I say dare) to flirt while you are dating an Arien. He will smoulder like lava at the minutest signs of betrayal. And don't get fooled by the passive Arien who appears to be 'super cool' every time your mobile phone buzzes with text messages from your male friends. Passive or aggressive notwithstanding...remember he is the possessive Arien first.

You can expect the same from him too. He is usually committed to a relationship as long as he is actually in love. His attention to you will largely depend on your 'interest holding potential'...the longer you sustain his interest, the stronger your bond will be.

And now here's a tip or two to make your love connection with an Arien an affair to remember. Our Aries man is a hard core, practical, business-minded, a man of the world. But when it comes to love, he is very much like a character from a Jane Austen novel...or better still, the best creation of the Bard himself; Romeo. His idea of romance is the fairy tale kind. He would expect you to be his princess perfect, one who goes to bed in elegant yet sexy nightgowns and wake up with a smile on her face. If he catches you in your 'hand me down' pyjamas, standing in front of the bathroom mirror frothing at your mouth with toothpaste, bid him goodbye right away. His idea of lady love is exactly that...a lady in love. And if you can't match up to his standards, all his love will go down the drain, literally.

He wants his woman to be extremely feminine and yet independent and strong. For example, he will want his wife to be ladylike on all occasions but take initiative in things guys do too, like playing squash or poker. That is because he would like his girl to also be his friend and not miss being with her, just because he has to be with his guy friends.

What does he look for in a partner?

A strong personality himself, an Aries man would never want a weakling for a partner. Be it casual dating or marriage, he would only be interested in someone who's a perfect blend of femininity and sheer fun. She would also have to sport brains (for intelligent conversation is the only way she can sustain his interest).

Dominating in style, he would prefer a partner who knows how to keep other suitors at bay, while giving him undivided attention. Inspite of being the kind of guy who turns green at the mere mention of another male, the Arien man wants a woman who would be willing to take his enquiries about his competition sportingly, allaying his fears with her genuine answers and love for him.

He aspires to settle down with someone who would be the perfect wife, mother and homemaker. He would want someone whom he could flaunt in front of the whole world, while declaring to the entire audience that you are 'his'!

While dating him, you should...

...play hard to get. The ram is a fighter, he craves for battles. Nothing could be more fun than challenging him to a game of chase. Top it off with the punch line 'catch me if you can'...and you will have him frantically looking for your phone number (secretly an Arien man wishes for his woman not to agree with him, as much as he wants to have his way). Don't overdo it though, because his ego/pride might stop him from pursuing you any further.

On your first date, let him do the talking. He likes to take control of things, so let him decide the venue, menu and the subject of conversation. Once you both are in a certain comfort zone you can get on with your opinions. An Aries man will always respect women with brains. Just because he is dominating doesn't mean he won't let you have your way. He has a unique way of making his date feel relaxed and on a first date you would feel like you have known each other for months or years.

Since he is a stickler for decorum, mind your manners carefully (slurping your coffee or talking incessantly won't help). Also dress up your fashionable best (subtle and elegant). The Aries man will appreciate all positive non-verbal vibrations coming from your end, more so if they are aesthetically pleasing.

While dating an Aries man, be sure you don't turn him off by looking at other men. He will not take it well at all.

If you think your dating is taking a serious turn and a long-term relationship is a credible idea, then you should know what an Aries man will expect from his girl. While he will charmingly help you put on your coat, don't expect him to take you grocery shopping all the time. Best way to impress him will be to take the car and drive to the store yourself, and the next time you might find him accompanying you on his own. In short he does not like be told, he prefers to do things like that by himself or be asked with a smile.

Dating an Aries man can be a funny, fulfilling and out-of-the-world experience. He will go out of his way to impress you, to be with you and make you do things his way. While he will dominate every aspect of the dating process, he will do it so charmingly that you won't be offended by it.

For an Arien, holding hands and a long look in your eyes is as much valuable as a kiss. Not one to foray into physical closeness at the first chance, the Aries man will never get intimate unless he is very sure of his love. In short, there are no 'one-night-stands' for him.

Intimacy without love is meaningless for him and he is not the kind of man to waste time on meaningless relationships. If he is convinced that you are the girl for him, he will make sure your passion and fervour matches up to his. But don't let this make you believe that he may not have done some 'net practice' or played a few games before the final match!

Compatibility quotient

Compatibility between two individuals depends on various factors and not just on their likes and dislikes. I have often found that persons of similar behavioural traits don't quite hit it off in the long run. For a long standing relationship, a balance between the aggressive and the passive traits of a personality is necessary. And more so in the case of Arien men!

Aries man and...

Aries woman: 3.5/10. An Arien woman is too similar to her male counterpart to make a relationship successful. Even the most passive types from the Arien men and women are dominating and overpowering. In such a case, who would dominate whom?

Taurus woman: 4/10. A Taurus woman will not be able to handle the Arien ego effectively. She is too practical to allow his impulsiveness and he is too fond of his freedom, to like her 'sticking together' ideas.

Gemini woman: 10/10. Gemini-Aries can paint the town red...with passion, love, fire or actual paint. With challenges and adventure at every step and each one ready for it, this relationship can be loads of fun and full of passionate conversations.

Cancer woman: 6/10. A balanced relationship can be had with much hard work at both ends. The Arien will need to keep his bluntness in check, while the Cancer girl will have to curb her 'mothering' behaviour. Both will have to bring their emotions on a mutual comfort level for the relationship to work.

Leo woman: 6/10. Great chemistry and a happy match, with full on emotions thrown in! But a word of caution here...too much of similarity can also bring the relationship to a dead end.

Virgo woman: 4/10. Not a very happy venture! The Arien will find it difficult to take orders from the 'preaching' Virgo woman. Their personalities are too contrasting to result in a healthy relationship.

Libra woman: 7/10. If there's something called love at first sight, this can be it. Each will be taken in by the other's intelligence but for things to steady, both will have to use patience and understanding.

Scorpio woman: 9/10. He has all the passion and masculinity that she's looking for and she has all the mystery and femininity that he's looking for. So far a perfect match! Only both may have to add a dash of respect for each other to sustain the relationship.

Sagittarius woman: 6/10. The Sagittarian woman will share a good deal of her love for adventure and travel, mingled with her sense of humour with the Arien. He in turn will impress her with his creativity and intelligence. This relationship can be for keeps if both are able to keep their bluntness in check.

Capricorn woman: 9/10. With the right amount of submissiveness, the Capricorn female can find a perfect match in an Arien. She may find it difficult to handle his ego and dominating nature, but has patience enough to be steady with him. He is able to provide her with the emotional and financial security she yearns for along with a dependable partner in him.

Aquarius woman: 7/10. The Aquarian girl has the right amount of independence and femininity to floor the Arien. She will be sporting enough to take his angry outbursts healthily and he will be caring enough to infuse their relationship with passion. But too much of dominance which an Aquarian woman displays from time to time could play spoilsport.

Pisces woman: 7/10. This combination can go either way. With the nagging Piscean woman and sarcastic Aries man, it can be a boat on the rocks. Or with the emotionally dependent Piscean and the masculine Arien, it can be a match made in heaven.

Famous Arien men personalities:

Arshad Warsi	Eddie Murphy
Jackie Chan	Marlon Brando

Aries woman

A shooting star leaving a blazing trail in the inky-blue sky: bright, packed with energy and the fire to achieve anything and everything; the Aries woman is all that and a lot more. Just like her male counterpart, an Aries woman has immense vigour and strength of character.

Although aggression too largely figures in her attitude, there are Aries women who are more placid. But both kinds (both are in existence equally, fifty-fifty) are like a shining star, unrivalled in its glory and complete in its own radiance.

Extremely conscious of her self, the Aries female is fearless, strong and egocentric. For her, the world revolves around her and her only. What she does or thinks is of utmost importance (with others being neglected or sidelined in the bargain).

She takes the term 'extreme' quite literally. She loves in extremes; she hates in extremes and generally lives life on the extreme. If she loves you, you will be the core of her existence, but if she dislikes you…nah! There's no word like 'dislike' in her dictionary…it's simple hatred…that's what I call living life in black and white!

How can you identify an Aries woman in a crowd?

With a body language that speaks of boldness, the Aries girl will talk with authority and look at you in the eye with unabashed confidence. Not one to mince words, it is easy to spot her in a social set-up as she will be the one most vocal with her opinions. She will also give you her undivided attention, but only as long as your conversation interests her; the minute she finds it boring, she will start looking around with impatience.

Another give away of the Aries female is her 'do-it-myself' stance. She will rush to get her own drink, pull up her own chair and carry her own bags without much ado (but that's not saying that she won't expect men around her to behave in a gentlemanly fashion), it's just that she is too independent to seek assistance, especially from men.

At a party, you will find her leading the way with her actions and speech. In a conversation she will be the chief talker and the first one to lead everyone to the dance floor. If she takes a fancy to you, she will immediately take you under her wing and from thereon you won't have a single dull moment to crib about.

What are the key features of her personality?

With the sensational election of Barack Obama as the first non-white President of US, the dream of America's first-ever woman president doesn't seem impossible anymore. And I am sure there are a lot of female Ariens out there aspiring to step into the White House. With a persistent urge to lead and be *numero uno* in everything, an Aries woman comes with a natural knack to be a leader. She will immediately take on the role at the helm of affairs...be it with her family, group of friends at college or business associates. She likes to lead with example and therefore you will find her energetic and full of vigour in everything she does. Arien girls are often heroines of inspirational sagas.

The same energy and vitality also make her restless. She is constantly on the lookout for new enterprises that can utilise her energy. With never a moment to spare she is on a whirlwind mission to complete tasks within the standards she has set for herself. Her aspirations are always high and she usually lands up expecting as much of others as she does from her own self.

While she is bubbling with energy, she is also like an emotionally charged atom. Any amateur psychologist can tell you what a fatal combination that is! But what lies on the surface is not emotion but sensitivity. Aries women are hypersensitive and are likely to flare up immediately when rubbed the wrong way.

An Aries female shows no trace of timidity...ever! She has complete confidence in herself. She takes each step with pride and self-assurance, be it her professional or personal life or merely the actual act of walking! Her frankness in speech and manner will floor you at first and disturb you later. Freedom of speech is dear to her heart and she will use it freely, sometimes crossing the thin line between openness and roughness. But one can't deny the fact that she is honest to the core in whatever she says or does. Her honesty makes her 'almost innocent' in worldly ways and guess what, like everything else, she expects the same from you.

How is an Aries woman on the following aspects?

Appearance: An Aries woman has sharp arresting features and a strong jawline. You will usually see her making a statement with her attire (with making a statement I don't mean she will always be dressed to kill, but whatever she wears will have a certain swagger to it). She is fond of dressing well and likes people to notice her style, but it won't necessarily be flashy clothes—her sense of style is very subtle yet effective.

I have observed that very often the more aggressive kinds of Arien women sport a tomboyish look, with short haircuts and a 'don't mess with me' look on the face; the passive kinds are more ladylike with long hair and girlie qualities and like to wear long flowing garments, for instance a dress or a skirt.

Ambition: On the ambition scale an Aries woman ranges between ambitious to being overambitious. Her love for challenges prods her into dreaming big and achieving bigger. An Aries woman is a dreamer and draws out fantastic plans for herself, both in the personal and professional life.

Her ambitious nature does not let her rest in her laurels. She believes in scaling new heights every day. Even in her successful role as a homemaker she will yearn to create a mark for herself. But to her credit, her ambitions are well-balanced, and she is almost always able to deal with work and home with unmatched equilibrium.

Ego/Self-respect: Both kinds of Aries women, the assertive and the passive, have tremendous self-respect and ego. While the passive Arien might be submissive most of the time, take care not to push her too far as her blazing ego is always lurking just beneath the surface.

Responsibility: Like her male counterpart, the Arien woman has an innate sense of responsibility and duty and aspires to excel at every given task, but her need to outshine in all her activities is more to prove her worth to herself than to the world.

Etiquettes: With an attitude tilting towards the casual, she makes no qualms in deviating from set social mannerisms. However, the passive Ariens tend to be perfectionists paying detailed attention to grooming and etiquettes.

What is her approach towards life?

Let me repeat myself here—she is a dreamer. She can weave yarns of fantasy and a golden future not just for herself but also for her loved ones. Her ambition and optimism tend to spread to include her family and friends. To her nothing is impossible, including miracles. Aye, miracle is a word this lady implicitly believes in!

Having said all the above, let me clarify that although she dreams big, she is never unrealistic in her approach. Her feet are firmly grounded and she knows the exact extent of her determination and efforts. Her energetic drive is however often glossed over by cynicism.

How does she score on the following points?

Cynicism: Both the assertive and passive kinds of Aries women display cynicism in varying proportions, with the aggressive ones walking away with the cake! On the other hand, cynicism in the passive kinds gets somewhat mellowed down by their optimism.

Suspicion/Jealousy: When it comes to suspicion, the Arien girl can sometimes go overboard. She is or likes to pretend (depending on the type you are pitted against) that she is trusting by nature and often thinks it below herself to get suspicious but there are very few cases in which she won't doubt her partner or his motives. But mark it, she abhors being suspected. Nothing will put-off an Arien girl more than sleuths on her trail. She believes that in a relationship, she should be trusted implicitly.

She can get jealous easily…and you really don't want to see that side of her. Unless she feels immensely secure in the relationship, she can be quite a monster. My advice to you is to underplay whatever you think might make her jealous.

Dishonesty/Infidelity: An Aries woman comes out with a clean chit on the count of infidelity. She will never be frivolous with her relationship. To her love is for keeps and she will fulfil her part of the commitment to the fullest. Only a completely out of hand situation can urge her to be promiscuous, and even that is a strong term for this girl.

Dishonesty too doesn't come easily to her. To put it plainly, an Aries woman finds it difficult to lie and when she does, it is a Herculean task for her to keep up the falsehood. Generally speaking, she might indulge in a little white lie now and then, but you can't stick the label 'dishonest' upon her. This might be amongst the few things she shares with her male counterpart.

Hardships: Buckling under duress, not this one! Women under no other sun sign display such strength of character and understanding as an Aries woman. She handles hardships with amazing practicality. Her love for challenges only makes her turn every adversity into a milestone and she will leave no stone unturned to overcome difficulties.

Success and failure: With success it's another story altogether: no subtlety or delicacy here. Aries women exhibit success in a moderate to loud manner. They make sure everyone hears and acknowledges their success and the louder, the better (this however may not apply to the passive Aries woman).

In spite of their ever-present optimism, both kinds usually take failures to heart. Failure can turn them into a self-critic. Given their sensitive nature, they blame themselves for their shortcomings (but that's only after they finish blaming everyone else!). But then again, pessimism is temporary in their nature. Given a chance, an Aries woman talks herself out of gloom and immediately starts looking out for the proverbial 'silver lining'.

Host: As hosts, Arien women show two distinct categories. One is like an Aries man, a stickler for details. Their parties will be elaborate affairs with everything from wine to cigars being served with finesse. And the other, show a completely casual attitude as hosts. If you ever land up at a party thrown by the second kind, don't be surprised to find home delivery parcels in the kitchen!

Guest: If there is a woman who likes attention and knows how to handle it, it's got to be an Arien. The lady in question likes to be at the centre of things. She demands and commands respect and attention, and if you are able to give her that, rest assured that your party is a runaway success.

How does she handle difficult situations?

My observations tell me that an Aries woman is quick at losing her temper, not because she is bad tempered, but because she is low on patience and tends to blow things out of proportion. Her flare-ups often result in arguments and debates that can end up in quarrels. It is difficult for both kinds of Aries women to maintain grace under fire—so insistent is her need to be right in everything that she will not fall short of using rough language to prove her point, and her excessive ego also makes it difficult for her to accept mistakes.

Though her outbursts are generally rather short-lived she tends to hold grudges. This arises from her judgmental and opinionated nature. Of course proper apologies can mend matters!

What is her characteristic weakness?

The very traits that set her apart when taken to the other extreme can bring about her downfall. For instance, her aggression often borders on crudeness while her ambition can make her seem heartless. In her obsession to succeed, she will leave behind those who can't catch up with her ambitious pace. Her low grace quotient, a by-product of her 'throw it in your face' attitude, can make her an eyesore in company. Second biggest weakness would be her constant mood swings. Once she loses her cool, it's difficult for her to stop. Her verbal barrages can drive people away, leaving her irritated and seething with anger. She also finds it hard to take criticism. Criticising her is a sure shot way of sending that lid up the roof!

Her strong sense of ego makes her myopic and she is not able to look beyond herself. She finds it difficult to bend her stance and apologising is clearly not her way of mending things.

Her possessiveness rating is slightly higher than ordinary, which makes her easily jealous. Moreover, her possessiveness comes with a catch. Though herself like this, she dislikes, no, hates this quality in others, especially her partner. She expects space from her spouse, but is not likely to give it to him as readily.

'Me' is a prominent factor for her. She is self-absorbed and often thinks only of her desires and needs and at times can turn hypocritical, especially to suit her needs. She has no qualms of 'fidgeting' with values and ethics to have her way.

Is there more to this energetic woman's persona?

I have come across Aries women who are highly focused on all fronts. At work they outshine others with their ambitious and competitive spirit. In the role of a homemaker, you will find them competent at just about anything, from personal hygiene to overseeing/supervising the cleaning of the house to doing the dishes and taking care of the family and pets. After all, she likes to be *in control*!

She also wants and yearns to be independent. Financial dependency can lead to frustration in an Aries woman. She likes to do things in her own way, especially those involving money. Apart from earning money, she is also enamoured by the fame attached to a work well done. Like in everything else, she is an early bird at earning a living as well. Don't be surprised if you see her doing odd jobs to earn a few extra bucks.

There are few things she will not take lying down and dishonesty and injustice are some of them, and not only to herself but to others too. She is quite capable of taking up your case and fighting till the finish if she feels you have been wronged. So for those who think you are more sinned against than sinning, an Aries woman will be an apt champion for your cause! She is also extremely compassionate.

Under all these fiery qualities lies an intuitive nature. An Arien female is extremely intuitive and believes in it too. I would like to add here that it is her intuition that makes her wary and therefore leads to suspiciousness in her character. This also makes her impulsive. Fearless and dauntless she is not afraid to take risks and plunge into things that her intuition says are right.

When it comes to higher callings, I have noticed Aries women swinging between two inclinations: either they are very spiritual or complete non-believers.

How should one deal effectively with an Aries woman?

With a lot of caution! Anything and everything can cause this firebrand lady to lose her cool. As long as you stay out of her hair, she'll be most helpful, courteous and charming to be with (of course, she'll still be wary of you and your intentions).

This lady craves for attention, and flattery is a tried-and-tested method of winning her. And yes! She would give you ample reasons to genuinely compliment her from time to time.

Since she likes being in control, she could sometimes go overboard with being helpful to the extent of being interfering. In such a scenario, be gentle in your reprimand, expressing gratitude for lending a helping hand, while at the same time delegating the task to someone else.

While dating one, make sure you don't get caught flirting around or cheating on her...she'll rip you apart! Be faithful and she'll shower you with more love and care than you could possibly imagine.

How does she handle money matters?

Hmmm...money and Aries women are best friends, although she assigns no value to it. Money for her is equivalent to her shopping bags. She can spend like there's no tomorrow (being a good spender she makes for jovial company as she is unbiased in spending money on family or friends).

Long-term financial planning is just not her forte. So be careful while sharing your bank account with her. In all likelihood her contribution would be to empty it. But, in hard times she is equally capable of buckling-up and making sure there is no waste of any sort.

How is she on the professional front?

Aggressive to the extent of being selfish and cruel, she is a woman on the fast track and draws delight from success like a junkie on hash. Her attraction for power borders on the obsessive and she will fight it out with anyone and everyone to win it.

But, the Arien can be quite a comforting friend and colleague to people who are important to her. However, this attribute would come into play only if you aren't in competition with her for the same plump post or project. She'll be a true friend only if she doesn't consider you as competition.

How is she in various relationship roles?

Excellent is an adjective which I will apply to all her roles as she is driven by her leadership quality and an urge to excel in everything. She will make sure she makes for a good daughter, wife and mother and not just for show but in earnest.

Since she is responsible and independent from an early age, she easily takes up the role of a caring daughter smoothly. She also shows great respect for her parents and elders.

As a sibling if you stay out of her business, she will be most loving, caring and affectionate.

If your wife is an Arien then respect from her has to be earned. She will not bestow it readily, but once convinced of her husband's true worth she will remain loyal and committed to him. With sheer strength of character she will stand by him in tough times. Remember, what you give to her in love will come back to you doubled, only...and this is important; make sure you voice your gratitude abundantly.

While she is extremely devoted, she lives in a fantasy world and often feels the urge to be experimental and flirtatious, which could either be very casual or very serious.

As a mother, she comes with low patience, but over time she realises she has little choice but to be patient. She will not unnecessarily pamper her children and would wish them to be independent (as herself) quickly. She can be found to be a little indifferent in teaching her children manners and public behaviour.

At work, her need to be perfect and efficient in every given task makes her a good employee. She likes earning laurels and will spare no hard work to do that. She can be extremely creative, responsible, sincere and hard-working. But on the flipside, she tends to be loud and centre of attraction. She likes to see people dependent on her and is also known to throw tantrums.

How is she when alone?

Her mind harbours a million thoughts on what she wants to achieve and how she wants to achieve it. She would plan (read 'plot') out her roadmap to success and re-consider options every time she is on her own, eliminating any ideas of failure.

When alone, her thoughts can often take on a negative shade, especially if she finds an object of jealousy...could be a professional rival, someone who's better than her at studies, or even her own siblings!

How is she when in love?

Before we delve further on this front, let me clarify that Aries women are extremely practical. Although they love the very concept of love (romance is the core of their belief system) their approach is governed by practicality. After an Arien has covered the grounds for education and career in life, her next priority is to find a compatible companion. And this search is likely to begin very early.

Being experimental and flirtatious, she goes through learning curves as she matures to understanding what she wants and what she doesn't. An Aries woman can cleverly hide her desires and want of material things. While she can stand by her companion through hardships and struggles, she will make sure she is not wasting her time with a loser.

Honesty of character upholds her in love as well. She will remain loyal and committed to her man, once convinced of him. Two timing is just not her cup of tea! She sees love only within the precincts of the term 'forever'. When in love she can be extremely passionate and open to sharing. But very often the streak of independence and dominance in an Aries woman creates a contrary impression of her needs. Even when she is at her bossiest, a hen-pecked husband /partner is not what she is looking for. She likes submissive people but not to the extent of their being wimps. She is most compatible with people who understand her needs and give her importance.

But when it comes to compatibility with her soulmate, the picture turns slightly different. She wants a man who stands up to her expectations, knows how to care and comfort her and shares her idea of everlasting romance. For peaceful co-existence with an Aries girl, it is also important to give her space and ample freedom. Be graceful while handling her possessiveness, but don't show yours. She will not like any infringement on her space. And if you try to dominate her, you will be shown the door in a flash!

If you are with the aggressive kind of Arien woman, you will be in for a lot of entertainment. She has a very good sense of humour and will envelope everyone around with her charming, yet reckless ways.

Once you fall in love with an Aries girl, for starters you have to accept the fact that she is a woman of the world. Your relationship will largely depend on your acceptance of this facet of her personality. She will forge head first in activities like listening to the woes of your parents, looking after your siblings, taking notes from some distant aunts on the phone, attending to your friends as well as being part of many social dos and shopping sprees. That is not to say she will neglect you, but once she is with you it will be your job to fit in as many romantic moments as you can. She will not be satisfied with falling in love with you alone. She will make it a point to gather your entire family in her love nest. That's an Arien girl for you!

What does she look for in a partner?

The Aries woman believes she's the best and wants her partner to be the best too! Tall, dark and handsome...she wants it all in her man. Throw in hordes of wealth, and she'll be squealing with glee (but that does not mean by any way that she is a gold digger). For the jealous Aries, becoming the object of envy is a big high. So if she finds someone who according to her is 'quite a catch', she'd be delighted beyond words.

While dating her, you should...

...get used to her dominant nature. That's a prerequisite! She won't leave anything to you or chance. She will supervise everything and a date with her will be a complete foolproof deal. A few meetings down the lane and she is likely to pop-in before a date to check what clothes you are planning to wear. But don't interfere too much in her plans. Let her have her space and you will be surprised to see how much she blossoms in it. The Aries woman is romantic and emotional, but to a degree. She doesn't like excessive closeness and clinginess. So don't appear needy while dating her. Show her how much you appreciate her (with a good amount of sincere compliments thrown in) and she will make your date the most memorable one of your life. Don't be too submissive either. She likes to boss around, but she will appreciate a man who is man enough to stick to his guns.

The Aries woman likes to take the lead in everything, dating being no exception. Don't be surprised if she asks you out first. Although she has a dominating persona, she isn't masculine or tomboyish. You will find her feminine in many subtle ways.

She loves the thrill and adventure, not to mention the risk of dangerous stuff. Dare her to a task and you will see the best in her. Since she likes challenges, it isn't a bad idea to invite her to a friendly game of go-carting. Although with her strong competitive streak, no game is ever going to be just friendly.

Her enthusiastic spirit never lags and you will have a ball of a time while dating her. She has good humour too, so you will enjoy your time with her.

Don't criticise or instruct her. It is also unwise to try her limited resource of patience, and don't be in a hurry to get that good night kiss. She won't like such advances but given her 'taking charge' nature, she is quite likely to initiate the first kiss herself.

And lastly, you won't have to wait long to know the result of your date with her. She will be frank enough to tell you whether you have made a place for yourself in her firebrand heart or it's 'exit' time for you. She is always vocal about her feelings and it easy to know if dating her is going to take you into a long-term relationship or not.

Finally to sum up...while dating an Aries girl wear smart clothes, play a little hard to get, be ready for surprises and book a table for two at the best exotic restaurant in town. I am sure you will love the experience. Happy dating!

Compatibility quotient:

They say one must fight fire with fire. I don't know how true that is technically but amongst zodiac signs too much of fire can have disastrous results. The fiery nature of the Aries girl needs a match that's cool and down to earth and yet one that has traits to equal her passionate nature.

But if she is a passive woman and meets an active/aggressive fire sign or if she is an active aggressive woman and meets a passive fire sign, opposites could work out really well.

Aries woman and...

Aries man: 3.5/10. There's just too much friction here for a long-term relationship to work out. With ego, dominating nature, temper and impatience in both, it is not a great match. Although like mentioned above opposite temperaments could work out well.

Taurus man: 6.5/10. This combination can work only if both are ready for compromises. She will have to curb her extrovert nature and unruly tongue, while he will have to learn to give her space. Money can be a bone of contention between these two as the Taurean is extremely cautious with it, while the Arien is extravagant.

Gemini man: 9/10. Here's a good one. Both are highly charged individuals. The Gemini man is intelligent enough to accept the free spirit of the Arien. She will be instantly floored with his charm and romantic disposition.

Cancer man: 7/10. This relationship can work out in a long run if both are able to check their obstinacy. The Aries girl will have to understand his moodiness and sedentary nature while the Cancer guy will have to respect her spirited and outgoing nature.

Leo man: 8/10. Great chemistry here! The Leo man has as much confidence and masculinity as required to impress the Arien girl. She is capable of taking care of his emotional needs and weak ego, while he is capable of giving her the luxuries of life.

Virgo man: 7/10. This match can go a long way in spite of the inherent differences. The Aries woman should learn to get used to his cautious and organised nature and also to keep her adventurous streak under check.

Libra man: 7/10. Again a good match in spite of the differences. The Arien will have to exercise the tiniest ounce of her patience to deal with the indecisiveness of the Libran man. But he is quite capable of taking care of her and his idea of romance is also likely to suit her.

Scorpio man: 6/10. The differences here are rather strong. The Scorpio man will not like her dominating nature while the Arien girl will not take his possessiveness too well. Although they will admire each other for some traits, it will take a lot of hard work from both ends to make this relationship last in the long run.

Sagittarius man: 9/10. A match well made! Both are attuned to each other's personality traits. Both are impulsive and adventure-loving. He has good humour to keep her interested and she has spontaneity to keep him impressed. The Arien may have to guard her tongue now and then, but apart from that they make a compatible pair.

Capricorn man: 7/10. Capricorn man and Aries woman are poles apart but opposites do attract. She is vivacious while he could be sombre; she is expressive while he is not. But patience and tolerance can work wonders for this relationship.

Aquarius man: 8/10. The Aquarius man is unconventional enough to suit the Arien taste. Her sharp and astute mind will prove to be a turn on for him. With a bit of understanding about each other's temperament and need for space, they can hit it off superbly.

Pisces man: 7/10. Although both are emotional, their emotional needs are quite different. Her aggressiveness might hurt the sensitive Piscean nature. She will like his mystic mind and with her intelligence can help him find his way in this materialistic world.

Famous Arien women personalities

Jaya Bachchan
Mariah Carey
Sarah Jessica Parker
Lara Dutta
Rani Mukerjee

Taurus

20 April-21 May

Taurus man

'Very cautious' is how I would describe a Taurus male. He is a level headed person, who likes to think over everything before taking a decision. His calm and composed demeanour conceals a fertile and active mind. One of the most industrious of zodiac signs, a Taurus man believes in himself and his ability to achieve everything with hard work.

Although patient most of the times, he can take on a stubborn stance if provoked. Make sure you don't rub him the wrong way and you will have the most patient and understanding man. Here's a male who understands his role as the head of the family and will do everything in his power to provide for the well-being of his loved ones. Trust him implicitly and you will win his trust and loyalty in return…for life.

How can you identify a Taurus man in a crowd?

It is easy to spot a Taurus man in a crowd as he is extremely animated in conversation and discussion. He will always try to dominate with his views, leaving very little room for suggestions or opinions from others. He has a hovering eye, checking out things and people.

Broadly speaking there are two types of Taurus men; 70 per cent of them are aggressive and 30 per cent passive.

While dressing up he definitely makes a classic statement with his clothes. Although there's nothing distinctive about his style, the way he dresses up and carries himself evokes a natural respect for this gentleman. A Taurus man is extremely flirtatious and not shy to strike conversations with strangers, particularly with women.

To Taurus men every situation is a battlefield where they have to win. Although many are able to hide it cleverly, they are self-obsessed and can be quite selfish at times. This doesn't mean that a Taurus man is not generous or compassionate because he is both, it just means, to him, he is the first priority.

What are the key features of his personality?

The Taurus male excels in the role of a provider. He is a thorough bred family man with a bachelor's heart. Confused? Well, here comes the explanation. His list of wants isn't too long. He would want things that are necessary to make life comfortable for himself and his family. Luxuries can wait. Of course the definition of luxury depends on his social status too. But overall you won't find a Taurean who is pining for opulence.

No matter how settled he is in his family life, the bachelor in him will often peep-out and make himself obvious. He enjoys the bouts of beer at the sports bar with his cronies. You may also catch him flirting harmlessly with his female colleagues. He will stay in touch with his college friends and probably do all the things he did in 'the days of yore' like clubbing, playing snooker and watching football matches with them. But come dinner time and he will amble home for a warm meal and a good night's sleep.

The Taurus man has strong likes and dislikes. And food being at the top of his 'likes' list, decide on dating him only if you are good at cooking. But don't expect him (or allow him) to try his hand at cooking. He is far too conservative to step into the predominantly 'feminine' territory. And if he does, be rest assured it would be a complete mess.

True to the symbol of his sun sign, the Taurus man is as stubborn as a bull. Once he has made-up his mind or formed an opinion about anyone, he is not likely to change it for the world. Same is the case with his decisions regarding life. If he has decided to pursue a particular path, no matter how hard you try to dissuade him, he won't budge an inch. Some bull I say!

However lean a bull may be physically, he can work like a Trojan. Same goes for the Taurus man! His ability to work remains unmatched with males from the other zodiac signs. Be it mental calculations or actual physical effort, for the Taurus guy it is all a day's work.

Usually not known to be satisfied with mediocre living, he yearns for a good life. But he is not greedy and once he has achieved what he started out for, he would be content with it. Not one to believe in the 'sky's the limit' motto; that's a Taurus man for you!

How is a Taurus man on the following aspects?

Appearance: Taurus men have sharp communicative eyes and usually a big face. They lead an active life and are into some kind of physical exercise; could be a sport, working out at a gym or yoga. Because of this they usually have a decently built body and a radiant glow about them. When it comes to clothes, he prefers to stick to classics. You will usually find him in Polo tees, checkered or striped shirts and in bright solid colours like orange.

Ambition: To a Taurus man ambition comes with the natural instinct to provide. Conservative in thought and action (especially concerning business), he is shrewd enough to attain success in whatever profession he chooses. Being self-disciplined, he takes work and subjects related to work very seriously.

Ego/Self-respect: Nobody has a bigger ego than the Taurus male. While he can come across as extremely humble, compassionate, caring and easy-going, the slightest of discomfort caused to this self-respecting egotistic man can make him launch-off at you.

Responsibility: Extremely responsible, a Taurus man is usually known to be a mama's boy. To him, his mother is 'the first lady' in every sense as he is able to relate to her contributions and sacrifices. He also learns to take on responsibility early in life. This is also because of his ego and the need to be financially independent.

Etiquettes: Being self-disciplined, a Taurus man wants to exercise right etiquettes at all times. But a certain part of him is extremely carefree and allows him to let down his guard and be casual. However, true to himself, he expects a lot of discipline from others too.

Taurus men are found to exercise chivalry from time to time, which to some could look pretentious and honestly, it could be so too!

What is his approach towards life?

Although a Taurus man is most of the times driven by his emotions and is also sentimental, he is level headed enough to be realistic in his approach towards life. He manages to keep a clear head, thanks to his pragmatic way of thinking. He also prefers to be a leader, which makes him a good entrepreneur.

The passive and sedate nature of a Taurean male allows him to have an easy-going attitude towards life, however, that by no way means he wouldn't want a set up that isn't near perfect. He likes to maintain a comfortable home for his family and himself, building on his wealth slowly and steadily. The Taurus man believes in maintaining a balance between work and family and would not be content with compromising on quality family time.

You'll rarely find a Taurus man who's gung-ho about being a part of the rat race. However, he draws great pleasure from acquiring the latest gadgets and gizmos. These possessions aren't for status symbol; you'll often find him splurging on them to satisfy the male Taurean's genuine interest in technology and new things.

How does he score on the following points?

Cynicism: A Taurus man can be overly cynical as he is known to have his way with most issues in life. If he cannot get things done his way, he will end up throwing tantrums and at times create unpleasant situations.

Another point that might mislead people into thinking of Taurus men as overly cynical is their habit of taking in every situation rather slowly. Given their cautious nature, they like to take stock of things and analyse any situation, person or problem at hand thoroughly. Lest they take a wrong decision or give an incorrect judgment, they think a lot before arriving at a solution. This might be mistaken for cynicism, whereas it is actually just extra carefulness on their part.

Although a positive thinker, he is always on the lookout for the devil's advocate. This wariness may make him come across as a pessimist.

Suspicion/Jealousy: This man is suspicious about everything—an attribute born out of his insecure nature. A Taurus man is the most insecure of all zodiac signs for unknown reasons. Though he camouflages his suspicion with words like intuition, instinct and sixth sense, he is actually suspicious about everything and everybody…family members, spouse, children, girlfriends, household help, drivers, etc.

Clubbed with his inherent suspicion, a Taurus man is overly possessive and therefore overly jealous too. However, his jealousy is reserved for matters of the heart and does not include success or material prosperity.

Himself usually very fair to every relationship, a Taurus man gives 100 per cent to them (well...maybe 90 is more reasonable), but he then expects people around to treat him with the same amount of dedication. It is strange how his measuring metre never matches up to his expectations. In his mind, a struggle is forever on between what he expects of you versus what you can do for him and you eventually lose. Don't take him to be unthankful. It's just that he wants more out of people all the time. When jealous or suspicious, he can make life miserable for people, create scenes, quarrel and be loud and aggressive.

Dishonesty/Infidelity: A Taurus man is not likely to take dishonesty and infidelity lying down. And since he is very trusting by nature (once he begins to trust you), the slightest of deviation in the dedication and loyalty of others can cause irreparable damage to his feelings.

Hardships: He takes hardships as challenges and always manages to bounce back from wherever he is. Since he is an earth sign, he needs to be grounded and requires a support system in times of hardships. If he is spiritually inclined and a believer, he will draw strength from his faith. But I have often found many a Taurus men falling victim to superstitions, rituals and beliefs during trying times.

Success and failure: In spite of being loud most of the times, Taurus men are subtle when it comes to success. I guess it goes with their conservative nature. They never gloat or bask in the glory of their success. To them, success is just another milestone and very likely after each such milestone, they ask themselves ...'what next?' Being great sportsmen, Taurus men take failure in good spirit. They believe in learning from their mistakes and are graceful in accepting failure. You will always find a Taurus man following the philosophy of 'let the best man win'. This should not be taken as a sign of weakness as he is a diehard competitor who is just as good at accepting failure as a lesson to better himself.

Host: Known to be very generous, a great percentage of Taurus men would invite people to dinner at the drop of a hat. While playing host they are detailed and like to see that everything is taken care of. They are also very attentive towards their guests.

Guest: As a guest, a Taurus man will generally make himself comfortable. Being a typical foodie, he will judge everything on the dining table from all possible perspectives—taste, quality, quantity, look and texture. While he can be really generous with compliments if he enjoys the food, he can also be extremely critical if he does not.

How does he handle difficult situations?

A Taurus man handles quarrels like a baby. He can be cranky, rebellious, loud, argumentative and generally obnoxious and this can last till he receives an apology. If not, then once calm, he will apologise willingly (in spite of his ego). This is when he is also likely to realise that he overplayed his part or overreacted to the situation at hand. An apology is the easiest way of sorting out matters for him as he cannot tolerate an unpleasant atmosphere around him for too long.

A Taurus is easily angered. When pushed beyond his limits, he can let his lid flip and you would then be witness to the darkest side of his personality—so dark you would wish the lid had never flipped in the first place.

What is his characteristic weakness?

If there is something that can weaken this man, it's emotion. And our man can get quite dramatic in that arena. When he has to take a decision, a Taurus man will always find himself in a cross fire between emotions (heart) and practicality (mind). Another of his shortcomings is his trusting nature. Once comfortable with somebody, he is known to trust that person implicitly. This for him is a weakness, especially since (in the long run) people tend to take undue advantage of his trust. But with maturity and experience a Taurus man learns to overcome this weakness.

Ego and anger are the two sides of a double-edged sword that Taurus men carry with themselves, very few Taurus men know how to deal with their ego and/or anger. Usually they end up doing more harm to themselves than others in moments of ego or anger display.

One of the funniest things I have noticed in Taurus men and deem it necessary to put under their weaknesses is the fact that they are incorrigible gossips. Gossiping is a habit they deplore in others, especially their better halves, yet they love to indulge in the same. Very likely they would carry out their gossiping sessions under the guise of 'information exchange'.

Is there something more to his persona?

The Taurus man is the perfect mascot for the dictum 'actions speak louder than words'. Passionate getaways, perfect sunsets, flowers and scented suites, this lover knows how to win and keep his lady's heart! The romance never ebbs out of a Taurean male's life, with gifts and outings playing an important part in his expression of gratitude to you for the efforts you put in to make this relationship work.

A Taurus man is known to be reliable and dependable. You can trust him with your darkest secret. But don't forget that he likes to gossip too. So let the secrets you share with him be less meaty else he might just get tempted to share them with the world. But on the whole, when it comes to work, duties and responsibilities, he is extremely dependable.

If anyone's averse to change, it's our Taurean male. He 'does not' like change. Be it his toothpaste brand or the arrangement of objects on his office table, he finds it difficult, nay almost impossible to accept change. And this stands true for his opinions also. Once a Taurus male has made up his mind it is very difficult to change it. And this is especially true of his opinions about certain people. He is also likely to hold grudges and not forget an unpleasant encounter very easily.

The Taurus man is one man who takes his gender very seriously. He is conservative in his outlook and somehow doesn't believe in equality when it comes to men and women and is very clear on certain things a man could/should do and things that a woman could/should do. Within the entire existence of Taurus men in the world, 80 per cent are conservative in their thinking, while only 20 per cent are able to follow the 'live and let live' maxim in the context of men-women equality.

Most Taurus men I have known are not necessarily opulent, but they are not the run-of-the-mill kind either. A Taurus man will build his assets, including money, as he climbs up the ladder in a steady and stable manner. He is in no hurry to be rich and would rather have a secure bank balance than high stakes in a risky business.

Another strange observation that I have made about Taurus men is their sense of humour. They thoroughly enjoy slapstick comedy, while one liners, graffiti and witticisms especially sarcastic ones are kind of lost on them. A Taurean man likes to make others laugh and will come up with millions of jokes and funny anecdotes, but you will rarely find him laughing at other people's jokes. Funny man, this one!

How should one deal effectively with a Taurus man?

A 'yes sir' person can do amazingly well with the Taurean male. However, one shouldn't stop at 'yes'; actual work should get done too.

Perhaps the best way of handling a Taurus man is by pleasing his palate. The saying 'the way to a man's heart is through his stomach' seems to have originated exclusively for Taurus men, so intense is their love for food!

The Taurus man is no exception to mood swings either. So if you catch him in a good mood, you can get whatever you want out of him. The reverse too is true though, so beware!

How does he handle money matters?

Most Taurus men are sincere and hard-working and for them money is a by-product of hard work and hence very dear to them. If he has access to considerable amounts of money or if he has had a windfall, a Taurus male will be generous with his spending. Similarly, in moderate or bad times he would turn extremely conservative and cautious with it. Taurus men are extremely good at managing finances and you can trust them to keep some extra bucks tucked away somewhere for the proverbial rainy day.

With money the Taurus man is far-sighted; he likes to save first and spend later. He will plan for his future as well as that of his family. His ideas about money tend to get conservative here and he would give similar advice to others too. The fear of being dependent on others in old age is another reason why the Taurus male wants to be backed by a strong bank balance.

How is a Taurus male on the professional front?

At work, a Taurus man is extremely aggressive and competitive. He is an achiever who carries in his head a go-getter attitude. He is also creative, sincere and hard-working. So if you are looking forward to working with a Taurus man, be sure you imbibe these qualities. Remember, he likes to have what he gives to the world. At work you will find him to be extremely meticulous and detailed. And when it comes to rewarding sincere efforts, he is not one to keep a tight hand.

While he can be a very generous and easy-going boss, when rubbed the wrong way or his work messed around with, he could instantly turn into a demon. In such a situation, he is not likely to stop at anything, including publicly humiliating his employees, but this usually comes after he has given a few warnings.

How is he in various relationship roles?

As a son, he will be devoted to his parents, especially his mother. But he would prefer to do his own thing and it will be quite a task for his parents to get him to do anything else. He shows signs of independence from an early age and this includes independent decision-making.

As a spouse he will be extremely supportive and his participation and contribution towards his family will be to the fullest. For him family comes first and he will give his 100 per cent to it in terms of effort, money, time, etc. Although he respects the capabilities of his spouse, he likes to be a step ahead of her. This goes back to his conservative thoughts on gender equality.

A Taurus man displays great responsibility towards his children. He is capable of forgoing the joys of life himself, but will make sure his wife and children are well taken care of. With a Taurean father, the children will have no dearth of toys and clothes as also his time and love. While he would indulge them and be patient with their childishness, he would expect them to learn the lessons of life too.

As a friend, a Taurus man is likely to outdo himself. He is very passionate about his friendships and believes implicitly in the adage 'a friend in need is a friend indeed'. He would have only a few select friends, but to him their friendship would be for a lifetime.

How is he when alone?

A Taurus man is no Robinson Crusoe. He hates being alone and if put in such a spot, will end up being cranky. Being a family-centric man, he likes to have people around him and will be seen chattering like a magpie most of the times. Given his high emotional quotient, he can also turn into an emotional wreck if left to his own devices for too long. So if your love interest is a Taurus man, make sure he gets abundant doses of your company as here is one man who just can't be on his own.

How is he when in love?

If you've dated a Taurean or are married to one, you'd agree that 'being made to feel really special' is one of this charmer's greatest talents. Though he might not be too expressive about his feelings for you initially (he is slow in falling in love), once he has your attention and knows that you're 'his', be ready for a lifetime of romance.

A Taurus man is romantic in a truly bookish sense. He is your knight in shining armour who would take delight in surprising you with gifts and flowers. Nothing pleases him more than clambering up to his girlfriend's balcony at midnight with a pastry in hand to wish her a happy birthday. Not one to shy away from expressing his love and 'possession', the Taurus male wouldn't hesitate in indulging in public display of affection either. When in love or out of it, he will write poems and sing songs. He is generous and extremely verbal with compliments when due. And yes, this one is a stickler for remembering dates, from your first movie together to your last fight, he will remember everything.

What does he look for in his partner?

Let me tell you what he looks for in his life partner—a lady! Yes, a Taurus man wants his girlfriend or wife to be a complete lady, in every sense of the term. He would prefer a homemaker who is an excellent cook.

Given his love for food and eye for detail, he would want a well set table to welcome him after a hard day at work. While he can be indulgent enough to accept undercooked pasta and overcooked spaghetti occasionally, you better not make it a habit. Like I mentioned earlier, he is extremely critical of food and your culinary skills will be forever put to test. Here's a good piece of advice...cook food like his mother prepares and your man will be as pleased as punch. As a homemaker, he will also expect his wife to keep a good house for him, one that is clean and warm and is a welcoming place for him, his family and his select group of friends.

With his penchant for hard work, a Taurus man likes to chill out at home. On his day off you will usually find him lazing around and hence he needs a partner who understands his need to rest. He looks for complete support and trust in his better half and is equally willing to give it to her too.

Like any other person, a Taurus male wants ample space for himself. Since he has clearly drawn charts regarding the duties and responsibilities of a man and a woman in his mind, he wants his partner to fall in step with these ideas. So if your man belongs to the sign of the bull don't ever be critical of him especially in public and respect his abilities to the fullest. Since he will trust you from the very core of his being, don't ever think of playing games with him...because the ensuing emotional outburst might damage your relationship forever.

While dating him, you should...

...be ultra feminine. He likes those knick-knacks you carry in your handbag, as also your silk scarf and diamond studs. While other males will size-up a girl with a sweeping glance, the typical Taurean will take delight in details. So be sure you are well groomed on your date with him. Nothing will miss his discerning eye, not even the subtle shade of your lip gloss. Dress up elegantly, wear mild perfume and carry accessories that make a statement. Club these personal charms with good food, warm ambience and stimulating conversation and your Taurus date will be enchanted.

One aspect of the Taurus male that comes across rather strongly is his sensuality. You can't miss it while dating him. He is extremely manly and his masculinity will be seen in the way he carries himself and takes charge of the situation. If you are meeting him at a restaurant or coffee shop, don't jump the line and place the order. You wouldn't earn any brownie points for that! He's the man here, at the helm of things and you better not forget it.

Also, don't be in a rush. Rushing won't help you at all. The Taurus guy will go at his own pace. For him, romance has to be relished and each day savoured like every bite of a chocolate chip ice cream.

But once your romance is underway, you will be blessed with the most caring boyfriend. Not only will you see the gentleman in him at its best, but he will also use his sensuality to floor you.

The Taurus male has a strong sense of aesthetics and adores music. You would need to take this into account while selecting gifts for him. He is also sentimental by nature and so his mailbox is quite likely to be full of your emails as his mobile phone would be with your text messages.

Go for a second date with this man only if you are sure you would want to continue seeing him for life. Yes, that's how sentimental a Taurean can be. He doesn't believe in make-shift relationships. He won't indulge in senseless dating or a meaningless relationship. If he is interested in you, it is likely to result in a proposal. His love is for life. His solid exterior hides a delicate heart and once broken it heals with great difficulty and then too the scars remain.

Compatibility quotient

Which sun sign can match up to the stubbornness of the bull? And which sun sign is smart enough to appreciate the qualities of the home loving Taurean? It is strange how one weak point in a man can outweigh his good qualities. But a discerning eye and a loving heart is all that counts to make two people compatible. With the Taurean good sense and love for security, it would be quite a treat for the ladies on the zodiac to be with this man.

Taurus man and...

Aries woman: 7/10. Essentially, these two have disparate qualities. He is too home bound and intense, while she is too outgoing and free spirited. But if both are able to adjust with each other, this relationship can work out pretty well. Given the fact that 50 per cent Aries women are submissive and easy-going, this could be worth exploring.

Taurus woman: 8/10. This relationship is bound to be love-saturated and sensuous. However, both are stubborn. Being a man, the Taurus male's stubbornness can take an upper hand, but if he learns to control it both the Taureans can be compatible.

Gemini woman: 8/10. Again a great combination, but one that will blossom only after adjustments. It would be important for the Taurus guy to give his Gemini partner ample space and freedom. He in turn can be an anchor to her vivacious mind.

Cancer woman: 9/10. Although I don't want to use this term, it is unavoidable here...these two are 'made for each other'. She is mysterious and entrancing and he is loving and caring. He has the ability to give her a secure life, while she is capable of being the perfect woman for him. The undeniable chemistry here could culminate in a lasting romance.

Leo woman: 7/10. This can be a relationship that's full of spark...and sometimes fireworks. Once the Leo girl gets used to the Taurean 'I wear the trousers' attitude and the Taurus guy accepts her extrovert nature, it would be a joyride for both. She will have to be more patient with him and he will have to show more understanding to avoid conflicts.

Virgo woman: 8/10. Another relationship that is likely to work wonders. The Virgo girl meets her match emotionally in the Taurean guy.

Also, he has the right amount of passion to influence her. She is feminine enough to suit his taste and he will be happy looking after her and her womanly needs.

Libra woman: 6/10. The basic interests of these two might clash. While the Libra girl will like his sensitive and sentimental nature, she will be put-off by his possessiveness. The Taurus guy, on the other hand, will find her need to be with friends intriguing and a little disconcerting.

Scorpio woman: 5/10. These two are too similar to each other, especially on the negative points. Both are stubborn, wanting to have the upper hand and are also possessive. A lot of compromises would be required at both ends to make this a happy relationship. Even with a spark of romance in the initial stages of this relationship, and it seeming to be headed in some direction, where exactly, would usually be unknown till both learn to adjust.

Sagittarius woman: 4/10. The Sagittarian girl will not like his bossiness as she dislikes taking orders from anyone. With her spirited approach to life, she would find his possessive demeanour an encroachment on her freedom. He on the other hand is way too inflexible to suit the taste of the swaying Sagittarian.

Capricorn woman: 9/10. Her femininity is sure to attract him. The Capricorn girl is responsible enough to take-up the role of the woman of the house, while she would thoroughly enjoy being looked after by her man...something the Taurus male loves to do.

Aquarius woman: 6/10. The compatibility quotient between these two is quite low. His conservative thinking can clash with her unconventional ways. In case of disagreements, it would be difficult to mend matters as both are willful and unbending.

Pisces woman: 9/10. This combination will work as both can balance each other beautifully. He is sensitive enough to handle her hypersensitivity, while she is romantic enough to deal with his sensuousness.

Famous Taurus men personalities:

Al Pacino	David Beckham
George Clooney	Pierce Brosnan
Sachin Tendulkar	Sri Sri Ravishankar

Taurus woman

The expression 'a sound head on her shoulders' was coined for the Taurean female spirit—she is a woman who knows how to balance her emotions, a woman who is a woman in every sense, who knows exactly what she wants in life...that's a typical Taurus woman for you.

Known for her stubborn yet affectionate nature, a true Taurean will find her way into your heart via two routes: either gliding sensuously into love or tickling your palate with her culinary skills. Either way, she will head for your heart!

There are two types of Taurus women and they are poles apart. About 60 per cent are aggressive with a strong streak of feminism in them. They like being dominant and belong to the liberated women's group. The remaining 40 per cent are true earth sign females—more submissive and easy-to-be with. But don't think they lack aggression. The passive kinds too have the vein of aggression in them, albeit a milder one.

How would you identify a Taurus woman in a crowd?

The aggressive Taurus woman is not too difficult to spot in a crowd. With her nose high up in the air, she is awfully opinionated. When in a conversation or discussion, she also displays certain masculine qualities like dominance and power play. Trying to control things around her is the core characteristic of this woman.

On the contrary, the passive Taurus female is a relief for sore eyes. She is warm, friendly and forever smiling. Neither an introvert nor an extrovert, she is a curious mix of both. She is also not likely to mingle in a crowd very easily, but you will find her approachable and friendly. Once she is comfortable with you, you will see her as a warm individual and a treat to be with.

What are the key features of her personality?

One of the highlights of a Taurus woman's personality (and perhaps a misguiding factor as well) is her relaxed demeanour. She appears to be outwardly calm and composed, but inside she is bubbling with restless emotions. She is much like a frozen river...icy cool on top and gurgling with action inside. The ice breaks very often and emotional outbursts are not uncommon.

Where the Taurus woman is concerned, remember, caution is her middle name. Be it the aggressive or the passive kind, she makes every move and every decision with great caution. With such a detailed thought process, she is either likely to arrive at absolutely correct decisions or come by them rather late so much so that sometimes her over-cautiousness makes her almost inactive.

Stemming from her cautious nature, is also her reluctance to accept change (she shares this quality with her male counterpart). Change of any kind, especially brought about by others, is a big no-no for a Taurus woman. So conservative is her attitude that she will never break away from the old order and will prefer to toe the traditional line.

The female Taurean has clear cut demarcation between people she likes and people she doesn't. She is very choosy about her friends, but those she befriends are lucky to have her friendship. She attaches great value to true friendship. To her it is everlasting! And with people she dislikes, she is rather curt at dismissing them. She has a special Taurus way of dealing with unpleasant people...she simply ignores them!

A Taurus woman is one woman who believes that she is born to receive. She expects life to keep giving. This doesn't mean she is incapable of hard work and sincere efforts, but very often what she expects is not in proportion with her efforts. She wants life to be fair all the time.

And she is definitely not satisfied with average living. She wants the very best for herself and her family. This woman belongs to the group of women who know exactly what they want, at least materialistically. You will not find her mulling over what her desires are. She has mentally sorted out everything from an early age. However, let me add that this clarity of thought is limited to material things only. Very often she is at a loss when it comes to more philosophical and idealistic matters of life.

She also has a unique approach towards life. To her, 'her way' is the realistic way. She prefers to lead and is a quick learner and a hard worker. While she is not afraid to put in efforts, she expects quick results.

I may have made them sound all intense and serious, but Taurus women have a unique sense of humour too. They are generally funny people and love to have a good laugh.

How is a Taurus woman on the following aspects?

Appearance: Taurus women have a very distinct combination of sharp and blunt features. They have sharp, expressive eyes. An odd observation, but I have found a small percentage of Taurus women to have well-shaped nose, with the majority possessing blunt noses. For a Taurus woman the highlight of her face is undoubtedly her lips, usually observed and found to be just perfect.

True to her earth sign, her taste in clothes too is earthy. She prefers clothes that are comfortable, generally in pastel shades and in soft fabrics like cottons, linen and denims. Since most Taurus women are creative and artistic, this is reflected in their dressing and you will find them wearing embroidered fabrics, or bold ones like batik and sometimes even whacky designs.

The Taurean girl has a knack for dressing up with femininity. But here again, practicality takes precedence. Although her taste in clothes would be expensive, it would be pragmatic to the core.

Ambition: Both kinds of Taurean women are highly ambitious. To them, growth and climbing-up the ladder, both monetarily and socially, is very important. They always aspire for top positions and work diligently towards their set targets.

You will get a better idea of her ambitiousness when I tell you how strongly it is backed by her stubborn will and her persistent need to be economically secure. It is almost impossible to get her to do what she doesn't want to do or stop her from doing what she has set out to do. She will firmly persevere in her efforts till she attains her targets. And in the process it is important for her to make money, which to her signifies purchasing power, stability and security.

Ego/Self-respect: An aggressive Taurus woman is driven by her ego, while hiding it behind the façade of self-respect. She will never accept her mistake and even if she is in the wrong will argue endlessly to prove her point.

If you ever find a Taurus woman being unbending in her stance, you can attribute it both to her ego and headstrong nature. And then there are certain issues (read 'feminist issues') that are close to her heart and she will show her egoistic standpoint while addressing them.

The passive Taurus woman is more accommodating and is open to accepting idiosyncrasies in others as well.

Responsibility: Although a Taurus woman usually has a good sense of duty, it comes with a condition tag. She is often found to be selfish and puts herself before her responsibilities. Because of this sometimes, her responsibilities take a backseat.

With the passive kind, who is more aware of her duties, fulfilling them to a T is a constant tug of war. She is always struggling to strike a balance between what her responsibility demands and what she owes to herself. But a Taurus woman, especially the passive kind, fullfils her responsibilities once she understands its true worth. For instance, when she understands the true value of her relationship with her husband, she will make sure she keeps an excellent house for him.

Etiquettes: Both kinds of Taurus women are extremely particular about everything regarding etiquettes, down to the minutest details. They expect a man to show chivalry and would themselves be chivalrous if the situation demands. Right manners at a party, at the dining table and overall at all occasions is a must with a Taurus woman.

What is her approach towards life?

True to the symbol of her sun sign, the Taurus woman is a strong willed individual, with a very practical take on life. She would stand tall amid utter chaos and not buckle under the most trying of circumstances, emerging from the conflicting situations with her dignity intact.

Bullish to the core, she could very often take on a stubborn stance and refuse to budge from her point of view. This could work out well, if she truly believes in what she's doing. However, it acts as a turn-off for those around her who find her unyielding behaviour disconcerting.

The passive female Taurean is not much concerned with worldly matters. Content if all is well with her and her loved ones, she would be delighted in attending to their needs, gladly sacrificing her own interests to serve her family.

How does she score on the following points?

Cynicism: I have found almost all Taurean women to be cynics to a great extent. Like their male counterparts, they are stubborn and need to have their way with everything. Although both kinds of Taurus women possess cynicism, their way of exhibiting the same is different. The aggressive Taurus female would put her foot down hard and do her will, while the passive one will be as stubborn, but in a more subtle manner.

Suspicion/Jealousy: Suspicion and Taurus women are inseparable with both the aggressive and passive types showing this trait. When in doubt they are capable of spying on people, especially their spouses. If you have a Taurus girlfriend or wife, be ready to be cross-questioned at the slightest misgiving and remember they will not be satisfied with excuses and explanations!

If their doubts are not satisfied, it leads to another trouble; their jealousy. They are likely to use their imagination and be jealous about things that might not have actually happened. Add to it their possessiveness and extremely passionate nature and they become easily jealous. Interestingly, their jealous disposition is not limited to relationships only—it also seeps into their professional lives.

Dishonesty/Infidelity: Taurus women are generally faithful and loyal but on the flipside they are no strangers to promiscuity. Being extremely passionate, as she ages/matures, a Taurus woman's desires seem to increase and she is usually found to be searching for a younger man to court.

But, when faced with promiscuity in her man, she will not spare him under any circumstances. Both kinds of Taurus women are likely to thrash out at their men, until their anger abates.

Hardships: A Taurus woman can't take hardships well. During difficult times, all her grace deserts her. She is most likely to take-up bitching and cribbing about her situation and lastly use the most effective weapon—blaming others.

Although she finds it difficult to deal with hardships, she is prudent enough to stand by her family, partner or friends during troubled times. This is where she will display her loyalty and faithfulness towards her loved ones.

Success and failure: Taurus women like to show their success but they are never loud about it. They would be satisfied once people know of it and have noticed their success.

When it comes to failures, as with hardships, they find it difficult to deal with it. This makes them bad losers, but they are blessed with a fighter spirit and won't give up on anything easily.

Host: A Taurus woman has the uncanny habit of making you comfortable and yet uncomfortable while playing host. She is meticulous and detailed to a great extent. But her dominant spirit can play down upon you. To explain it; as a host you will find her hovering above you, trying to make you comfortable, but this over-graciousness in her makes her seem overpowering.

However, I must add here that she is very good at handling her guests. No matter how big the guest list, she will make sure everyone is well taken care of. At her parties, you will generally find her standing next to her husband/partner beaming with satisfaction.

The passive kind, however, lets people get comfortable on their own through her warmth as a host.

Guest: Being a perfect host herself, as a guest she would expect the same of you. She likes to go to social dos that are painstakingly planned and neatly executed. But a slight slip (which can be something as unimportant as the colour of serviettes) will turn her into a snub and send her nose up in the air in a sniff. She is capable of being all sugar and honey while conversing with you and bitch about everything behind your back.

The passive kind here too is at ease. She may or may not have expectations as a guest but won't fret too much about it.

How does she handle difficult situations?

To begin with, I have often noticed that both kinds of Taurus women are capable of great self-control and possess a good patience level. So it is quite a task to get them into a difficult situation or get them riled up. Like her male counterpart, she gets livid only when provoked to the extreme. But once she has been pushed too far, there is no stopping her. With the fierceness of her zodiac symbol, she will charge ahead, fully giving vent to her anger.

With an aggressive Taurus woman, a difficult situation is a very difficult situation. She refuses to own up to her mistakes and goes on the defensive if fingers are pointed at her. You will generally find her raving and ranting to cover-up her inconsistencies. I am yet to meet an aggressive Taurus woman who knows how to apologise gracefully.

The passive woman is more flexible and knows how to handle complicated situations. She is more open to discussions and communication and shows inclination towards resolving issues.

What is her characteristic weakness?

The core weakness of a Taurus woman is her high sentimental quotient. Even the aggressive kind, who shows a strong exterior, is sentimental within. Another shortcoming of the Taurus woman is her high expectation from life, society and people around her. She believes everyone and everything around her is for her service. She would put little effort and expect the world in return.

Her stubbornness can also come in her way, and in her headstrong moods, it is difficult to make her see reason.

Is there more to this resolute woman's persona?

One of the finest traits that I have noticed in Taurean females is their capacity to be feminine without being sissy. At least emotionally, deep inside, she is as solid as a rock.

She is also quite independent. I don't mean it in a manly sense but she likes to take things in control and manages tasks related to herself with efficiency.

The one sense a Taurean girl has in abundance is common sense. She sees everything from a practical standpoint. You won't catch her wasting anything, be it money or emotion, without a reason. Because of this trait she always gets to the crux of the matter directly and doesn't believe in philosophical, intellectual or verbal meanderings. However, this does not imply that she is not smart. Her intelligence is directed towards making the most of this practical world.

At times the bullish attribute of her sun sign makes itself obvious and you may catch a Taurus woman being inordinately stubborn. She will refuse to bend her stance. During such times it is best to let her be. Now I would request you to take this advice seriously...when I say let her be, I mean it. She has loads of patience but it isn't endless and once it snaps there is no restraining her. When rubbed the wrong way or provoked beyond endurance, she can get into a blinding rage. Then on...there's no stopping her. Like a bull in a Spanish bullfight, she will ransack everything around. And you've got to be an expert matador to be able to control her. So beware of that Taurean temper!

With the occasional sighting of the red flag, the Taurus girl usually sees things in black and white. To her the world is made up of friends and enemies. Her friends are treated with love and affection, while her enemies are merely ignored. So if you find a Taurean girl giving you the cold shoulder, be rest assured that she has you on her 'black list'.

If emotionally she is made of steel, then her will is made of iron. She has tremendous capacity for hard work, which includes physical strength. You won't find her buckling under stress or giving up a fight due to lack of resilience.

Another aspect of the Taurean personality (which I have been witness to) is her love for aesthetics. She appreciates beautiful things, from artefacts to art works. She also finds herself drawn to the fine arts with painting, music and dance forms appealing to her. And to get the best out of her, she should be taken to her original habitat—the lap of Nature.

How should one deal effectively with a Taurus woman?

The feminist part of the Taurus woman expects her man to treat her equally, but the woman in her wants a man of strength to dominate her. With the aggressive Taurus woman, a man needs to strike a balance between submissiveness and dominance. While he can let her have her way sometimes, in situations of tantrums and emotional dramas, it is important for him to dominate.

A Taurus woman basically needs an assurance that she is strong and independent. Once she is assured of this and if you have succeeded in winning her heart, she will live with you with great comfort and ease.

Whether with friendship or with love, she thinks in terms of 'forever'. There are no temporary relations for her. If she befriends you, she will remain by your side through thick and thin. And if she is in love with you, you will get all the attention of a devoted girlfriend or wife from her end. But all this is not unconditional. She will expect loyalty and dedication or more in return. And any hitch in either is usually not tolerated.

This woman dislikes hypocrites so while dealing with her make sure you mean everything you say. She is shrewd enough to see through you and if she uncovers hypocrisy in your motives, then it may as well be goodbye forever!

Also remember that she is highly emotional. While in a way it is her weakness, it is also her greatest strength. She draws power from her emotions and can battle it out in turbulent times with the sheer force of her emotional prowess.

Overall, a Taurus woman is dependable and caring. She will also be trustworthy and trusting of you once she is comfortable with you.

How does she handle money matters?

A Taurus woman, in general, is careful with her money. No one understands the power of money better than her.

While she is not exactly a miser, she likes to save money. She can be quite resourceful in investing her income safely, usually for old age. Not one to gamble with money, she relies totally on the security that money offers and would rather do with a little extra cash at home than wait for windfall gains.

Given her cautious nature, you can trust her with your credit card. She is not one to go on a spending spree. Though she likes material comforts, she is very practical in her spending. But, when it comes to herself and her loved ones and friends, she can be very generous, yet very conservative.

The Taurean also has a smart head regarding investments and accounts. She knows where to put her money to make it grow.

How is a Taurus woman on the professional front?

Taurus women are extremely competitive, with the aggressive kind tending to be tactful and shrewd. If need be she will not shy away from using her femininity to get her work done.

She is a hard worker and will put in sincere efforts in her work. Of course what she expects out of it might be way beyond what she deserves. She is also a quick learner and a jolly person, which not only makes her extremely competent but also easy to work with.

She falls in the category of achievers and is extremely creative too. Always in a hurry to achieve success, at times she has to be patient but eventually she gets what she wants.

How is she in various relationship roles?

The aggressive Taurus woman treats her home like her office and therefore needs a more passive man to strike the right balance. She likes to chart out her territory in her house and creates clear demarcations for everything including TV hours, household chores, etc.

The passive kind is fabulous as a homemaker and excels in the role of a working woman too. She has all the qualities a man looks for in a wife. She is affectionate and caring, will never make you feel unwanted and knows how to make her man feel happy, excited and sensual.

In return for all her efforts at being a good wife she will expect loyalty from you and unconditional support, especially in public. She will want her partner to hold up her views in front of others and if you contradict her or prove her wrong, be ready for fireworks at home.

She yearns for independence and makes a great show of being dominant. But secretly she desires a man who knows how to control her. So treat your Taurus wife like a queen—fullfil all her demands and be submissive when she is stubborn, but also learn the tact of holding the reins and pulling them at the right time.

The aggressive Taurus women are disciplinarians, especially with their children. As mothers, they can be fun to be with but equally strict. To them, raising children is like running a military school. The passive Taurus woman can make a great mother as she is patient and loving. She can be a good friend to her children and they will find her easy to be with.

If you have a Taurus woman for a boss, the easiest way to be with her is to say what she wants to hear...'yes madam'. Since she is meticulous and detailed in everything, she expects the same of you and as your boss she would know how to get things done her way as well.

As a friend, she will remain forever committed to friendship. Like I had mentioned earlier, she has select friends but those are very dear to her. She will be an excellent ally, holding their hand through good times and bad, and like everything else will expect the same in return.

How is she when alone?

Given her high emotional needs, a Taurus woman can be miserable when alone. Although the aggressive kind likes to be independent, her emotions need constant support and hence she is never happy when left alone. However, this does not mean that she likes crowds. She prefers her select group of friends and her party list is not likely to exceed fifteen people.

How is a Taurus woman when in love?

The Taurean love is not just love...it's a complete package. She will be a lover, wife, friend and guide to you. She will be wife-like even though you are not married, which means she will take care of you and your needs as a wife would. She would also be a guide to you and give you wise, practical tips on how to get along with life.

Like I had mentioned earlier, the Taurean is possessive by nature. It is advisable not to make her jealous or suspicious. Since she trusts easily, she finds it difficult to handle breach of trust. Another reason to avoid provoking her is her destructive anger. Very often she is not able to control her anger and it rages on like a storm, destroying everything in its vicinity.

When in love perhaps the most outstanding of her traits would be her sensuality. The Taurus girl will tread the path of love rather slowly. She will size you up completely before going ahead. But once things get underway, romance will be in the air forever...it would be a natural part of her aura.

Her sensuality is a double-edged sword. She is quite aware of it most of the times and thus practices restrain. She needs a man who appreciates her sensuous charm as well as knows how to keep a tab on her.

Moreover, a Taurus woman looks for an emotional anchor in her boyfriend or husband. In cases where she is married and the emotional quotient in her marital relationship is lacking, she is quite capable of outsourcing the same.

To conclude, I would say the Taurus girl is the kind of person you can take home to meet your parents. What makes her more interesting is her/how chauvinistic penchant for cooking and housekeeping.

What does she look for in her partner?

Most Taurean women are quite picky when it comes to selecting a partner for themselves. Pragmatic in their outlook towards life, they'd easily write-off a man who is too emotionally vocal, as mere sissy.

The female Taurean desires a partner who is financially and emotionally sound. Since she herself has a very practical attitude, she seeks a like-minded individual who shares her interests...reading, watching movies, visiting places of archaeological importance and the like.

This however, does not mean that she wants someone who's indifferent towards the romantic yearnings of a woman. She would love the occasional long stemmed roses and would be delighted if her partner surprises her with a very romantic candle lit dinner for two.

While dating her, you should...

...get her an expensive (but practical) gift, buy her flowers and take her to a fine dine restaurant. The gift will assure her of your love, flowers would delight her and good food will do the trick for you.

The Taurean female is a woman of taste...and I mean it literally. She likes good cuisine and the right mix of spices and flavours can make her go home with her head full of thoughts of you. If you can pull up a faire extraordinaire, it wouldn't be a bad idea to invite her to your place for a quiet dinner. And when it is her turn to return the compliment, you can be rest assured it would be a meal you won't forget for a long time, as the lady in question also happens to be an excellent cook.

Remember, a Taurean is very selective about whom she dates. So if she has agreed to meet you it is after careful consideration and whether a second date would follow depends largely on how you excel at the first one. First impressions mean a lot to her. Although she has patience, she won't necessarily exercise this virtue in case of dating. But once she commits herself it would be for keeps.

All this does not mean she will hang around your neck like a lovesick puppy. The Taurus woman likes to take charge of her emotions and you will find her pretty much in control. Dating her will be a slick affair, with a lot of feeling and sensuality and totally devoid of the messy and mushy stuff.

Though she has agreed to date you, it is advisable to give her time. She would like to go through the details of her relationship with you and only then would decide upon the future course. Don't rush her into things, she might think you to be too fast and back out right away.

Another absolute no while dating the Taurus woman is attempting to take the bull by its horns. The bull, especially the aggressive one, is quite egoistic. If you try to meddle with her way of working or criticise her, the wall of her patience may crumble. Moreover, she hates being contradicted, especially before acquaintances. While you need not be a 'yes madam' man, you will have to master the art of understating, (remember she does not like sissies. She needs a man with a strong shoulder to lean on and stronger arms to carry her in).

Once you are in the second phase of dating a Taurean girl, you are very likely to see her sensuousness. It's not an 'in your face' kind of appeal, rather it is subtle and sometimes provocative but always governed by love. No Taurean will get into the 'step two' zone without being sure of a long standing relation. The best way to flatter her is to tell her how beautiful she is, to charm her with your caresses and let her know that she is the best thing that's happened to you...and none of this, by the way, would be untrue.

Compatibility quotient

While the typical Taurean isn't exactly sweet tempered, she is a complete woman in every other way. What's more, she is in a way aware of her shortcomings and knows how to keep them in check. In spite of being strong willed, she needs a man who can take care of her. In such a scenario who would be the most compatible man for her? Let's find out!

Taurus woman and...

Aries man: 5/10. His passion can get things started but it won't necessarily stand the test of time. She is way too practical to suit his impulsiveness. With a woman with such an independent streak, the Aries man might feel tied down and think his freedom under threat.

Taurus man: 8/10. This combination can hit the bull's-eye...no pun intended. The Taurus man's stability can impress his female counterpart, whereas her penchant for good housekeeping can keep his comfort levels high. But both will have to learn to keep their obstinacy under check.

Gemini man: 4/10. The compatibility quotient between these two is rather low. The Gemini male is adventurous and impatient, not to mention reckless at times. A Taurean will find these aspects too much to adjust with, while he may take her staid nature as kind of boring.

Cancer man: 9/10. There will be no dearth of warmth and romance in this relationship. The Taurean would know how to deal with his mood swings with patience, while the Cancer man would know how to appreciate her womanly qualities.

Leo man: 7/10. With a little bit of hard work, this relationship can turn out pretty well. The Taurean will have to learn to handle the Leo ego with grace and he would need to be more appreciative of her love.

Virgo man: 8/10. Security is the key word in this relationship. She will be able to draw out the romantic in him, while he will undoubtedly appreciate her pragmatism. Both will be able to satisfy each others' demands for commitment and devotion.

Libra man: 7/10. Again, a lot of hard work would be needed to make this relationship tick, not to mention lot of compromises. The Taurean will have to be less clingy and needy of a commitment. The Libran guy on the other hand should learn to give her the security she yearns for.

Scorpio man: 6/10. This one would be a really tough one to pull off! The Scorpio man's secretiveness won't go down well with the Taurean, making the mercury of her suspicion soar. Both might also get too headstrong for each other to handle.

Sagittarius man: 6/10. If the law 'opposites attract' can sustain over a long-term, this combination is likely to survive. She would be floored by his adventurous spirit and he will like the idea of returning to a warm home after a hard day's work. But to really make this work, she will have to tone down her need for security, while he will have to be more 'home bound'.

Capricorn man: 9.5/10. The Capricorn man is the best match for the Taurus girl. With her loyalty, the Capricorn guy will learn to let his guard down and be more expressive of his feelings. She would also know how to bring his humourous side to the fore. She will always have a strong shoulder to lean on and never feel bored in his company.

Aquarius man: 7/10. If both are ready to learn, they can teach each other a few good lessons in life. She can be an anchor to his wild nature and he can show her how a few laughs can brighten life. These two can together strike a balance between the intense and lighter sides of life.

Pisces man: 9/10. The Piscean's dreams will get staunch support from the practical Taurean. The Taurus girl is loyal and the Piscean will appreciate this quality in her. She will also show him how to realise his dreams in a practical manner. The Piscean will impress her with his spiritual leaning and intellectual mind.

Famous Taurus women personalities:

Audrey Hepburn
Kate Blanchet
Uma Thurman
Janet Jackson
Madhuri Dixit

Gemini

22 May-21 June

Gemini man

Two-faced, flirtatious, reckless, restless, experimental, enigmatic...the list of attributes associated with a Gemini man is endless. With a million facets to his personality, the male of this seductive sun sign is all of the above, yet none of it. His two faces are not any different from the masks each one of us dons in our day-to-day life, (thankfully with a Gemini there are only two faces) but, the duality in his nature is genuine and you'll rarely find him trying to hide it.

And whether he is flirtatious, reckless and restless depends largely on his age and social status. Young Geminis tend to be more restless than mature ones. But when it comes to the company of the fairer sex, a true Gemini, no matter what his age, will be partial towards them, but this sociable being conducts all his affairs with amazing masculine grace. When you're with him be ready to be floored as this charmer knows how to make his woman go all weak in the knees!

He has a head full of fantastic ideas that makes life with a Gemini a roller coaster ride with constant change in scenarios and frequent ups and downs.

How can you identify a Gemini man in a crowd?

Unless you spend a lot of time studying people, it's not easy to spot a Gemini man in a crowd. In a given situation like a party, if you keenly observe you might find him looking at or flirting with the prettiest face around (no wonder he earned the tag of Casanova), but he will flirt in the most subtle manner, as if he doesn't care for the result, (of the little that I know of women, they usually find this fascinating and often fall for the bait).

This is the only sun sign that leaves me confused as I am not able to classify Gemini men into either aggressive or passive kinds. After having met many Gemini men, the only thing I have concluded is that they are highest on energy levels.

What are the key features of his personality?

Generally, the first reaction one gets upon meeting a Gemini man is that he is two-faced. This can be attributed to the symbol assigned to this sun sign, but I strongly feel that if not all, a lot of us are two-faced; it's just that this trait is stronger in Gemini men. And because of this, you will find diverse qualities co-existing in Gemini men.

Being a convincing talker and a knowledgeable man, women often find a Gemini male appealing but not someone who'll settle down soon. Though fond of female company, he is wary of commitments and hence in spite of having been with many women, settling down doesn't come easy to him.

A Gemini man is intelligent and likes challenges, be it in love, business or career. He is also versatile and since he likes talking, he can usually be found amongst people, if not in a crowd. A people's person, he likes parties and social dos. You are likely to see the best side of him at a social event.

In his quest for knowledge, the two things that help the Gemini get more out of life are experience and travel. He loves travelling and entertainment. Known to enjoy life to the fullest, he is also extremely adventurous. However, 20 odd per cent of them are introverts and have select friends.

The Gemini male is inordinately interested in observing human nature. I guess it arises from his voracious thirst for knowledge. To him any individual is like a mystery, which he has to unravel. Once it is solved, he moves on to the next one (this may be one reason why he is fond of dating many women). There is also something of a wanderer in him. He likes change and like a butterfly will flit from one bunch of flowers to another. With this statement I don't imply only women, but this holds true for any aspect of life. Given his multifaceted personality, he adapts himself to any situation and gets the best out of it.

A Gemini man is usually very self-obsessed and at times even selfish. You might not see or feel it but you have to experience it to know how smoothly he gets away with what he wants. This attitude often makes people feel that he lacks emotional intensity.

I have also found a quality in Gemini men that is rather uncommon... common sense. Combined with his deep knowledge, this makes him an intelligent companion to be with.

How is he on the following aspects?

Appearance: Most Gemini men I have met have mischievous, playful eyes. They come across as extremely intense yet fun-loving. They have a great sense of fashion and you'll always find them updated on latest trends and styles, easily adapting to change. There are very few exceptions of the ultra casual type in Geminis.

Ambition: For a Gemini man who is motivated by the acquisition of materialistic objects, enough is never enough! There is this certain percentage of Gemini men who will put in a lot of hard work and sincerity in their work or in creating a business empire, but the majority of them want to work little but make pots and pots of money and have maximum fun.

Ego/Self-respect: I would say 80 per cent are governed by their egos while 20 per cent have some sense of humility. This doesn't make them necessarily bad, it is just an attitude. Being selfish, they are usually found donning the mask of self-respect or being diplomatic, but if you observe closely you will notice they are actually led by their egos.

Responsibility: The best and easiest way to be around with a Gemini man is to expect the least. While he can show he is responsible and dependable, due to his habit of over committing or a general lack of interest, he is mostly never able to meet his responsibilities. This should not be taken as a comment on his ability or intention; it's just that he wants to do too many things or nothing at all and is unable to convey the same.

Etiquettes: A Gemini man can be a good match between extremely formal and extremely casual when it comes to etiquettes. Since he is very adaptable, he can adjust to any kind of environ and follow the right etiquettes to suit the occasion.

What is his approach towards life?

Most Gemini have an amazingly materialistic bent of mind. Acquisition being their key motivator, they work relentlessly towards whatever they set their eyes upon, till they 'conquer' it (the same applies to their attitude towards the opposite sex).

To a typical Gemini male, life is all about the chase! Once the chase is over, he loses all interest in man (read 'woman') and material. He would then move on to his next target, investing great time and effort in planning out his plans of plunder.

This nomad is usually found exploring new places and interests from time to time. He will invest time and money in keeping himself occupied and in the company of others (especially those whom he can impress with his display of knowledge and charm). Given to making impromptu plans, the adventurous Gemini man exhibits a distinctive charm in his approach towards life. He comes across as a blend of James Bond (suave and sophisticated) and Indiana Jones (adventurous).

How does a Gemini man score on the following points?

Cynicism: A Gemini man can come across as extremely cynical but on close observation you will realise he knows exactly what he is doing. He will be unsettled till he finds what he is looking for. Having dealt with many Gemini men at work and as friends, I feel the phrase 'have your cake and eat it too' was coined solely for them.

Suspicion/Jealousy: Gemini men expect a lot of space in relationships and hence are capable of giving it too and this generally makes them non-suspicious. But if you try to imitate his nature, of being flirtatious or give him reason to be suspicious, he will not take it kindly.

A Gemini man may not show jealousy in relationships but his competitive spirit often gets the better of him and he can go green.

Dishonesty/Infidelity: A Gemini man enjoys a very good rapport with women, but commits rather late in life and so very often he marries at a mature age. Having the experience of 'been there, done that', he tends to remain loyal to his chosen life partner. Of course, his flirtatious streak may come to the front now and then, but it's nothing serious.

As I mentioned before, since he expects and gives a lot of space in a relationship on account of trust, infidelity or dishonesty from his partner can hurt him a lot.

Hardship: As much as they would like an easy life and easy money, Gemini men are very capable of facing and taking hardships in life (although this quality comes with the rider of excessive cribbing) in the right spirit.

Success and failure: When a Gemini man tastes success, he likes to relish it by himself. He will not be loud about it and it will be celebrated with a select few. Even the most extrovert Gemini man would keep to himself.

When failure comes his way, a Gemini man most likely has himself to blame. Due to his over commitments and need to multitask, he often loses focus of what he sets out to do, but instead of realising his error, he ends up blaming others or circumstances for his failures.

Host: A very casual host, a Gemini man will prepare for a hospitable ambience and leave the rest to you. It's upto you how comfortable you can make yourself at his party. This does not imply he will not be warm, welcoming or courteous.

Guest: As a guest, a Gemini man is observant to a great extent, but if in an unfamiliar environment, you will usually find him keeping to himself and doing his own thing.

How does he handle difficult situations?

When in conflict, he tends to be diplomatic and casual as though nothing has happened. Thanks to his gift of the gab, he finds it easy to communicate and you will find him ready to talk things over and iron out differences. Unless he is extremely hurt or angry, a Gemini man will easily patch up after any fallout. He is not shy to apologise when at fault and expects to be forgiven easily.

What is his characteristic weakness?

His weaknesses are indecisiveness, restlessness and inconsistency. Now you might think this listing of his shortcomings is plain vanilla, but with this guy these flaws are interconnected and critical to his demeanour.

A Gemini man is most indecisive by nature. He can't decide on the spur of the moment and you will find him in two minds about everything. This leads us to his restlessness. As described earlier, he likes challenges. And as soon as any challenge fails to hold his interest anymore the Gemini man will be impatient to move on. But again, he is not sure where to move to, as he has too many options and likes to keep them open. This applies to relationships, career decisions or something as simple as planning his day-to-day schedule. If you ever come across a man who is mulling for hours over what to wear, where to go and what to do...you can double check and see if he is a Gemini or a Virgo.

This brings us to his third shortcoming—inconsistency. His indecisiveness and restlessness make him inconsistent too. You will often come across a Gemini who plans on something but ends up doing something else. Also, in a well-sketched out plan, his self might interfere and make him change the course of things. His multifaceted personality can lead one to believe that he is a different man everyday...inconsistent or variety, you will have to figure it out yourself!

He can be quite a 'yes man' to everybody. He will say yes to everybody and every idea, leaving people around him confused about what he exactly wants to do.

Is there more to his persona?

Given the complex times we live in and the diverse traits of this man's personality, if you dig deeper you'll find lots more. And here I would like to reveal more about a Gemini man, as per my observations.

There maybe exceptions out there but I would never trust a Gemini man with a secret. This purely comes from my personal experience with them across the ages of twenty and seventy-five. And boy! They can't keep their mouth shut! I have not been able to understand why they do this, but they do it nevertheless.

Lest the reader thinks that I am too critical of the Gemini man, let me introduce a finer aspect of his personality. He has the ability to think from a second person's point of view. This quality makes him intuitive and receptive to other people's opinions and needs. He is also known to go with the flow, which makes him a comfortable person to be with.

A Gemini man wants to partake of all the good things in life. Materialistic to a great extent, he will put in the required efforts to make it big. He wants to achieve too much in too little a time. Also, given the restlessness in his nature, he will be in a hurry to climb on to the next rung of the ladder, many times without getting a firm grip of the lower rung.

A Gemini man is emotional and sentimental about matters concerning him, but with others his emotional quotient takes a slight dip. He is a dreamer and an achiever in numerous ways. He is one man who can excel in professions as varied as banking, food and beverage industry, mixing music to playing in a rock band.

I have also found that energy is a driving force for Gemini men and based on this quality a classification can be made amongst Geminis. There are two types of Gemini males. Type A knows how to handle their vivacious and energetic personalities and tend to utilise these qualities to the best. They are more organised, hard-working, goal-oriented and resolute. Type B Gemini men are weak and slapdash as they don't know how to put their innate energy and intelligence to good use. Such men are often found pursuing mundane tasks and being weak-kneed about adventures and challenges. In short, Type A is more aggressive and forthcoming, while Type B is less masculine and less responsible.

To a great extent, there is something of a trickster in the Gemini male. I have seen this surfacing when self obsession washes over his better qualities. He can trick people to achieve his ends, which may not necessarily be monetary.

I would like to explain this point with a personal example. In one of my real estate deals I was approached by a Gemini man and appointed as the sole broker to either rent or sell his property. The man is a renowned architect and one took his word when he said, 'Even if I sell or rent it to someone I know, you will be involved and covered always.' This was repeated by him several times over a period of one year when the market conditions were not that good and it took a while to find buyers. He wished to dispose off two apartments in a three-storey building he owned. I found him a serious buyer for the third floor apartment and started negotiation, and in the same span of time, got him a well known client for the apartment on the second floor as well. Everything was finalised between him and my client and the sale was about to go through.

Unexpectedly, the deal with the buyer for the third floor apartment fell through. He knew that the second client I had got for him initially had wanted the third floor apartment, and so he called them up directly, without my knowledge, to ask if they were still interested, since the place was now available. Naturally, they said yes and the deal was then struck for the third floor apartment instead.

After all the paperwork was done, I got a call from this Gemini gentleman informing me that since my client did not buy the second floor house but bought the third floor one instead, I was out of the picture and he was not liable to pay for any services rendered by me. Imagine my indignation! I gave him a piece of my mind in the choicest of words and hung up on him.

A few months down the line, he had no qualms about walking upto me and greeting me at a party and discussing his property again. So much for some of the unique work experience with a Gemini man!

How should one deal effectively with a Gemini man?

After having dealt with Gemini men I realise that they have to be handled with a lot of tact. He is not the kind of man to whom you can open all your cards, otherwise he will walk all over you.

If you are looking forward to dating a Gemini man or marrying him, you will have to strike a balance between playing hard to get and keeping him interested. As much as he likes to chase, if you play too hard, his ego won't permit him to go further.

You would also require high amount of patience to deal with his impatience, inconsistencies and indecisiveness. If you can cope with that you will have a good friend by your side.

How does he handle money matters?

A Gemini man is extremely shrewd with money. Smart and innovative, he is capable of making money one way or the other. He can be both a high spender and a miser, but without any correlation with his bank balance. Another pointer of the typical Gemini shrewdness is the fact that regarding money matters they can't be cheated or deceived easily and are very good at negotiations.

How is he on the professional front?

The Gemini male's inability to stay focused for long periods of time can land him in trouble. Since he loses interest in people, places and generally in everything else too soon, he has a tendency to leave a trail of unfinished business upon exit.

On the positive side, our man has a knack of motivating people with his infectious enthusiasm. He thus makes an excellent leader as well as an effective team worker. Knowing how to convince others with his words, this manipulative smooth talker can excel in professions revolving around sales and marketing or public relations. Given their shrewd business acumen and insight in matters of finance, the more entrepreneurial kinds of Gemini men are generally found dabbling in the stock market or related fields. They can also get impulsive with their investment decisions.

How is he in various relationship roles?

Much can be drawn from how a Gemini man behaves during courtship. Once his attitude towards love and marriage is clear, it will be easy to anticipate how he would be in the role of a husband. As a husband, a Gemini man can be attentive, loving and caring, and would give lots of space and respect to his wife. But if he is closeted with too many marital responsibilities, you will end up walking into a brick wall. Also, keep a look out for the inevitable fickleness in a Gemini man, that will surface every now and then.

As a father, he will be a friend and a guide to his children. He is likely to spoil his kids with excessive cuddling and will also be protective of them at all times. He has the ability to charm children with his stories. The gift of thinking like them makes it easy for him to befriend them. However, he scores low on the discipline front...so if children are assigned exclusively to a Gemini man's care, they are likely to end up as spoilt brats. As a friend (not casual acquaintance), a Gemini man is helpful, warm and friendly. Although he is friendly with many, he has few friends. Since he likes change, you will often find him leaving his old friends behind and moving on to new ones.

How is he when alone?

A Gemini man needs to be constantly involved in something. He usually does not want to be by himself, and likes company or prefers to be part of some activity. After having keenly observed my Gemini friends, I have realised that 70 per cent of them have literally a handful of friends only. They are not capable of initiating meetings or programmes but are always willing to participate in ones initiated by others. This is where I find myself confused—is it his ego that stops him or pure laziness? Hence I find it difficult to generalise and categorise and would like to maintain that these observations are purely mine.

How is a Gemini man in love?

Discussing this most sought after question in the context of a Gemini man can be quite a task, but I am going to attempt it nevertheless. I have explained earlier how his restless and indecisive nature keeps him from settling down early in life (while women can take this as a warning if dating him, a Gemini man himself can take this as a cue and make wise decisions about relationships and marriage).

However, this is not to be interpreted as a red signal to stay away from a Gemini man. On the contrary, he can be a very attentive lover. Being a good conversationalist, there will never be any dearth of communication and interesting exchange of information, this also explains why a Gemini man is on a look out for a receptive and informative girlfriend.

The Gemini man can be mischievous, notorious, crazy and even kinky. He can enjoy one or multiple relationships that match his desires. But for settling in the long-term, he looks for simplicity in his partner and is quite conservative when choosing one.

Since he likes to remain unattached for as long as he can, if you have met him early in life my advice to you would be to stick to enjoying his company to the fullest. The minute you try to attach strings, you will find him disappearing faster than you can imagine...unless he is completely in love.

A Gemini man can be extremely warm, affectionate, loving and compassionate, which can make any woman feel 'he is the one' and believe me all these qualities in him are genuine but it's just that his personality is so dynamic that one fine day you may not see any of them in him. This has often led many people to conclude that a Gemini man lacks emotional stability.

A Gemini man is not meant for a sensitive woman. So all ladies out there looking for assurance and security of undying love, or stability of relationship...think again! This man's love is as true as the next one's but his personality traits can make it quite a struggle to remain in love with him.

Although I have explicitly talked about his gossiping nature, I would like to add that he is quite secretive about his personal matters. If you think he will share everything with you, you are wrong...so very wrong!

In the initial stages of a relationship or in the early years of adulthood, a Gemini man will not be able to provide stability to a relationship. His fickle nature will be a hindrance here. But once he has had everything and he is doing too much of everything, he would need the very stability he had been shunning. The stability and security of a long lasting relationship is likely to rein in the fickleness of his nature and tame his inconsistencies.

What does he look for in a partner?

Most Geminis would naturally be propelled towards courting women who are conventionally good-looking, and have a sensible head on their shoulders. Even with beauty being an important consideration, a Gemini male would write-off any woman who can't carry an intelligent conversation. He would also be desirous of finding a mate that responds to his spontaneity with the same passion.

Gemini men are known for their exploits of the carnal variety. Our ladies' man would appreciate a partner who reciprocates the same sensuality or is at least willing to experiment and learn with time.

While dating him, you should...

...read newspapers regularly. Shocked? What's dating got to do with newspapers, you may ask. In the case of a Gemini man...lots! Here's a guy who is steeped in current affairs. If you want to make the right impression on him, brush up your know-how about the world around you.

He is intensely interested in everything that's happening around. The key here is 'interesting'. Once you are able to gauge what interests your Gemini date, it would be easier to deal with him. He likes intelligent stimulating conversations and that is the best way to get things started. He likes to talk but he also likes to listen. Choose topics that would excite him and you won't realise how the evening went by in his pleasing company.

The Gemini guy is not your staid and composed gentleman; he is a whirlwind that will sweep you off your feet without him as much as blinking an eye. Keep a knapsack ready at home as he is given to impromptu travel plans and if he asks you to join him, don't miss it for the world.

A Gemini man has a lot of panache and this will be evident in the way he courts and dates you. On a date, be your appealing best. The Gemini man appreciates feminine charms. But mere good looks and grooming won't take you beyond a first date with him. Remember it is important to hold his interest if you want to make any inroads to his heart.

As you go down the dating path with him, you will have to learn to give him space. The moment you show possessiveness or jealousy, he will disappear in a flash! You will also have to adjust with his hovering eye and inconsistent nature. Giving him space also means not pushing him for commitment or marriage. Gemini men usually take their own sweet time in deciding matters of the heart. Notice him admiring the solitaire ring at the jeweller's display window? Don't get your hopes up as that ring would take at least a year or two to find its way to your finger.

Be as mysterious with him as possible. Once the Gemini has unravelled you, he will lose his interest and get impatient to move on.

A word of caution...date a Gemini man only if you love adventure and completely understand the expression 'spur of the moment'!

Compatibility quotient

The hovering eye and restless nature of a Gemini man are much talked about issues. But these aspects are mere personality traits and not the deciding factors of his character. After all, the measure of a person's 'negativity' depends on his situation in life, his upbringing and individual mindset. Gemini men are sociable, charming, adventurous and fun-loving and they share a common bond with many women on the zodiac.

Gemini man and...

Aries woman: 9/10. This relationship is 'happening' on a number of levels. Both have energetic and vibrant personalities. He has a commanding presence without being too dominating, while she has the adventurous streak to match his fervour. However, both will have to learn to curb their possessive nature and let things take their own course.

Taurus woman: 4/10. Not likely to work well, this relationship has too many 'opposites' to deal with. The outgoing, reckless Gemini will find the intense and steady Taurean rather boring. Moreover, his flirtatious nature will drive her nuts.

Gemini woman: 7/10. A bonding between the two Geminis will result in excellent rapport and highly charged tête-à-têtes, not to mention some adventurous escapades and a lot of partying. But on the flipside, both might get tired of each other pretty soon. They would need to take each other's specific needs into account and make adjustments accordingly.

Cancer woman: 8/10. Once the Gemini guy masters the art of dealing with a completely feminine woman, this relationship can go places. The Gemini has the exact dose of verve and passion to interest the Cancer woman, while she has charm and mysticism to intrigue him. But, the Cancer woman will have to learn to keep her emotions in check to be able to adjust with a Gemini.

Leo woman: 8/10. The Gemini is quite compatible with the lioness. Both would enjoy each other's company and conversation. Since the Leo girl is also adventure loving and a party person, she will have a rocking time with the Gemini guy. Of course before the fun begins she will have to give him ample space, while he will have to refrain from his wandering ways.

Virgo woman: 7/10. Although this combination has chances of success, it would largely depend on the way these two adjust with each other. It would be advisable for the Gemini guy not to make the Virgo girl jealous. On the other hand, she should refrain from criticising him too much, as he is not likely to take it sportingly.

Libra woman: 9/10. Great chemistry here! This relationship will be full of liveliness, adventure, passion and charm. She will be impressed with his intelligence; the Gemini man will be lured into a commitment by the compelling charm of the Libran and will stick with her in a long-term relationship.

Scorpio woman: 6/10. The one thing both have in common is passion. And there ends the similarity. However, similarity is not actually a necessity. These two can use their disparate natures to their advantage. The Gemini guy will have to give her commitment and security, while keeping a tight rein over his flirtatious nature.

Sagittarius woman: 8/10. If both can treat each other with caution, this relationship can stand the test of time. Both are outgoing people and party lovers, but the Sagittarian also needs a comfortable home to get back to. His 'common sense' and intellectual behaviour might over awe her. Both would need to mellow down their spirits in order to coexist in bliss.

Capricorn woman: 5/10. A difficult match! The Capricorn woman's sensitivity is too fragile for the dashing Gemini spirit. She is warm and tender hearted and he would find it difficult to adjust with such a person. Moreover, he won't be able to provide her with the security that she desires. But she will be able to give him as much space as he needs and he can teach her how to be flexible in life.

Aquarius woman: 9/10. Both are likely to hit it off from day one. The vivacious Aquarian meets her match in the energetic Gemini. These two can easily forge a deep friendship and thereon their relationship can be a joyride full of conversation, adventure and new experiences.

Pisces woman: 6/10. Emotions can be the bone of contention here. The Piscean girl is hypersensitive and extremely emotional, while the Gemini guy hates to be tied down with emotions. He might hurt her easily with his blunt tongue and her passive stance would not appeal to his egoistic nature.

Famous Gemini men personalities:

Bob Dylan	Clint Eastwood
Donald Trump	Johnny Depp

Gemini woman

The Gemini woman is beautiful. Please don't misconstrue this as a biased opinion; it is more than an opinion...it's an observation. Even if she is not beautiful in the conventional sort of way there is an inner beauty that she possesses, which gets reflected on her face as you come to know her better.

And her face...or faces! Is she really two-faced? I don't think so. This woman has a multifaceted personality and knows the art of adapting herself to any given situation. If this trait can be labelled as 'two-faced', then so be it!

A woman of intellect and boundless charm, the Gemini always leaves a trail of peppiness and fun behind her. Given her penchant for multitasking, she is usually found to be overcommitted and running from pillar to post to achieve her targets.

Having a Gemini female as a friend or a girlfriend is a delightful experience as with her around life is full of stimulating conversations and tinkling laughter.

How can you identify a Gemini woman in a crowd?

If you ever come across a woman who has a store of intelligent questions on the most diversified subjects and at the same time is an amazing listener...you can be sure she is a Gemini. At any social event, you will find her moving from one group of friends to another with unmatched grace and a warm innocent smile on her face.

While most attributes discussed here will apply to all kinds of Gemini women, there are two categories amongst them with behavioural differences. I would divide Gemini women into 70 per cent passive and 30 per cent aggressive.

A good percentage of Gemini women are charismatic and stunning in their appearance, with an equal amount of intellect backing them up. And those Gemini females who are not-so-great looking (as per conventional standards) seem equally beautiful once you get to know them. This is chiefly because of their distinct ability to emote.

A Gemini woman will not let her looks do the work for her and would like you to appreciate her brains rather than her beauty (they share this quality with Capricorn women).

What are the key features of her personality?

When people who have considerable knowledge of zodiac signs encounter Gemini women, they usually have a comment or two to make on their dual personality or the famous (or infamous) Janus-faced characteristic. Through my personal observations and interaction with Gemini friends and workmates, I would give 80 per cent of Gemini women a clean chit on this. However, people who think otherwise have possibly been misled firstly because of the symbol assigned to this sun sign and secondly due to the multiple roles that a Gemini woman can juggle with easy grace. A Gemini woman can fit into as many roles as life demands but don't think that she is merely a good actor because she usually is as genuine as they come.

No matter to which age group she belongs to, a Gemini female is curious. She is the one with questions, questions and more questions on everything under the sun. And if with this statement you are rethinking of calling up the attractive Gemini girl you met the other day to match your wits against...don't! Curious she may be, but all her questions are intelligent and relevant.

She won't settle for anything less than a good lifestyle. A Gemini female will put-up with average living only if she is struggling, but her aim would always be to achieve quality life for herself and her family. And given her determination and ambition, she usually gets what she aims for.

Going back to my categories of aggressive and passive Gemini women, I would like to talk about the personality trait of the 30 per cent aggressive Gemini women. An aggressive Gemini female would be extremely bossy, forceful in speech and behaviour, argumentative, short-tempered and someone who always wants to have her way. However, the good news is that the 70 per cent passive (conventional) kind are not that crazy.

How is she on the following aspects?

Appearance: Don't let her dressing style fool you. A Gemini woman is driven by her mood swings and will dress up accordingly. An amusing observation I have made is that she is one of the three women who love to use men's cologne if given a choice...the other two being Scorpio and Capricorn. And believe me this is the only touch of masculinity you will find in her! They love keeping pace with new trends in fashion and accessories. They also love gadgets.

Ambition: Extremely ambitious, this lady is raring to go, but what actually drives a Gemini woman is the search for inner satisfaction rather than money. That doesn't mean money is not important, but to her satisfaction in what she is doing is more important.

A Gemini woman is exceedingly committed towards her work but is likely to get bored if she remains in one industry or profession for too long. Since she pursues satisfaction, she can move onto another terrain to get the kind of growth she wants. Her need to innovate and be creative can drive her to an either affiliated industry or to a totally contrasting field of work.

Her greatest strength lies in the 100 per cent effort she puts in adapting herself to her new work profile and with it she manages to develop a sense of comfort or discomfort in the very early stages.

Ego/Self-respect: A Gemini woman is governed 70 per cent by her self-respect and 30 per cent by her ego. If you are dealing with the conventional kind, don't let her submissive and compassionate nature mislead you into thinking that she can be walked over. With the aggressive kind you won't know what's hitting you; all you will be looking out for is an escape route.

Responsibility: Gemini women are extremely responsible and dependable. In life there is a distinct difference between how close you feel to somebody and how close that somebody feels to you. Once a Gemini woman gets close to you...as a friend, workmate or lover, she is as dependable as a ₹1000 note!

Etiquettes: Although she comes across as friendly and easy-going, don't think she lacks etiquettes or doesn't expect the same from you. From a man, she would expect chivalry and to be treated like a lady and from friends she would expect civilised behaviour to say the least.

What is her approach towards life?

In any given situation, a Gemini woman will follow a realistic path. Driven by her intellect she will always be guided by her acumen and make choices accordingly.

My study of Gemini women across all ages has allowed me to conclude that once over thirty, a Gemini woman will use her sixth sense, experience and maturity while taking decisions. But this too will be in consultation with her grey cells!

She is also a dreamer and believes in her ideals. This is one woman who can be an excellent follower. She is not in a hurry to lead. But given her core characteristic, she can turn out to be a natural leader.

How does she score on the following points?

Cynicism: Unless she becomes really stubborn about getting something (which we all do at some point of time or the other), the passive kind of Gemini woman is not cynical. But the aggressive kind may come across as very cynical. Their doings only make sense to them.

Suspicion/Jealousy: This is one woman who is absolutely blind when in love. Unless provided with a valid reason she is not the suspicious types; she believes in the maxim, live and let live. She will give you as much space as you want and expect the same from you. But if provoked, she can get possessive and jealous too, especially if it is about the one relationship that's meaningful in her life.

The aggressive kind although can be totally opposite. She can be jealous, suspicious and under such influence make life miserable for the person in question.

Dishonesty/Infidelity: Promiscuity and infidelity are touchy issues with a Gemini girl. Being committed and loyal to her loved ones she expects exactly the same or more (this particular topic if discussed about a friend or with friends elicits a similar response from her). Only in her calm moments can you communicate reasons for infidelity and get your point across. Being driven by her intellect primarily, she is as capable of taking decisions with her head as with her heart when in a calm mood.

Although Gemini women can be flirts, they are not usually capable of deceit or having multiple relationships. So if you are with a Gemini woman who loves you, you should have no reason to be insecure.

Hardship: The aggressive Gemini woman is likely to crib in times of adversity, while the passive one will learn from her mistakes and try her best to get on with life.

Success and failure: Here again the two kinds would show a marked difference: the aggressive kind would show off their success, while the passive kind would be more modest about their achievement and share it with family and friends only. But whatever the type, all Gemini women put in a wholehearted effort in whatever they do. If they fail at what they set out to do, they can get extremely emotional. The bright side though is that in a week or so you will see them back in action, emerging wiser from their failures.

Host: Depending on what her age is or the social strata she belongs to, you will find a Gemini host either calling for home delivery or organising a five course meal. Whichever way it goes, she is a generous and detailed host.

Guest: A lot depends on her moods, which tend to swing quite often. But overall a Gemini woman is not very fussy as a guest.

How does she handle difficult situations?

In a difficult situation like a quarrel she can be quite stubborn because she too doesn't like to admit her fault (even when she knows she in the wrong). But the saving grace here is that she is open to communication. However, on the flipside you will have to give her two to three days by herself to cool down. If you are up against the aggressive kind, my advice is to concede or give up and move on: either she will come around on her own or not at all.

What is her characteristic weakness?

Over the years I have observed that Gemini women are extremely detailed and meticulous. A Gemini woman will apply these qualities to most aspects of her life, namely: work, home, kitchen, relationships and love. Add to that her multitasking abilities and her disability to say no to people (which again load her up with multiple things to do) and she ends up being overcommitted and short on time, much like her male counterpart.

The passive Gemini would know how to prioritise her tasks and will effectively multitask with grace and ease. On the other hand, the aggressive Gemini would do more or less the same thing, but with full effects of a soap opera.

Is there more to this spirited lady's persona?

Oh yes! She has many facets to her personality. You will find a Gemini woman restless and cranky only if she has unfinished business, otherwise she is quite composed. You may also find her confused and indecisive at times, but mostly she is quite clear about what she wants.

A Gemini woman is more sensitive than sentimental, unless it concerns her immediate family or a loved one. But under certain odd situations you will find her developing deep attachment to small things like a gift from an old friend, a birthday or greeting card, etc.

She is charm personified. Although Gemini women portray a strong exterior, they are all femininity inside. They would always try to show that they don't break down easily and in fact, they really don't, but they are not bereft of feminine weaknesses. And they know how to use their femininity to their advantage, if the situation demands.

A Gemini woman is also very adventurous and believes in trying out everything at least once, which could be anything from an international cuisine to sky walking. This attribute also stems from her undying curiosity, for instance at a party she wouldn't mind having a tequila shot or a swig of vodka although her usual vice may be wine or whisky. In another extreme case, she would take-up yoga classes or spiritual sessions.

The Gemini lady is known for her spontaneity. With a good deal of intellect thrown in, she does of course control her impulsive side, yet, with her inability to turn people down, you would often find her making impromptu plans.

Given her strong streak of independence, the Gemini woman is usually career-minded. She would like to establish herself as an identity to reckon with, apart from her family or husband's name. In fact you may come across Gemini women who switch over effortlessly between their career and domestic life.

How should one deal effectively with a Gemini woman?

Oscillating from one point of view to the other, a Gemini woman often provides enough ammunition for people to brand her as two-faced. But as I said earlier, this is just her way of adapting to situations. She would constantly be coming up with new, innovative and exciting ideas to implement and if you're willing to appreciate her enterprise, you would surely earn brownie points from our talented Gemini lady.

Since she likes to get things in motion and making her presence felt, she enjoys being in the limelight and bonds with people who allow her that margin. Also, with her being a fountain of energy, you would need to match up to her energy levels in order to communicate on the same plane with her.

Though she seldom loses her cool, our Gemini woman can often indulge in brooding and wailing about her woes. At such time, it'll be best to leave her to her own company, giving her ample time to cool down before trying to lighten the mood or trying to set things right with her. She really wouldn't care for your opinion when she's upset with you and it would be sheer stupidity to invite her not-so-pleasant comments, since she can be rather vindictive if pushed up the wall.

Certain Gemini women are incorrigible flirts and they would make a play for your partner right under your nose. Though they don't subscribe to the idea of extramarital liaisons, they are comfortable with exchanging flirtatious glances and sweet talks with their friends' partners. If you're the kind of person who just can't digest anyone toying with your guy, I'd say...keep him away from this seductress!

A Gemini woman can prove to be a bankable partner in the long run. She's there by your side whenever you're in need and will always be willing to go the extra mile just to put the smile back on your face. Though she wouldn't be too dependent on her friends to reciprocate in the same way, she would expect her man to treat her in a similar manner. At the same time, it would be important for you not to come across as too 'clingy' for this vivacious lady hates being confined or tied down.

How does she handle money matters?

Like everyone else, money is important to a Gemini woman too. At work don't let her submissive and easy-going nature fool you. She does understand the maths when it comes to effort versus reward. Many Gemini women have shown shrewd business sense and acumen at investing money wisely. Again their habit of multitasking will egg them on to dabble in varied and often risky projects.

Another unique quality about a Gemini woman and her money is... she likes to share. She won't hesitate to help anyone in need as for her money is a tool and not an end in itself. She can be quite a spendthrift, while spending on herself and her loved ones.

How is she on the professional front?

I have observed six out of every ten Gemini women to be part of the media industry be it films, TV or print. Her need to be in this industry very likely comes from her inherent curiosity to know things. Being in professions like news reporting, content writing and research and development, satiates her quest for knowledge and allows her to constantly be in a creative environment. Or her natural multitasking ability gives her the drive to work as different characters in a role.

It would be needless to add here that her ability to prioritise her work and multitask makes her a very competitive worker who is also hard-working.

How is she in various relationship roles?

My advice to parents with a Gemini daughter would be to keep an encyclopedia handy, for their girl will squeeze every iota of information out of them regarding anything and everything around her. But when she asks questions, she should be encouraged as it will help her fertile mind to grow in the proper direction.

Being determined and stubborn, she can come across as rebellious in her relationship with her parents but if you befriend her and give into her 'reasonable' demands, she can be the most devoted of daughters.

If given ample space and treated with respect, a Gemini woman can be a wonderful wife. She needs to have proper share in the decision-making when it comes to domestic life and also freedom to operate as she wishes, within her domain. But as with everything else she will be good at keeping house and with her multitasking abilities, will be a good wife, daughter-in-law (don't want to guarantee this one) and mother...all at one go.

As a mother, a Gemini woman shows great balance between being a friend and a disciplinarian. Since usually her nature is 'to give', unless rubbed the wrong way, she will be a fabulous mother to her children.

How is she when alone?

Geminis do not like to be alone. They are social animals who like to be on the go and thrive on being in the company of people they like. The female of this sun sign loves to talk and can deliver discourse after discourse, often digressing from the topic at hand.

You would find her on her own only in three cases. One: when she's mad at you and wants time to simmer down. Two: when it's self-imposed. For example while playing the perfect host, a female Gemini would spend hours alone, without complaining, painstakingly checking on the minutest of details for her elaborate lunch or dinner party. Three: if she is in the mood to read a book alone and is simply looking for a retreat or space for herself.

How is she when in love?

A Gemini woman is typically an independent thinker and having dug up answers to most questions early in life, she is quite aware of what she wants from an early age...sometimes as early as sixteen or seventeen. So if you are planning on wooing a Gemini girl, you have a daunting task ahead.

But here's help. I know the secret to a Gemini woman's heart and I'm letting it out right here...to win the irresistible heart of a Gemini female let your guard down and be absolutely unpretentious. She hates pretense of any kind and is smart enough to see through any games you try to play with her. So just be yourself and show your love and she will be ready to be wooed. But also remember she is an intelligent woman and likes her man to be a man and not a spineless junkie.

She is rather slow at commitments when it comes to love and marriage and with good enough reasons. Being a keen observer of human nature and understanding the crests and troughs of long-term relationships, this cautious lady likes to wait for the right moment before committing herself. Add to that her long list of 'must haves' in her beau, and it leaves her indecisive.

So if you are in a relationship with a Gemini girl and know that a commitment is in the offing, just take care of two things. Firstly be dead sure about your own decisions (no backing off at the last minute please!) and give your lady love the assurance she needs...that you are the one for her and that things will work out just right.

What does she look for in her partner?

The first thing any Gemini woman will look for in a man is intelligence. She cannot accept stupidity or silliness of any kind, (most Gemini women I have met are often drawn to their male counterpart, the Gemini man, who possess similar or higher intellect level). Secondly, she will look deeper for humility but with the right amount of pride. She is quite capable of getting involved with 'her type of men', who are artistic, creative, thinkers, philosophers and writers.

I have discerned that Gemini women eventually settle down with passive men. Since you already know by now that she is full of variety and excellent at dealing with a million tasks at one go, it's also important to know that she is very passionate and can get crazy and kinky (again depending on her mood and age). While she is capable of doing all this, she does expect her man to be equally passionate, full of variety and surprises to keep her passion going.

She is full of desires and wants and can keep most of it to herself unless probed. Most of the time she ends up surprising herself at what she is capable of doing...she is constantly in the process of discovering and rediscovering herself.

In spite of all this she is extremely malleable and submissive and usually would put her partner's needs, be it emotional or physical, before hers. This particular quality of giving is actually what keeps most relationships alive. If you simply go by the saying you will get what you give, you can allow your mind to race with a Gemini partner.

While dating her, you should…

…win her heart! And if you are smirking right now thinking it's a child's play, first look around her and count her admirers. You have tough competition buddy! A Gemini girl is generally surrounded by people (read boys!) who are floored with her intellectual charm and are chasing her with their hearts on their sleeves. With such a situation at hand, the only way for you is to match her grey cells.

A Gemini woman appreciates intelligence like nothing else. She will never date someone who is silly or frivolous or thinks her to be so. She likes men who respect women and acknowledge their equality. She's not a feminist in the same way like some Aquarians can be, but her sharp mind understands the need for an equal footing in a relationship.

On your first date with a Gemini girl, be ready with an updated report on current affairs. Here's a woman who is insightful, curious and eager to learn more and more about the world around her. If you can satisfy her curiosity, you can pronounce your date to be a success.

Your date is likely to be full of conversation as the Gemini girl loves to talk from varied subjects ranging from history, to war, to the charity organisation that she is a part of. She also likes smart peppy talk…so make sure you have brushed up your one-liners. And don't even think of using your whacky sense of humour here. She likes simple, entertaining humour… so keep your slapstick comic jokes at home when you come to meet her.

Come smartly dressed. It doesn't matter if your attire isn't exactly the latest thing in, but as long as it is elegant it would have the desired effect. If you are planning on getting her a gift, let it be something practical and sophisticated. Don't waste your time (and money) on those mushy cards and impractical gifts. Can't think of anything better? Just go with a head-full of ideas and an easy laugh…she'll love it!

Remember your Gemini date has a daring heart and an adventurous spirit. She won't balk at the idea of trying something new…so you can experiment with your ideas and have a blast!

Give her as well as your relationship some time before entering the intimate zone. Once you are steady with her and think she is the girl for you, you can get close and cozy with her. She likes the transition from dating to love to be subtle...full of delicateness and interesting intimate moments but whatever you do, be direct. It is more likely that the Gemini girl will sense what's on your mind.

Compatibility quotient

Given her zest for life and quest for knowledge, dating a Gemini woman is fun. But is that enough to sustain a long-term relationship? It is quite a task to manage an overcommitted Gemini and break through the myth of her 'dual' personality. Unless you are equipped with a good deal of common sense, getting along with the vivacious Gemini can be a hard bargain.

Gemini woman and...

Aries man: 10/10. Wow! And double wow! This relationship sizzles! The Gemini girl is the ideal match for an Arien guy. An Arien's love for conversation is the answer to Gemini's curiosity, while Gemini's spirit is the answer to Arien's passion. Of course, the Aries man will have to balance his arrogance and ego around her and she will have to swallow her pride to put-up with his super blunt nature.

Taurus man: 8/10. With the right kind of adjustments, this combination can work out well. Once the Taurean learns to give the Gemini woman enough space, he will have a fun-loving and practical partner by his side and for life. In return, his steady nature would be a good anchor to her liveliness. He can be a dependable partner and can provide the emotional security she secretly yearns for.

Gemini man: 7/10. Since both share a love for good stimulating conversations, they might start off on a pleasant note, but then they will have to make an effort to sustain the other's curiosity. Once the course of conversation is run, they might grow weary of each other. This relationship requires more than 'lip service' to work in its favour.

Cancer man: 5/10. The free Gemini spirit might not be able to offer the Cancer man the love and security he needs, neither will she be able to give him undivided attention. His serious demeanour might put-off the vivacious Gemini mind. If this relationship is to work successfully, a lot of adjustments are required at both ends.

Leo man: 8/10. The sociable nature of both these individuals can be a key to the success of this relationship. With her around, their relationship will never lack romance or passion and with him in charge, it will be full of good humour and generosity. The only hitch here being that they can end up offending each other's egos.

Virgo man: 8/10. With a bit of fine-tuning, this relationship can go a long way. For starters, both have an understanding nature and an identical emotional quotient. The Virgo guy however will have to bridle his critical attitude, while the Gemini girl will have to keep her tactless tongue under control.

Libra man: 9/10. Another great combination! Both are sociable and party-lovers. There would be enough passion and romance in this relationship to keep the two going. The Libran wit and the Gemini liveliness would only add to the fervour. The only issue that could crop up is that they both love their independence and space. If they are in opposite zones and unable to connect, then it could mean trouble.

Scorpio man: 5/10. What might start off on a promising note is likely to meet with major roadblocks. The Scorpio man might get smitten by the Gemini passion and she by his persuasive charm, but in the long run he won't be able to put-up with her inconsistent nature. She will find it difficult to cope with his demanding and dominating nature, not to mention his possessive attitude.

Sagittarius man: 7/10. Both are on the same wavelength intellectually, but their emotions tend to be out of sync. Her flirtatiousness can make him feel insecure, while he is too undemonstrative to suit her taste. But if both are in love, these differences can be overcome with some amount of hard work and this relationship could actually work.

Capricorn man: 5/10. This one can swing either way! If they both learn to appreciate each other's good qualities, this relationship might work. Otherwise the Gemini's modern outlook will not go down well with the conservative Capricorn man.

Aquarius man: 8/10. Since both share common traits like non-conformist behaviour, love for adventure and spontaneity, this relationship is likely to work in the long run. There would be understanding in both and each seeks change and variety in life.

Pisces man: 5/10. Not a very happening combination! The Gemini girl is way too pragmatic to suit the lifestyle of the dreamy Piscean. It is also a balancing act between her blunt tongue and his sensitive heart. This relationship calls for a lot of compromises.

Famous Gemini women personalities:

Angelina Jolie
Naomi Campbell
Shilpa Shetty
Brooke Shields
Nicole Kidman
Sonam Kapoor

Cancer

22 June-23 July

Cancer man

Forgot who said what and when? Or what you may have worn on the first date? Ask your Cancerian partner and he will rattle it all off in a single breath. His memory can be compared to a great tusker. There's very little that he doesn't store in the deep recesses of his mind.

With moods that swing like a pendulum, the Cancer guy can dip low or rise high in a matter of minutes. Sensitive to the core, a harsh word or a careless gesture is enough to hurt him.

But he also comes armed with an easy-going nature that appeals to all. Not to forget his quirky sense of humour that makes being with him such a whole lot of fun.

While his love for travel can take him places, he always wants to come back to a warm abode...his 'den', an affectionate wife and obedient children. And if his mother is staying with him, he is likely to come home double quick!

How can you identify a Cancer man in a crowd?

This is one of those zodiac signs where it is impossible to categorise people as aggressive or passive. There are distinct percentages of introvert and extrovert kinds under the sign of the crab, but the sociability of even the most extroverted Cancer men stays within limits. Although outgoing, he will have only a few select friends (this may be because Cancerians tend to get picky with their preferences as they mature).

A Cancer man is adventurous and likes to hit the road. His easy-going nature makes him adjust to various situations with grace...he can stay at a five-star hotel or a local guest house with equal comfort.

Don't be surprised if you see him on a luxury cruise liner one day and on a backpacking spree the next!

Cancerian men are driven by emotions. Like their female counterpart, they are also hypersensitive, emotional and very sentimental. It has not been easy for me to spot Cancer men in a crowd.

What are the key features of his personality?

Like I said before, a Cancer man's outgoing nature stays within boundaries. This is probably because the assertive side of his personality is tethered to shyness, insecurity and ego. This often stops him from opening up in front of people, especially strangers. But there is a positive outcome of this too...most, not all Cancer men know how to mind their own business.

One of the major highlights of a Cancer male's personality is his mood swings...rather, constant mood swings. He is in a perpetual state of transition and can be seen in different avatars in the span of a day. He is much like a baby...sleeping one moment and awake the next, laughing one moment and crying the next. But these mood changes are not personality changes and as his frame of mind returns to normal, he gets back to being his usual self. His moods range from restless to hyperactive, stubborn to easy-going and 'gnashing your teeth' to 'happy-go-lucky'. So much so for a Cancer man in a day!

He is also a perfectionist...but not in the general sense of the term. To him being a perfectionist means having everything around him in order. He likes to keep his accessories on display and in perfect array. Anything out of sort can rock his boat!

A Cancer male likes to wear a mask of indifference and sometimes of mysteriousness. This enables him to hide his true emotions. But this façade camouflages an emotional heart, which is also kind and affectionate. This man is honest about his feelings. Be it anger, love or hatred...he means every word he says. He is also understanding, compassionate and sympathetic and 'usually' never hurts others intentionally.

How is he on the following aspects?

Appearance: I have found most Cancer men to be extremely casual. When it comes to fashion and clothes they do admire the good things in life but it is not a 'must have' for them. However, I am not saying this for the ones who have made it big in life. A Cancer man, if his monetary condition permits, will have all things stylish and will devote both time and money in maintaining sophistication in everything.

Ambition: A Cancer man is known to be extremely ambitious. Yet home is where his heart is. Given a choice he wouldn't want to work more than six to eight hours a day unless he has nothing to go back home to.

The Cancerians I have known have sharp business acumen and are very enterprising. However, a certain lack of initiative can prove to be a deterrent to their ambition. Also, some Cancer men tend to be lazy, which affects the career growth curve.

Ego/Self-respect: A Cancer man would come across as a regular guy. He is not overly warm or friendly. This is mainly because he is selective about what company he keeps. Besides being picky, this may also be because he is governed by his ego but unless you have a keen eye for observation you will never come to know about it.

Responsibility: Like most of us the Cancer man too likes his independence. As much as he can manage, he would avoid living in anybody's shadow. This shows that he is capable of taking responsibilities. But there's a catch! He can be very dependent on his family for emotional support.

Having achieved independence and made a living that he yearned for, he will make it a point to take care of his parents if he is on good terms with them. But, this may not apply to all Cancer men, as they can be quite selfish and self-obsessed.

For a Cancer man, responsibility towards his spouse is generally conditional. As much as he can be loving and caring, he can be driven by certain mood swings and turn cynical.

Etiquettes: A Cancer man is known to be casual and laid-back, yet at the same time quite proper, if the situation demands. You cannot call him a stickler for etiquettes, but he will show impeccable manners while in public. Here again his upbringing and social status play an important role.

What is his approach towards life?

Amongst Cancer men, 50 per cent are realistic and practical while the rest are not. Once again it is ironic how the Cancer man's status and money determines, at times, how he behaves and what he does.

He is not just emotional and sentimental…he goes overboard in that department. Touchy like a mimosa, a Cancer man can be a difficult client if his emotions are trifled with or sentiments ignored.

Most Cancer men I have met prefer to be leaders than followers but usually need to analyse their risks beforehand. Unless fiercely independent, they also look for support from family and friends while taking any initiative.

How does a Cancer man score on the following points?

Cynicism: As per my observation, about 30 per cent of Cancer men are cynical, although you might not notice this in your early interactions with them. The remaining 70 per cent can get equally cynical but only under exceptional circumstances or when provoked or cornered.

Suspicion/Jealousy: I am yet to come across a Cancer man who is not suspicious and jealous by nature. The odds are one against thousand… one peculiar Cancer guy may come across as unsuspicious but there again it maybe because he is up to something sneaky himself.

Dishonesty/Infidelity: A Cancer man is usually committed, yet a flirt at heart. Like most men, he regards occasional diversions as his right but he is not liable to promiscuity while in a loving and satisfying relationship. But infidelity in his partner will not be taken lying down …no way!

Hardships: If faced with hardship, a Cancer man can be dominated by his emotions and moods instead of his intellect. He is not known to give up easily but would rarely put in more effort than required. Some Cancer males can be quite a cry baby and play the blame game to avoid taking responsibility.

Success and failure: Most Cancer males I have met are conservative and hence something like success will be shared only with their loved ones or people they feel close to.

Given their emotional nature, most Cancerian men find it difficult to deal with failure in a sensible manner. They take matters to heart and would brood and clam-up, without specifying what exactly upset them. However, they have a tendency to recharge themselves (especially drawing emotional strength from their loved ones) and get back to the task at hand with a positive attitude.

Host: He can be casual and also adaptive depending on whom he has invited. For instance a Cancer friend of mine would create a formal atmosphere, order the best wine/beer if he were to invite me home. He revealed himself when he admitted that he took all these pains to make me comfortable because he gets similar treatment from me when he is invited over. The inside story is, he would be casual with people who are not as fussy as me.

Guest: Mostly adaptive, a Cancer man when invited over, can be quite adjusting and easy-going...unless he has gotten himself into a 'criticising mood'.

How does he handle difficult situations?

From what I have seen, known and heard, in a situation like a quarrel, there is a clear divide on how different Cancerians behave differently. While a certain percentage of them can stay composed, some of them can get really aggressive (because of their extremely possessive and insecure nature). Due to this when in a torrential mood, a few are even capable of manhandling the woman they love.

What is his characteristic weakness?

I believe the negative or positive qualities of someone are a matter of perception. But there are some traits that are undoubtedly jarring in an otherwise pleasing personality. And in Cancer men such traits are rather prominent.

Foremost is a Cancer man's retentive memory. He will remember every minute incident or happening in his life, especially related to his childhood and anecdotes from his experiences will keep cropping up in every conversation. His memory is all the more sharp in keeping a tab on others' mistakes. He is so engrossed in his ledgers of errors that he often misses out on the goodness of other people...and also the good things life has given him. A Cancer man can forgive (not so readily though!) but he will never forget. This can cause unpleasantness around him and discomfort to his loved ones.

Some Cancer males also suffer from a sort of inferiority complex. This makes them narrow minded about their approach towards others. Basically, not all Cancer men are people-centric and all these inhibitions trouble them a lot while dealing with others. His opinionated nature makes him stick to his guns, I mean his views, with unrelenting obstinacy. He then believes his opinions are gospel truths and should never be questioned.

Another behavioural pattern I have noticed among Cancer men is fatalism. A Cancer man tends to be fatalistic about life and its outcomes. Nothing wrong with this attitude as at times it helps you prepare for failures and setbacks. But a Cancer man tends to carry it a bit further and applies it to everything in life. A Cancer male lives life on the extremes... every emotion, every feeling is taken rather seriously (read over-seriously). Sometimes to the extent of being ridiculous (if a Cancer guy comes down with an ordinary flu, he would kick such a ruckus one might think him to be in some grave medical danger).

Much like his female counterpart, a Cancer man suffers from the drawbacks of hypersensitivity. You will usually find him high on emotions and the smallest of provocation can send him into a flying rage or in the throes of misery.

Is there something more to his persona?

Yes...there are more characteristics of a Cancer man that are evident only to a discerning eye.

A Cancer male can be a good mix between being satisfied with what he has and aspiring for more. Depending on his standard of living and status he can grow from moderately ambitious to overly ambitious. Although he flaunts a casual attitude, he is usually not satisfied with mediocre living, but whereas he aspires for good things in life, he is not dependent on them.

A Cancer man craves for security...be it emotional or financial. He is so fond of saving things for tomorrow, that it is almost an obsession. There is an underlying fear of being destitute or helpless in most Cancer men, which leads them to think of future as 'full of tragedy' and therefore take every precaution to provide for the future...and that includes huge savings in the bank and hoarding his refrigerator! Okay, maybe I exaggerated a little!

Cancer men are secretive to the core. Although they might be privy to their friends' secrets, they won't be quick to confide their own. Herein again lies the insecurity that someone might take advantage of their situation. This trait is also the cause of their innate shyness.

This man likes to treasure everything from 'the days of yore': his baseball cap, his kid sister's hand-painted greeting card, his mother's gifts, all find a place in his cupboard. Don't let the box of his treasures be a part of your spring cleaning...if you throw any of his old stuff you are likely to face his wrath and see him sulk for days on end.

In spite of his rather serious and at times morbid nature, the Cancer man has a peculiar sense of humour. He enjoys a good joke now and then and is also capable of cracking one himself. His quiet exterior hides a rather funny face. Don't expect mimes, slapstick or stand-up comedy from him; he is more likely to make sophisticated jokes that inspire quiet laughter. Very often he sees humour in situations when others don't.

A Cancer man has a mind of his own and his innate sense of understanding does not necessarily match with those around him. While he may understand people and things, it can be from a totally different perspective. Hence I have concluded that it takes time to convince him as he does not readily agree to things.

He is not one to make an effort to start conversations/discussions but is also not incapable of participating. Through my observation I have known Cancer men to keep themselves abreast with news and happenings and therefore usually come across as knowledgeable during conversations.

How should one deal effectively with a Cancer man?

The only condition applicable while dealing with a Cancer man is...none whatsoever.

When it comes to work he is extremely shrewd so keep it simple. With love and emotions, he can get very demanding when it comes to a relationship. He requires constant attention and constant assurance of your love. So be there when he needs you and you will find a most loving and caring life partner in him. And knowing his homely nature, make sure you keep a good house and a warm heart for him.

How does he handle money matters?

This is one man who is not at all casual when it comes to his money. A very careful spender, he can be shrewd and even stingy in money matters. But if the situation demands he can spend on family and friends.

He is also very particular about managing his finances. He is the one whose bills are paid on time, whose bank balance is regularly updated and whose investments are only with blue chip companies. Better safe than sorry when it comes to money!

But he is not one to compromise on his standard of living and will not shy away from spending wherever necessary to maintain that.

How is a Cancer man on the professional front?

Given a choice, a Cancer male would not like to work much. Being conservative, he is slow and careful in making new commitments. I am not saying he is not risk-taking types, but nothing he does is done without consultation. Overall easy to work with, I would give him an eight on ten as a colleague at work. As a boss, a Cancer male can be very generous, both in terms of money and leniency.

How is he in various relationship roles?

A Cancer man likes to talk about his parents. I see that as a good quality. If he has had the right kind of relationship with his parents, you will often find him talking about them. He is especially attached to his mother and tends to hold extreme emotions for her…either utmost love or utter indifference. However, more often than not, it is love. For him his mother is a shining example of womanhood and he loves to talk about her… especially to his girlfriend or wife. In my opinion, this is not a problem. Wouldn't you like it if your kid spoke of you with pride?

Going by the people I have met and observed, the Cancer man can be very protective and doting as a husband. As a father, he is a disciplinarian to a great extent. He would excel in his role as a provider and head of the family.

How is he when alone?

The hermit, you'll often find a Cancer male by himself. This emerges as a typical trait, probably owing to his suspicious attitude towards others that stops him from befriending too many people. The handful of friends he will have will be people whom he finds completely bankable.

Since he restricts himself to just a few people, he often finds himself lacking in company to hang out with. His lack of expression and blunt utterances too act as deterrents.

The Cancerian male feels quite at ease in his own company and would gladly spend his day watching some odd movie and dining out on his own, taking in the visual delight of the city. But this might not hold true for the very social and active kind of Cancerian male. He would reach out to his friends, and their friends if he is travelling alone or out alone, (although his self-respect does not allow him to show his desperation to have company).

How is he when in love?

Remember your school days, when you were caught napping in class and your teacher asked you to write 'I won't sleep in class' fifty times on the blackboard? Well, being in love with a Cancer guy is akin to that, the only difference being here that you might have to repeat 'I love you' a hundred times a day. And I am not kidding when I say this. The sense of insecurity is so strong amongst some Cancer men that it becomes important for them to receive repeated assurances of love. In any case, when in love they would expect their partner to be vocal and expressive about her love.

Words like commitment, trust and loyalty mean a lot to a Cancer man. He won't stand infidelity or dishonesty of any kind. Given his sensitive nature, he is likely to be deeply hurt at the smallest sign of any of these traits in his partner. On his own part, you won't find him flirting with other women after having committed himself. Whatever interaction he may have with other females would be restricted to social dos and professional circles. Quite a 'one woman man' this!

A Cancer guy in love can be very romantic, caring and attentive. Once he is able to come out of his shell, he will show a warm and affectionate heart. He will shower you with gifts and take you to fantastic, yet undiscovered, places. About 40 per cent of them are different from the way the majority appear here; what I mean is, they are easy-going, cool and fun partners to have as a friend and a lover.

When in love, the Cancer guy will be fiercely possessive as his love is driven by a sense of insecurity that the person he loves and is emotionally dependant upon might leave him. And that is why assurances of love are very important to him, as he feels relieved at being the sole interest in his partner's life.

And lastly, if you are in love with a Cancer man, here is the master key to his heart. Learn to cook and keep a house like his mother. Most Cancer men adore their mothers. Nothing pleases a Cancerian better than a spouse that takes after his mother. And though he may not own up to it, he likes to be pampered and petted by his partner, 'just like how mamma used to do'.

What does he look for in his partner?

I have already stressed on the Cancerian male's severe insecurity syndrome and from it stems his clinginess. If there's one man who can be really clingy, our man takes the cake! Petrified of being betrayed, the Cancer man will hold on really tight, rather too tight, to his partner, sometimes to a suffocating extent. He seeks someone who can constantly assure him of her love, support and security.

He wants a woman who loves him unconditionally, has a practical approach towards life and most importantly…can keep his home beautifully! Nothing pleases him more than a neat and tidy home, where he's served food on time.

As I mentioned earlier, the Cancer man does not like his ideology to be questioned and would stick to his opinion, however redundant or narrow minded his approach may be. With his temperament, he would want someone who holds his opinion as precious, someone who wouldn't challenge his point of view and would appreciate his knowledge and outlook.

While dating him, you should…

…tackle his shyness first If he is the shy type! It is important to understand this basic trait of his personality before you date him. The Cancer guy can be extremely introvert and cautious. He won't tread the path of love and dating till he is 100 per cent sure he has got the right person. Given his sensitive heart, he is afraid of getting into a relationship as that might result in heartbreak. If you have to get things started with a Cancer guy, first earn his trust. Once you inspire in him this confidence, he would go all out to prove his love for you.

You may have to work hard on certain aspects like penetrating his hard cocoon. While dating him you will have to draw him out and make him feel comfortable. As he gets familiar with you and the surroundings, you will see him opening up in the most wonderful manner. Down the line, you would also get a taste of his exquisite sense of humour.

Like I have said earlier, if you are planning a long-term dating scene with a Cancerian man, it is best to give cooking a shot. If you are able to strike the right chord with his mother, he would be as pleased as punch.

As you get ready for your date with the Cancer man, don your most feminine and graceful attire. The Cancerian loves those soft, womanly touches. Be easy-going and your charming best. The ideal way of beginning your date is a good conversation amidst an ambient setting. The Cancer guy is a very good talker (although a reluctant one initially), once he finds an eager listener, he would churn out beautiful tales from the treasure of his memory.

And be prepared that while dating him you will have to adjust to his mood swings (though it isn't a very overpowering trait, it can get a bit tiresome, given the Cancerian's innate pessimism).

And whatever you do, don't invoke his over-possessiveness. You may feel looked after and well cared for initially, but he can take this trait of his rather seriously and you may have to face the fallouts of his suspicious and jealous disposition. Show him how warm and affectionate you are and once he feels secure he lets go of his over-acquisitiveness, if he is that type.

Compatibility quotient

What do you need to be compatible with a sensitive creature like the Cancer guy? Love without understanding can mean very little for a Cancer man. Given his need to be in a secure relationship, finding the right soulmate can be a tough job for him. Let's find out who amongst the twelve zodiac ladies can best cope with the candid Cancerian.

Cancer man and...

Aries woman: 7/10. With understanding and a little bit of adjustment, this relationship can go a long way. The Arien will have to understand his mood swings and sedentary nature, while the Cancerian will have to give space to her outgoing nature and independent thinking. Both will have to keep their stubbornness under strict check.

Taurus woman: 9/10. Great chemistry! While both would know how to keep the romance going, their mutual understanding adds to it; she will know how to manage his mood swings patiently, while he will find her femininity appealing.

Gemini woman: 5/10. This combination might result in clashes. The free spirited Gemini would find the Cancerian conservatism irksome. He is too serious and intense to suit her vivacious nature.

Cancer woman: 8/10. There will be no dearth of love and care in this relationship. But both suffer from mood swings and hence the relationship can suffer if the moods are not bright. However, if one of the two Cancerian is emotionally more secure, this relationship can work wonderfully in the long run.

Leo woman: 8/10. Once the Leo female learns to control her blunt tongue, this relationship can rock. She would have to adjust with the Cancerian's hypersensitive nature. In return, she would get his loyalty, love and ample care.

Virgo woman: 9/10. These two can strike a very good bond. The Virgo girl would know how to draw out the Cancer man from his reserve with her love and affection. He would respect her femininity and protect and provide for her in the most affectionate manner.

Libra woman: 7/10. This relationship won't work without understanding. His lack of emotional expression might leave her feeling high and dry, while she may find his ideas of scraping and saving too much to digest.

Scorpio woman: 9.5/10. Rocking chemistry here! A Scorpio is a perfect match for the Cancer guy. This would be an emotionally-charged relationship as they would understand each other's emotional needs perfectly.

Sagittarius woman: 5/10. Lot of hard work will be required to make this relationship work. The Sagittarian would have to curb her 'out of the house' behaviour and concentrate more on homemaking. He would have to get a bit adventurous and treat her to the thrills of life every now and then. But with the right kind of adjustments, this can work just fine.

Capricorn woman: 6/10. Once they learn to respect each other's opinions and emotions, this combination can work. However, here the equation is reversed as the Cancer guy would need to teach the Capricorn woman to display her emotions. Although both are emotional, their emotional quotient is quite different and they would need to develop an understanding in this sphere.

Aquarius woman: 4/10. A difficult matter! The Aquarian might not be ready to give the Cancerian 100 per cent of her time and love. She lacks the depth that he is looking for. Similarly, he won't be able to meet up with her demands of highly intellectual conversations and would be at a loss to appease her questioning mind.

Pisces woman: 9/10. Perfect! The Piscean girl has just the right amount of womanly charm to floor the Cancerian, while he has a warm and affectionate heart to offer to her. Since both are understanding and sensitive, they will appreciate these qualities in each other.

Famous Cancerian men personalities:

George Michael
Saurav Ganguly
Naseeruddin Shah
Sunil Gavaskar

Cancer Woman

I would like to introduce the Cancerian woman with five Cs—crazy, creative, calculative, compassionate and confused. The Cancer woman displays sudden mood swings. She can be happy as a lark one minute and down in deep dumps the next, but mind you, each mood would be as genuine as the next (governed largely by her impulsive, crazy or, in an extreme case depressive thoughts). The Cancer girl nevertheless has a soulful laughter and a good sense of humour. But her sensitivity is the hallmark of her personality.

There is a crab-like trait in her too. Innately shy and reserved, a Cancer woman would 'rarely' make the first move...in love, business or any walk of life. If at all she has to move, it would be sideways (just as a crab does) and never straight ahead. She needs an understanding partner to draw her out and help her emote well.

Even the most career-oriented Cancer woman has her heart at home. A complete 'home' person, cooking and keeping her house in order constitute her favourite activities. She likes to pamper her loved ones thanks to her warm and affectionate nature. You can trust her to bundle you off to bed with a mug of hot chocolate on a cold winter night.

Extremely careful with her money, the Cancer girl likes nothing more than a fat bank balance and a protective man in her life. She has a thing for security, be it emotional or financial, that almost borders on obsession with her.

How can you identify a Cancer woman in a crowd?

This may sound funny but I have observed a good number of Cancer women have an almond shaped face and small, deep set eyes. Most Cancerian women are friendly and in a crowd likely to be the most popular person on the scene.

Most Cancerian women I have met or observed are extremely particular about their dressing. Coordinating their clothes with accessories like hand bags, belts and shoes is a must for Cancer women.

What are the key features of her personality?

There are two types of Cancer women—30 per cent aggressive and 70 per cent passive. The aggressive kind is extremely competitive and loud. She always wants to be on top of everything and can also be overly demanding and ambitious. Completely unpredictable by nature, some are found pursuing careers in the television or film industry. These women can be very blunt and forthright and their sharp tongues can often end up hurting people's feelings (although none of them would intentionally want to hurt others). Also, these Cancerians are usually achievers and will relentlessly pursue what they set their mind on. They are not shy to use their femininity to their advantage as and when the situation demands.

The passive kind of Cancer women too are unpredictable and very moody but what sets them apart is that they are essentially romantic at heart and could go to any end to get what they want in the romance zone. The passive Cancerian is very emotional, sentimental and hypersensitive. Being with her can be a tight rope walk.

Amongst all the twelve signs it is easiest to read the face of a Cancer woman. She has a very expressive face though, you will usually find her unsuccessfully trying to hide her emotions behind a mask of indifference.

A Cancer woman likes to display a strong façade but since she is governed by her emotions what is seen on the outside is usually different from what's happening inside her. A lot of things are going on in her head at any given point of time, so either she ends up finishing her job and a little bit more or ends up doing nothing. This typically arises from her desire to do more and get more.

To a great extent she is practical but her high emotional sense and hypersensitivity often become a hurdle for her. On a day-to-day basis when a Cancerian is confronted with situations that affect her sensitivity, she would turn into an emotional live wire and this usually gets her into trouble but on the bright side, also gets her what she wants.

One unique observation I have made over the years is that no matter how good your friendship with her is, she does this unique disappearing act when she would vanish for days, weeks or months to later reappear as though nothing happened or that she was always around. And when she reappears she wants to catch up and meet with you on such an urgent basis that you will be forced to think that she has something really important to share.

How is she on the following aspects?

Appearance: Women of this zodiac sign usually have an oval (almond shape) face, with a pleasant smile adorning it. They are fond of keeping themselves well groomed and are usually obsessed with their appearance. You will find them splurging on clothes, shoes and other accessories to get that 'perfect' look.

Ambition: Most Cancerian women are ambitious. They yearn to be independent but are not shy to be dependent either. They are comfortable being a homemaker when given the right kind of respect and control at home. In short, they like being in charge of everything.

Ego/Self-respect: Quick to react to people and situations, the Cancer woman scores high on ego and self-respect. Though she won't pick a fight with anyone unless pushed, once riled up, her ego won't allow her to give in easily either. Her typical Cancerian trait of opining (thanks to her practical bent of mind) doesn't always go down well with people around her. Yet, she would defend her stand tooth and nail, taking it as an attack on her ego and self-respect.

Although most Cancer women will not accept it, they do have a big ego. A Cancer woman is unable to take any form of criticism and would take shelter under being hypersensitive. She rarely will accept she is wrong, even though she knows she is. Since she is vulnerable to criticism and it can blow her lid off...it's better to avoid it.

Responsibility: As young girls, Cancer females can be quite stubborn. In circumstances where her relationship with her parents turns out to be unpleasant, a Cancer woman could be quite a rebel too. Other than that she can be a very responsible woman, provided she is given her space.

When in love a Cancer woman can be extremely submissive and as her relationship grows she'll take-up lot of responsibilities too (but if things were to change, she could react differently). Towards her children her behaviour is friendly; she could be a great mother and a great friend at the same time. One unique observation though—her children will mature with age, only to have their space taken up by their mum, who will continue behaving in a childlike manner and throw her occasional tantrums.

Etiquettes: There are very few exceptions in this case and generally a Cancer woman scores nine on ten on etiquettes, as she is a stickler for mannerisms and code of conduct.

What is her approach towards life?

Her approach to life is a delicate balance between being unrealistic and being practical. She is a dreamer and an idealistic person at the same time. Her emotional and sensitive nature often overrules her pragmatism. If things go her way, she will prefer to be a leader.

How does a Cancer woman score on the following aspects?

Cynicism: A Cancer woman can get cynical but only to an extent (and this will last till she gets what she wants). If she sets out to achieve something, she will go for it with icy cold cynicism. And if betrayed in love or insecure in a relationship, a Cancer woman can turn into a cynic easily.

Suspicion/Jealousy: A Cancer woman is quite suspicious by nature. She may not show it but she is always on her guard. Since she is extremely possessive, she can be quite jealous as well.

Dishonesty/Infidelity: It won't be fair of me to say this and it does not hold true for all Cancerian women but I have realised that the Cancer women can lie very easily. As much as they are sincere and dependable, they can be dishonest and even promiscuous; sometimes for a reason and sometimes just for the heck of it. But if thrown in a situation I have also known Cancerian women who are clear-headed enough to sit and talk it over with their partner and move on with life.

To a Cancer woman, trust is very important in a relationship. Being extremely possessive, she finds it difficult to accept infidelity from her partner. On her part, once she is assured of true love, she will be completely devoted and submissive towards her partner.

Therefore, her feelings should not to be trifled with. Hypersensitive by nature, a Cancer woman's reactions, when emotionally hurt, can stir up a storm in a teacup. She is extremely vengeful and not likely to forget wrongs done to her. She will not rest until she makes you pay for them. Her revenge can be seen in the form of sulking, heated arguments...and escalated credit card bills.

Hardships: This woman is not shy of hard work. The competitive spirit in her keeps her going. But when faced with extreme hardship, a Cancer woman is also likely to have nervous breakdowns.

Success and failure: With Cancer women success is displayed in different ways depending upon their temperament. The aggressive women will be loud and showy about their success, while the passive will be more contained and graceful in their celebrations.

I think most women don't take failure very well and a Cancer woman is no exception. I say this not to demean women but to justify the disappointment they feel when they fail because, I believe, their sincerity quotient is higher than that of men.

Host: Being detailed as hosts, Cancer women will put in their best effort when organising a party or event. One step into the ambience they have created and you would know the party is a happening do and the invitation came straight from her heart.

Guest: As a guest, a Cancer woman can be anything between easy-going and friendly to being picky, observant and critical. Overall, she would maintain grace and her conduct towards others would be as warm as her personality.

How does she handle difficult situations?

Situations like a quarrel are not pleasant with a Cancer woman as her agenda is to win every round, every battle and finally the war itself. She can scream, shout, hit out and throw stuff about to get her message across. Being stubborn, once she has taken a stand on something, she sticks to it.

On very rare occasions would she give in or give up. Mostly she will go on and on about it in her head, but it is all very subjective and depends on the gravity of the situation.

What is her characteristic weakness?

I would call a Cancer woman an extremist by nature. In both love or hate, she will go overboard with her emotions (but no matter which way her emotions swing her stance is absolutely genuine. There is nothing fake about her). This extremity in emotions stem from her hypersensitive bent of mind and disability to rein her overflowing feelings. She is also prone to tears. But I have seen Cancer women overcome these shortcomings with maturity and sometimes with the help of spirituality.

But till the time a Cancer woman learns to handle her hypersensitive nature, it is quite a task to deal with her. In spite of her brilliant wit, she often turns gloomy and introspective. Such moments leave her displeased, and sometimes disappointed, with herself. A Cancer woman also takes everything personally. This makes her an easy victim to self-pity.

Her other major weakness is the tendency to become a self-styled/ appointed leader. Add to that her non-stop talks and endless speeches. She has the ability to go on and on about herself, her life, her miseries and more. Usually this is a one way interaction where she is the only one who gets to talk and you get to nod or get your few lines in.

Is there more to this sensitive lady's persona?

The 'more' in her personality is actually the 'less'. What I mean is that she has less of the unsightly traits that are prominent in women of other signs. For instance she isn't bossy or outspoken or fickle-minded or proud. She is your simple girl-next-door who has a thing for sentiments.

A Cancer woman can be very practical and is usually very graceful in getting her demands fulfilled. She can be patient yet watchful if it is something that she desires/fancies and will make sure she gets it. In order to achieve what she wants she can be quite manipulative and devious (especially if a personal plan is at stake). She is not one to hesitate in using other people's weaknesses to her advantage. But, in a situation of genuine delay, she might even let go of it.

But sometimes, in spite of usually being sure about what she wants, a Cancer woman can be quite indecisive. Although she may do exactly what she decided to do, she looks for support/opinion.

I would like to share an interesting anecdote about a Cancer woman, which led me to a funny conclusion—the childishness in her nature often puts her in a tight spot with people (of course, let me clarify this does not apply to all Cancer women).

Here is my story: A forty-five-year old Cancer woman was watching a rather melodramatic soap opera one day. Her newly married daughter, who had come to stay with her for a few days commented on her choice of show. That was it! The Cancer woman flew into a rage and a tirade of angry words came gushing from her. The shell-shocked daughter stood amazed, wondering what got into her otherwise warm and friendly mother. But unmindful of her daughter's reaction, the lady went on and on about meaningless things, hurting her daughter deeply.

When the daughter narrated this incident to me, I got a chance to explain the core characteristics of her mother to her. A Cancer woman likes to mark out her territory and any intrusion is not taken kindly (in this case it was the TV soap) and she can turn from a crab to a tigress for the silliest of reasons.

From time to time she can be quite introspective. Whenever she feels disappointed with the world, she submerges herself again into her bottomless thoughts and spends hours contemplating.

As much as I may have made her sound intense, serious and an emotional fool, almost every Cancerian woman I have met has a great sense of humour. Her philosophy in life is to have fun and be happy. She has the unique ability to blend in as a friend with both men and women. Although ultra feminine, she can make the boys feel she is one of them.

Being extremely adventurous, a romantic at heart and a woman full of desires she can be quite a rebel. In order to fulfil her desire to have fun, she is capable of doing things that are usually not acceptable in the world, without giving a damn about them. She is extremely creative and has a great imagination and usually lives in her own fantasy world. At the same time, she is firmly grounded in matters concerning her family and work. Much like a Capricorn woman, she is very protective of the people she loves.

How should one deal effectively with a Cancer woman?

A Cancer woman is one person I have observed who behaves childishly throughout her life, and especially when it comes to her stubbornness. In standing contrast to this is her extremely sensuous nature. She is quite capable of making the first move if she meets an intelligent and powerful man. To cope with such extremes, her man needs to be romantic, practical and easy-going. But that doesn't mean she'll settle for anyone. She also needs a man who is mentally strong and can dominate her.

A Cancer woman is usually very sharp, smart and has an eye for detail. In order to deal with her you actually have to let her see your real self. Once she knows who you really are, you will find her easy-going to be with. She finds it easier to be around people who speak their mind and are comfortable in their skin, just as she is.

One last tip—flattery will help you score a home run with a Cancer woman.

How does she handle money matters?

Money is important to her but it is not the sole objective of living. Ruled by emotions and given her compassionate nature, she can be very generous and at times gets short-changed in money matters by family and friends. Otherwise, she is quite careful with her money. She likes to maintain a balance between extravagance and stinginess. And as mentioned earlier, given her sentimental nature, she likes to save everything that can be reused...gifts, greeting cards or old clothes.

Money holds another meaning for her as well. It denotes security. In spite of being fond of decorating her home, a Cancer woman would much rather have a healthy bank account than expensive home décor products.

How is she on the professional front?

Cancerian women come across as pleasant co-workers thanks to their easy-going nature. Not ones to get angry easily, they maintain an icy-cool composure on the work front.

Though reserved initially, the Cancer woman is quite a charmer once she gets to know people around her and can let her hair down. But don't let this friendly demeanour fool you. Step on her toes, and you're dead meat! Treat her with dignity and you'll have a very supportive co-worker/boss; question her integrity or thought process and you're in for big trouble!

How is she in various relationship roles?

As a daughter, the Cancer woman is usually attached to her parents, but this attachment diminishes as she matures, with her exhibiting a growing need to establish her independence. She bonds well with her siblings and they often turn to her for her opinion and advice.

As a wife, the Cancerian is utterly devoted to her husband, and very often submissive. She believes in keeping her man well-fed and spends a good deal of time in the kitchen, readying her hubby's favourite cuisine.

A devoted mother, she's a friend to her children—the child in her helps her build a connection with them. She would offer them advice when solicited, though sometimes it would also be forced even when they wouldn't want it.

She is extremely protective and possessive about her family. No matter which way things go in her life, she will stand by her family at all times. So it is advisable not to mess around or crack jokes about her family or loved ones unless you are looking for trouble.

Where the Cancer woman is concerned, friendship is for keeps. She is a loyal friend who would do anything in her power to help out a friend in need. As long as her ego isn't messed with, she would stay by her friends' side, supporting them in every way possible (emotionally, financially), offering advice, sharing knowledge and being the perfect 'agony aunt'.

How is she when alone?

A Cancer woman if left alone for long can get insecure. I have found this in Cancer women at an advanced age too. Even after experience and maturity of years, they need the emotional bonding and support of a partner and/or friends. And this can easily be attributed to her emotional state of mind.

How is she when in love?

Love can bring out the best in this woman. The amazing feel and pride of true love gets reflected on her face and you would instantly know how deeply she cherishes it. Although as usual, she will be reserved about her feelings, yet the frequent happy moods that she finds herself in, would be instant giveaways.

While in love, she would literally lay her heart out for her lover. Nothing about her is shallow or casual and hence she would not only take her love affair very seriously, but also walk the extra mile to make it happening.

A Cancer woman is quite romantic in the conventional sense of the term and once you get used to her hypersensitivity, your love journey with her will be a pleasant one. She will shower you with gifts and praises, cook your favourite food and take care of you very much like your mother. Her love is for keeps and she will never give you a chance to get suspicious or jealous. Her actions, gestures and words will all proclaim her love for you...and she would mean it too.

But naturally she would expect you to keep your part of the bargain too. Constant assurances of love may be required to get rid of her nagging insecurity. You will have to be careful, especially with your words, not to hurt her, else she will recoil in her shell and you will have a tough time getting her out of it. Be supportive of her and she would stand by you through thick and thin.

What does she look for in her partner:

Maybe it's too clichéd but a Cancerian woman looks for a friend in her partner. Someone who is adventurous and is upto doing the craziest things she wants, for example, mountain climbing or scuba diving. She looks for a warm and friendly yet dominating partner who she respects and looks upto. If she had her way she would custom order a man for her.

While dating her, you should...

...be chivalrous. The Cancer girl is romantic, albeit in a very traditional sense. She would expect her date to be gentlemanly and courteous, if not the actual knight in shining armour.

Like I had mentioned before, you should be careful with your words while dating her as she takes offence easily. Given her rather high emotional quotient it is advisable to plunge into a relationship with her only if you are thinking of long-term bonding. A short fling or a passing affair is a term unknown to a true Cancerian (unless she herself is looking at it to get over an earlier break up or just for the sake of fun)...a few dates down, and you will have to either go ahead or back off completely.

Take her to a restaurant with excellent food and beautiful ambience. Nothing will evoke the romantic more in her than good music, cuisine and sweet nothings whispered into her ear. Draw her out of her shell and let her talk. Once she is in the comfort zone with you, she will fill your heart with warmth and the room with her tinkling laughter. She can talk eloquently when she chooses too, so give her space and time to open up and you will be spending your date with a most wonderful companion.

A Cancer woman loves sophistication. While dating her let all your gestures have touches of elegance. Don't just buy a gift and send it by courier. Gift wrap it in her favourite colours and hand it to her the next time you meet her. Trust me this gesture won't be lost on her. Take her to beautiful places, especially those with a history. The Cancer girl will love it better for the air of nostalgia attached to it.

To take the relationship to the next level, you will have to gain her confidence and trust. She would never be open or forthcoming about her feelings for you and you may have to help her along. To win her heart, you will have to show how true, sincere and affectionate your love for her is. The best way is to draw her close to you and hum the song *I'll be there for you* softly in her ear...and mean it too!

Don't and I repeat don't think of getting intimate if you are not serious about this relationship. After the level of intimacy has increased, the Cancerian would be too emotionally involved to back out. And then if you decide against dating her, she might end up an emotional wreck.

Compatibility quotient

Dealing with sensitivity and putting up with nagging or coming back from work to a warm, glowing home and a dining table full of wonderful aroma...which one's for you? I know everyone would jump at the latter, but dear reader you will get both sides of the bargain when you date or marry a Cancerian girl. Find out who amongst the zodiac is best suited to the emotionally charged Cancerian.

Cancer woman and...

Aries man: 6/10. This relationship can work well if both are able to keep certain personality traits under check. The Aries man will not like being constantly pampered or treated like a child, while the Cancer woman is not capable of standing the blunt and straightforward words of the Arien.

Taurus man: 9/10. This combination can hit the bull's eye. He has the ability to love and care for her and most importantly give her the security she craves for. On the other hand, she is the perfect mate for him as she can cook well and keep a good house for him... things that are important to the Taurean as well.

Gemini man: 9/10. The Gemini with his usual panache can do wonders to this relationship. He has the vivacity to attract and draw the reclusive Cancer out of her shell, while she has the feminine charm to impress his manly heart. The Cancerian however will have to keep her hypersensitivity under check.

Cancer man: 8/10. The success of this relationship will largely depend on the emotional security that both the crabs have. If one of them is able to take stock of the emotional balance, this bonding can go a long way. Moreover, both will have to keep their mood swings under control.

Leo man: 9/10. This relationship is a perfect blend of loyalty and love. Since the Cancerian will remain committed towards the Leo, he would be more than happy in her company. Moreover she would let him be in charge and load him with motherly care and attention, something the Leo guy won't be able to resist.

Virgo man: 9/10. Another relationship that can stand the test of time! Both are equally romantic as well as dependable and sincere. Although the Virgo lacks interest on the home front, the Cancerian has enough culinary talent to make him stay back with her at home.

Libra man: 6/10. This combination can swing either way. If both show understanding of each other's basic needs, this relationship can work out better. The Libran will have to go slow on his intellectual trips while the Cancerian will have to learn to be less emotionally dependant.

Scorpio man: 8/10. She is romantic and he is passionate. He is masculine and she is feminine. And both are almost faithful and sincere. This relationship has the potential of going a long way.

Sagittarius man: 4/10. The Sagittarian outspokenness may not go down too well with the Cancerian sensitivity. After the initial attraction, things might get a bit difficult as he will dislike being tied down and she will object to his flirtatious ways.

Capricorn man: 7/10. A difficult yet not impossible combination! The Cancerian for once will have to make the first move and draw the Capricorn out of his reserve. The Capricorn on the other hand will have to adjust to the excessive emotional demands of the Cancerian.

Aquarius man: 5/10. This is a case of opposites and although opposites attract they are not necessarily compatible. She would interpret his freedom as negligence while he would think her emotional bonding as excessive neediness. It can be a clash between emotion and intellect.

Pisces man: 9.5/10. This combination is near perfect. His imaginative mind is a true match to her feminine heart. He will shower her with love, affection and care and give her the support and security she needs. The Cancerian can make her world revolve around the Piscean—believe in his dreams, be supportive and make him feel 'he's the only one'.

Famous Cancer women personalities:

Karishma Kapoor
Pamela Anderson
Priyanka Chopra
Meryl Streep
Late Princess Diana

Leo

24 July-23 August

Leo man

He would roar like a lion: interpret that as a signal to attract attention; he would purr in contention: that's his way of saying he is satisfied; he would growl with impatience when his ego is hurt; that's the Leo man for you. He is the most assertive of all zodiac signs and loves to be the centre of attention.

Every time he enters a party scene, it is with much fanfare. He wants people to sit-up and take notice, be courteous towards him and generally consider his presence a 'huge favour'. Two minutes into a conversation with him and you will know how full of 'me, myself and I' your conventional Leo male is!

He also has an irresistible charm about him, thanks to his extreme passion. He is romantic in every sense of the term; he won't shy off from stopping at the traffic signal to buy flowers for his girlfriend or leave work early to catch up with her over a cup of coffee...all these romantic interludes however come at a price—his impatience. But, once you know how to deal with it, you will have a rather mellow Leo at your side. With good amount of love and trust, you can have the lion eating out of your hand!

How can you identify a Leo man in a crowd?

Here I am in a fix! Identifying a Leo man in a crowd is pretty easy, but explaining how to do that is kind of difficult. I will tell you why. Based on my observations I have inferred that amongst Leo men 60 per cent are conventional (read 'aggressive') type and 40 per cent are passive. However, this differentiation in Leos is not that simple. The passive kind of Leo men also possess a belligerent streak, but well under control. So, in appearance and behaviour the passive Leo male will appear as composed as they come.

The conventional Leo will also appear outwardly calm and composed and it is only after you interact with him that his true nature and assertive manners come to the fore. This is the chief difference between these two kinds of Leo men.

It is not at all difficult to spot a conventional Leo man especially if you both are part of the same conversation. This type is prone to exaggeration, particularly regarding numbers and figures, you will usually catch him showing off his assets, either subtly or loudly depending on his mood and the environment, but show off he will! For instance, if a Leo man who owns two cars is asked how many vehicles he has, he is very likely to say he has five. This is the kind of self-adulation he prefers, (I have also noticed this trait in many Aries, Capricorn and few Sagittarius men). This category of Leo male fraternity is also noticeable through its aggressive body language and animated demeanour in a conversation.

On the other hand, the passive type of Leo male is usually quiet and intense. He is more easy-going, warm and friendly. Although he prefers to speak only when spoken to, he is a good conversationalist too. He will display his assertiveness through forcefulness of ideas and opinions (more in words than in actions), but without going over-the-top.

What are the key features of his personality?

True to the qualities of the majestic symbol of this zodiac, Leo men exhibit a keen taste for luxury and grandeur. More often than not, they are not able to differentiate between wishful thinking and dreaming big. This stems from a lack of pragmatism. They want everything to be larger than life.

Another interesting quality I have noticed in Leo men is that they are like children through most of their lives. I say this because they want to have everything they see. No matter what age, experience or maturity he is at, a Leo male will keep yearning for material things just like a five-year-old yearns for his first bike. In fact, his list of desires keeps growing with age.

Even within the 40 per cent passive Leo men, 15 per cent possess this characteristic. Anything with a luxury tag or any brand spelling grandeur usually catches his eye. I have known some Leo men who are determined to achieve success only to be able to fulfil their desire list. I think this is a great motivation to work.

Another peculiar trait and one that often works to his disadvantage is a Leo man's love for flattery. Flattery is the easiest way to a Leo man's heart. It is usually nothing but an ego boost for him and as soon as he hears a compliment or sweet talk about himself his brain sends a message saying this person is likeable (not that he can't tell fake from real). It is also very easy to stir up a Leo male emotionally. He can get easily influenced by the genuine and the not-so-genuine stories and is capable of acting upon them without any verification.

It won't be fair on my part to call 'all' Leo males pseudo-chivalrous. I am sure there are many who are genuine too, but by and large a Leo man's chivalry is a matter of doubt. It's not that he lacks courtesy but his gallantry is usually ego driven and hence conceited to a great extent. No offence, but I have to conclude that this habit makes Leo men come across as vain and arrogant sometimes.

Majority (almost 90 per cent) of Leo men are low on patience. So don't expect your man to wait patiently in the car while you finish your make-up...he is more likely to wake up the neighbourhood with his honking. They are also temperamental and prone to becoming cynical or pessimistic, not to mention their short temper that can at times take a serious turn. Such temperamental nature is more pronounced amongst the conventional kind of Leo men. The passive kind is much more mellow and will not display these tendencies unless provoked repeatedly.

Going back to their being pessimists, for Leo men the glass is forever half empty and the pastures are always greener on the other side. This incorrigible pessimism in them arises from their insecure and unsure nature. For the same reason most Leo men I have met, have displayed only marginal amounts of optimism.

Diplomacy is a skill most passive Leo men and very few conventional ones possess. While they are known to be blunt, curt and straightforward in their speech, some of them can be quite diplomatic. Although they don't believe in mincing words, they can play it up to anyone to get their work done. Compromising on values to suit their needs is not an unknown tact to Leo men.

In spite of a few issues, a Leo man is a man of honour. When he makes a promise he abides by his word as he believes it's a matter of prestige to do so. Very rarely will a Leo male not keep his word, especially if it is a promise he made to his loved ones. However, few of them feel no such compulsions in business deals. With such Leo men, it is better to double check on his assurances before you sign on that dotted line. Once again, he is not exactly a shady character and don't benchmark him against this, there are exceptions.

How is he on the following aspects?

Appearance: Most Leo men I have met have a very prominent jawline. Some men have deep set eyes, that look very soulful, while some have very fiery and mischievous eyes.

Regarding his dressing style, a Leo male prefers to stick to solid colours. The passive kind will very often be seen in blue jeans and black and white shirts...primarily just basic classics with black being the favourite colour of both kinds of Leo men. The conventional Leo has similar taste in clothes, but he also likes to experiment a lot. Depending on his mood and the occasion, but once in a while, he will try out bright flashy colours and extravagant designs.

Ambition: I have observed this across a good number of males of the lion sign that they are moderately ambitious. Leo men are constantly in a tug-of-war between work and play. They want to progress in their work or business and at the same time have lots of fun too. They like new challenges to keep them going and enjoy being creative and innovative in their field of work, in order to achieve their goals and ambitions.

Ego/Self-respect: The conventional kind of Leo males are completely self driven. Most of them are usually on a trip of their own. They can also come across as extremely arrogant and cold, but in spite of all this they still have a number of friends.

The passive kind is the surprise package here. He is a complete contrast to his conventional counterpart. He is more practical, approachable, relaxed, calm, composed and easy-going. The content expression on his face makes you feel he has found inner peace. This should not be misinterpreted as lack of self-respect, for he does possess immense self-respect and just the right amount of ego as well and knows when and where to use it. The passive Leo males make great friends and are dependable too. This also makes them loyal to a great extent.

Responsibility: The passive kind is extremely responsible and dependable. For all relationship roles, the passive Leo man will score a nine on ten for responsibility and reliability whereas the conventional one will get a six only.

Etiquettes: Here's where they reverse their roles. The passive kind is casual in his approach towards social etiquettes and I would give him a six on ten for it. The conventional Leo male who has great regard for decorum gets an eight.

What is his approach towards life?

A far cry from being realistic and practical, the Leo male is largely governed by his emotions and sentiments. Moreover, he is hypersensitive. The smallest of emotional drama can send him into throes of agony.

Most Leo men would prefer to lead, as they possess natural leadership qualities. But if provided with the right kind of inspiration and motivation, they will not hesitate in following people they idolise.

Like most people a Leo male too wants the best from life (obviously a commonplace life is something that won't satisfy him). Since he likes to have all the comforts about him, a Leo man definitely yearns for a higher quality of living. To add to this, he is also idealistic and a dreamer.

How does he score on the following points?

Cynicism: Under the 60 per cent conventional kind of Leo men, 100 per cent of them are cynical, whereas under the 40 per cent passive kind, 25 per cent are cynical. I would say their cynicism has been grown on their self-doubting nature and also the general misgivings they harbour for everyone. Only a few Leo males would know how to make this cynicism work in their favour. Usually, it leads to pessimism and more self-distrust.

Suspicion/Jealousy: Almost all Leo men, irrespective of what category they belong to, are suspicious. This suspicious, doubting nature is the direct result of their insecurities in life. If you are dating a Leo man it is best not to give him reasons to doubt you, otherwise a good part of your courtship period will be lost in convincing him. And if you are in a relationship with him, make sure your mobile phone is never 'unreachable' or switched off as that might make his thoughts run haywire.

Being possessive, protective and competitive, a Leo man can be jealous, both in relationships and at work, (but depending on the situation, most Leo males won't show that they are jealous because of their pride). In a relationship, a Leo man will get easily jealous even if his girlfriend or wife so much as looks at another man. And in a professional set up, the success of his colleague or business rival can get his green horns up!

Dishonesty/Infidelity: He is not able to tolerate dishonesty and infidelity, but in rare cases does reserve the right to do so himself. But overall he is not promiscuous and hence will generally be caught only looking happily at attractive heads rather than doing something sinful.

Hardships: Most Leo men take hardships with a pinch of salt. They can have an occasional breakdown but usually bounce back roaring with fresh vigour. But to do so they need proper amount of support and backing from family and friends.

Success/Failure: The conventional kind would gloat in their success; perhaps even put it on display. Their success stories should make it to the headlines, something to be noticed and talked about by the people he knows. While the passive kind of Leo male would be a lot more graceful and subtle about showing off his success...even his exhibit will have a decent dose of humility and refinement.

Failure is one area where the Leo man loses face. No Leo man I have known has been able to take failure well. The males of the lion sign tend to moan and groan about their setbacks sometimes even for weeks. And it is not just the immediate losing-out on something that causes this mourning, most of the times failure makes them question their own capabilities. For instance, if a Leo male who is an excellent batsman were to get out for duck in a game of cricket, he would lose all confidence in himself and his capability as a good player. So intense would be his introspection that he would even consider a change in profession. That's how tragic Leo males can get!

But the bright side is that with a good cushioning of moral support and counselling they are able to spring back with renewed zest.

Host: Like all fire signs the Leo man likes everything to be extravagant. If his monetary status permits, he will go all out and be a very generous host. In case he is not cash rich, he would make-up for this deficiency with his grace, charm and finesse. He would be extremely hospitable and would make sure all his guests are comfortable and well looked after.

Guest: As a guest he believes he is a lion in the truest sense. No Leo man would like to be neglected in the slightest degree when invited as a guest. He would want to be the centre of attraction at any party where he has been invited. His hosts should be around to look after his every comfort and the party should be a well-executed affair from cuisine to entertainment. The passive kind however is more relaxed and easy-going as a guest.

How does he handle difficult situations?

A conventional Leo male in a quarrel is like a warrior on a warship, with orders to fire all cylinders. He is like a machine gun on an auto-mode firing rounds non-stop. With him, anger knows no restraints and he can even get violent, both verbally and physically.

While the passive kind can also turn aggressive in quarrelsome situations, he generally tends to rationalise and act accordingly. To put it briefly, he is not likely to go over-the-top.

The conventional Leo male will rarely accept his mistake and would go on arguing endlessly to avoid being blamed. The passive kind could and would accept mistakes as and when necessary.

What is his characteristic weakness?

In case of Leo men I have often found their lack of self-confidence or their over confidence to be their weakest point. They are so full of themselves, or full of doubts about themselves, their capabilities and about others, that they fail in carrying out tasks with usual efficiency.

Some being insecure and unsure of themselves, find it difficult to achieve their set goals in life. One reason for this is the high expectation level and targets that the Leo man sets for himself. These targets and benchmarks are often higher than his capabilities and if he is unable to achieve those, he falls into doubt about his skills and competence. But I have also observed that those Leo men who learn from their mistakes are able to overcome this weakness and turn out to be super achievers too.

Is there more to his persona?

I have found that there is something of an actor in a Leo male. Whether he is in his boyhood or beyond sixty, the child in him forever makes him take-up play-acting. On the surface, he can play the mimic to a hilt. And deeper still he can don masks to get things done his way. Like I had mentioned before, he takes up the role of a gallant to prove his chivalry, which may be just a façade to mislead people around him. I am not implying he is fake all the time, but he also has the capacity to 'act' in order to fulfill his secret agenda.

Here is a man who understands the meaning of power like no other. Power means everything to him. He is very conscious of the importance power plays in his life...be it monetary, physical, psychological, social or political. Akin to his Aries counterpart, a Leo man has a strong dictatorship quality. While this makes him an excellent leader, it also makes him stress on power more than ever.

How should one deal effectively with a Leo man?

My answer to this question would be—with caution. Never let a Leo male take you for granted. Once you do that he will walk all over you...with his patent leather shoes with thick soles. The crux of this whole dealing business is that no matter how much you do for a Leo man, he will remain unappreciative of your contributions and will keep expecting more from you. It is therefore important that you define your role and draw a line in the early stages of your interaction with a Leo male.

Another important point to remember when you are in a relationship with him: never and I mean 'never' try to dominate him. Any attempt to govern him will instantly turn him off and might even send him into a flying rage. Be or pretend to be submissive and you will learn how to tame this majestic beast.

You would also need loads of patience when dealing with him. Generally, a Leo male finds it difficult to take anything seriously, which can be an annoying habit to put-up with.

I would also advise you to be more vocal and clear in your

communication with him rather than leaving things to imagination... which with a Leo man is kind of scanty!

How does he handle money matters?

With money the passive and conventional kinds of Leo men show some differences. The passive types tend to focus on earning a good living. They are capable of spending as much as saving but being emotional they also end up lending money to friends and family. As compassionate as he is, the passive Leo male also partakes in charitable work and making donations.

The conventional kind too is good with his money. He too is focused on earning but very often due to his risk-taking nature and egoistic attitude, he faces hurdles. He has a freehand in spending but if guided correctly he is also capable of saving and learning how to save well. He is very shrewd in matters of lending and recovering. With subjects concerning charity, he is as compassionate as his passive counterpart.

On the whole, with money matters, a Leo male usually requires guidance and a stabilising support...his impulsive spending and occasional gambling streak can leave his or your bank balance empty!

How is he on the professional front?

Aggressive! Very aggressive! Born with a penchant to lead, the Leo male believes in being an engine, not a caboose. Since he hates being told what to do and how to do it, he finds it difficult to conform to norms and tends to be a rebel.

However, in the case of his being higher up in the hierarchy, the Leo man will be motivated to create an environment which is conducive to the working of his seniors, peers and subordinates, working dedicatedly towards the achievement of goals. This however would be more to meet his own ends, for he lives for adulation and knows that recognition would come only through his work being in proper order. For this he would leave no stone unturned in achieving the same.

Fun to hang out with, the Leo male can be quite a prankster, even at work. His laughter is infectious, and he would have most people around him in splits with his witty comments and wisecracks. Not one to accept defeat, this competitive man can wreak havoc on your professional and personal life if you try to deceive or backstab him or unwittingly step on his toes.

How is he in various relationship roles?

Being responsible, the passive kind of Leo man is dependable as a son, but with the conventional kind it is advisable to teach him obedience from an early age. Given his dominating nature and ego-driven attitude, he can prove to be quite a handful to manage (with maturity and experience, he is likely to fulfill his duties).

As a husband, he will be loving and caring. It would actually be upto you to keep him interested to any degree of love and care. As long as the fires of romance are glowing and he is assured of his position in your life, he would be amazing as a husband, companion and provider.

With children he will be warm and friendly. He would dote upon them but as always will expect something in return. Akin to the female of his sign, he would want his children to have impeccable manners and high respect towards him. Due to his insecure nature, he fears being ridiculed and any disrespect shown either by his wife or kids can hurt both his ego and emotions. Fatherhood is a role he will take very seriously and you will never have to worry about your kids' school preparations, parents-teachers meet and extra-curricular activities. Just teach them to love and respect him and you will see what an excellent husband and father your Leo man turns out to be.

How is he when alone?

A Leo man will rarely be found and should rarely be left alone. He always needs company. When idle, his mind tends to wander into dark areas where it really isn't advisable for him to be, with him conjuring up the oddest, most negative thoughts about people and situations (I guess most Leo men realise this and hence will seldom be alone). They like an action-packed life and usually look for reasons to stay away from home. This can be interpreted in light of many diversions men like to indulge in to get a dose of adventure and action in their lives.

How is a Leo man in love?

Very, very romantic and very, very passionate! A Leo man loves the very concept of love.

With the kind of romance that he believes in, it is easy to get a Leo man to fall in love. Moonlight walks, candle-light dinners, romantic movies and sweet nothings over long telephonic conversations can do the trick. He enjoys the attention and pampering that is associated with being in love. When in love, he needs constant assurances from his lady love and will not hesitate to give the same in return.

He is also quite devoted and faithful. But in return, he demands unremitting attention. So if you are planning to marry a Leo male, be sure you know how to handle his constant need for attention…homemaking, in-laws, kids and other household chores notwithstanding.

He will put in plenty of efforts to woo you and will continue with his romantic endeavours even after marriage. But in return he would want you to appreciate his efforts. Like I said before, flattery will help you here. Also remember that he is one hell of a possessive guy, so once you have walked into his lair there is no glancing over the shoulder at other faces! He would want to be in complete control of you, your life and your emotions.

Although I have often heard them being called playboys, Leo men are not so. In rare cases wherein he is rich and carefree will a Leo male indulge in that kind of flirting.

What does he look for in a partner?

Fiercely aggressive and ready to pounce at the drop of a hat, shrewd, manipulative and rebellious our king of the zodiac is but a child at heart. He is just as vulnerable as any other guy and yearns for undivided attention, praise and appreciation. It is imperative for him to find a partner who understands this attribute and provides him with the emotional support that he so desires, without his asking for it. Oh no! The royal Leo will never 'state' that he wants anything. He would expect his partner to read between the lines and be ready with whatever his big, affectionate heart desires.

Leo males are probably amongst the most romantic men on the zodiac. They'd go to any extent just to prove their love or impress the object of their affection and seek a woman who appreciates his huge efforts and expresses her gratitude through actions or words.

Since our royal friend doesn't take well to criticism, he would be delighted to spend his life with a woman who is not prone to chiding him about his shortcomings. Leo men despise women who are too aggressive (as life partners), as they believe in keeping the reins of control in their hands.

Prone to bouts of self-doubt and lack of confidence when faced with failure, a Leo man needs a woman who can be his pillar of strength in times of strife. The child in him loves being mothered (a trait that is well exhibited by Sagittarius and Gemini women). He would lay his life down for someone who besides loving him can also keep his house spick and span (not to miss the impressive décor!) and most importantly…knows how to cook! Yes! The way to a Leo man's heart is definitely through his stomach! This is one man who is known for his gastronomical weakness. If you know how to toss up a mean meal (read 'tasty, loaded with love, and fattening'), you'll find a permanent place in this die-hard romantic's heart.

Passionate with a capital P, our man is known for his prowess in the art of seduction. Not one to settle for the size zero variety, our Don Juan likes a woman who's made for comfort, not speed. The Leo male would be on the prowl for a worthy quarry, someone who satisfies his passion with equal madness…someone who is willing to surrender completely to the desires of the roaring beast with amour and undying loyalty.

While dating him, you should…

…play the damsel in distress! Sounds fun? It is fun. Believe me nothing will please the Leo guy more than a game of 'slay the dragon and save the princess', as it allows him to display his chivalry. However, you must learn to take it at face value. There is no real depth to his gallantry; he would use it just to impress you. Once he knows you are suitably impressed, it would be folded and stowed away like old clothes.

But nevertheless, the Leo guy likes a girl who is dependent on him for most things (read all things). He would complain and complain about his responsibilities but would secretly enjoy working around the house, doing the 'manly' stuff and even accompanying you grocery shopping.

Coming back to the debatable point of 'dating', the first step with a Leo man is grooming. Dress up to kill! Your attitude and style will be properly noticed and commented upon and the more feminine you look, the more pleased your lion would be.

Keep the spotlight on him! Don't ever forget that attention is very important to him and he can go to great lengths to get it…which includes pretending illness. While on a date, let him do the talking and support the conversation with witty one-liners and remarks. Not to forget, loading him with compliments and flattering him. But it is not a good idea to criticise him, as the Leo man will not take it sportingly. He might think it to be your way of putting him down and that might hurt his ego.

As the course of dating progresses, show him your loyalty and commitment. The Leo is quite possessive and it is not a good idea to evoke his jealousy or rage.

And a final word of advice...don't ever get in the opposition mode with a Leo guy. If you are presenting opposing views or contradicting him, he won't like it at all. You will have to deal with him with tact and diplomacy. Be extremely womanly about everything you say and do, that's the best way to tame the king of the jungle.

However, the Leo guy is romantic to the core. While dating him you are likely to spend some of the most beautiful moments—a mix of tender love and fiery passion. He will make each date an affair to remember and you will find yourself being gladdened by his love-filled words and tingled by his sensual touch.

Compatibility quotient

He roars when he is angry and purrs when content...he is the Leo man. And do you need to be the lioness to get along with him? Not necessarily, but there are certain 'must haves' that a woman requires to be able to etch out a long-term relationship with him. Let's find out what these prerequisites are and who amongst the zodiac is better able to fulfill them.

Leo man and...

Aries woman: 8/10. Very near being the perfect match, the Arien woman can get along very well with the Leo man. His romantic nature and charismatic personality will floor the Arien, while the Leo guy will find her liveliness and independent streak quite appealing.

Taurus woman: 7/10. Both will have to put in efforts to make this work. The Leo guy will have to be considerate towards the Taurean's simple love, while she will have to handle his ego with diplomacy.

Gemini woman: 8/10. This relationship can be quite a sizzling affair. Both are equally romantic and sensual to fill up their relationship with passion. And then there are traits like generosity, good humour and adventurous spirit that add further zing to this combination.

Cancer woman: 9/10. The Cancer woman is capable of giving the Leo man what he needs the most—attention. Her undivided attention and motherly affection would do a world of good to the Leo's sensibility. In return he would provide her with security and loyalty.

Leo woman: 6/10. This relationship can swing either way. They would either end up loving each other fiercely or hating each other ferociously. If this combination has to work in the long-term, one of them will have to learn to take a backseat. Both of them are incapable of sharing spotlight and their attention-seeking nature might be too much of a hindrance for this relationship to work.

Virgo woman: 6/10. Lots of compromises will go in to making this combination work. The Virgo woman is a homely person who keeps everything neat and tidy. But the Leo man is slow in giving appreciation. She is also terribly critical, which is not a good sign for the compliment-craving lion.

Libra woman: 9/10. A perfect match! The typical Libran indecisiveness will go down well with the assertive Leo. Moreover, both have similar tastes as both love to socialise, are adventurous, romantic and passionate.

Scorpio woman: 5/10. Not a very good match. Since both are assertive, there would always be a clash of ego and interests in this relationship. While he is more inclined towards sensuality in a relationship, she needs intensity. Moreover, she would hate his constant need to be in the limelight and disregard all his public display of affection as fake.

Sagittarius woman: 7/10. This relationship can work wonderfully after a few adjustments. Both like adventure and are outgoing by nature. But they will have to mutually decide on sharing attention, as well as giving each other enough attention, for their relationship to work in the long run.

Capricorn woman: 6/10. If both are able to understand each other perfectly, this combination will succeed. He will have to be more understanding of her lack of expression while she will have to be more accommodating of his attention-seeking nature.

Aquarius woman: 5/10. A lot of hard work will be required to make this relationship work. The Aquarian woman will have to concentrate her energies more on the Leo guy rather than the outside world. And the Leo will have to learn to think more about his Aquarian partner than himself.

Pisces woman: 8/10. The Piscean woman can be the feminine alter ego of the Leo man. She can give him stability and emotional understanding as well as offer him the leadership role on a platter. However, he would have to keep his bluntness under control to get along with the sensitive Piscean.

Famous Leo men personalities:

Antonio Banderas	Arnold Schwarzenegger
Bill Clinton	Rajiv Gandhi
Sanjay Dutt	

Leo woman

Razor sharp, golden eyes glittering in the dark, watching each and every movement of the quarry, every muscle tense, every sinew packed with power waiting to be unleashed as she prepares to move in for the kill…

An embodiment of grace, energy, talent and unlimited potential, the majestic Leo woman is Jacqueline Onassis meets Mata Hari. An odd mix of pride and amity, loyalty and coyness, and passion and compassion, the Leo girl craves for spotlight. Known to making 'bang-on' appearances, the lioness in a human garb is hard to miss.

How can you identify a Leo woman in a crowd?

When it comes to Leo women, the aggressive and passive categories are in a 4:1 ratio, with both types being extremely assertive who love to have their way with things. They would give in or be submissive to someone only if they are deeply in love with that person or have great respect for him.

It is not difficult to spot a Leo woman in a crowd. A Leo woman will possess unmatched style and panache. You are also likely to see her talking endlessly, mostly about herself. When in a group, she will be the principal talker and the conversation will usually revolve around her.

I've observed that most Leo women have a rather prominent jawline. Madonna, Jennifer Lopez, Sridevi, Manisha Koirala...get the point? One peculiar thing I have noticed is the shape of their eyes...they are mostly almond shaped, with somewhat heavy eyelids. Quite like a Gothic painting! Commanding, questioning, yet friendly, her eyes will follow you everywhere, forcing you to take notice of her.

They have a unique sense of smell and if your aftershave or cologne is right, it does help to a great extent. Things like aromatherapy were either created by her or for her.

What are the key features of her personality?

A Leo woman is materialistic hence will not be satisfied with ordinary living. She will of course make do if the situation demands but her eyes will be set on a glitzy lifestyle.

While describing her behaviour in a crowd, I have mentioned that she likes to talk and is also an attention seeker. But I would also like to add here that she is not a senseless talker and definitely not a chin wagger. In spite of being outspoken and straightforward (read blunt), unless she is very comfortable with people around her, a Leo girl can be quite reserved. Her ego often stops her from breaking the ice, while she can also be reticent to open up until she has reached a stage of compatibility with people around her. She needs to be at ease and in command of the situation and people at hand. But don't let her initial reticence fool you. This lady is anything but shy. She is only sizing up the situation and waiting to get into the comfort zone before making her move.

I think I have harped enough on a Leo female's desire for materialistic pleasures. Let me add that her every material comfort comes with a grandeur tag. Remember the lioness! Everything that she does, from clothes to home décor is done on a majestic scale. If you ask me, she scores a ten on ten for grandiosity and if her bank balance permits her, her opulence would know no bounds.

Another strong characteristic of a Leo woman is that she prefers admirers to friends. To a great extent, it is easy to get close to her via flattery and admiration. Also, as she always wants to be in control, she finds it easier to be around people who constantly agree with her. You will sometimes find her getting carried away with excessive praise and even thinking on the lines 'who needs friends when there are followers'.

But she is in no way stupid or shallow. A Leo woman knows how to make friends and respect them. She is aware that good friends are always around to hear her innermost thoughts and share her secrets. On her own part, if she learns to control her blunt tongue, she would indeed make a very good friend.

A common trait that I have noticed in the 80 per cent aggressive Leo females is arrogance or pride. Beauty, appearance and popularity can make her think too highly of herself. A combination of arrogant attitude and acerbic speech can make her one haughty woman. Sometimes you will find a Leo girl taking too much pride in her wealth (either self-made or inherited). The only saving grace here is self-awareness, which instills a certain amount of humility in her.

Like I mentioned before, a Leo female has innate leadership qualities. This can also be attributed to her desire to hold things at her command—situations and people alike. She is usually sure about what she wants and how to get it. Also she is clever enough to use her personality to get things done, which makes her come across as a leader.

On the flipside, a Leo woman can be very unforgiving and even vengeful. If you are ever involved in a tussle of any kind with her, be sure she will not rest until she has set the scores even with you. She is especially touchy about matters of the heart and you can't ditch her in love and get away with it. This lioness will be on the prowl till she has her revenge.

But revenge or anger never makes her blind. She is shrewd and calculating and will not plunge into any aggressive action without weighing the pros and cons of it. She is catty enough to realise that if her adversary is someone powerful (financially, socially or physically), she might as well bury the hatchet.

Moreover, there is a marked difference between the way an inexperienced Leo girl behaves and the conduct of a mature Leo woman. Experience and maturity teaches her to be less self-centred and demanding. Once she learns how to cope with her desire to receive attention, she grows more generous and attentive towards her loved ones and as life progresses she also realises that she has a natural charisma of attracting people and grows more subtle in her demand for attention. Her appearance and gait also complement her regal mien and she commands respect like no other woman.

Leo is one zodiac sign which is known for its boundless energy. Leo woman naturally endorse this trait. A Leo female has a large fuel reservoir and is high on energy levels. You will always find her leading a spirited, active and cheerful life. She is warm towards her friends and loved ones and her exuberance is seen through her spontaneity and creativity. With a Leo girl you are sure to have a lively and fun-filled time.

How is she on the following aspects?

Appearance: As far as physical features go, I have already mentioned the prominent jawline. When it comes to dressing up, a Leo woman leads the pack. She has an original sense of style and an eye for new trends. She is quick to adapt to anything new on the fashion front and is not shy to imitate others. For example, if she sees another woman with a handbag or shoe that catches her fancy, she wouldn't hesitate in going and buying the same for herself.

Another peculiarity that I have noticed in Leo females is their penchant for displaying their 'feline' self through their choice of clothing. You are likely to catch her in a leopard-print outfit or sporting a tiger-striped handbag or scarf. Just like the Leo male, she too prefers black and white as her colours.

Ambition: When Madonna sang *I'm a material girl* she so meant it! Leo women are driven by their materialistic desires—it forms the very basis of their ambitious self. It is because of the need to fulfill these yearnings that a Leo female will excel in her chosen career. She would strive to reach the top and put in sincere efforts to be the best and make a mark in her field of work. But she will also make a lot of noise on her way up so that people around sit-up and notice. However, to achieve their material desires, some Leo women are quite likely to find a rich, good-looking man and marry him…an unfailing get-rich-quick scheme.

Ego/Self-respect: I have observed that amongst all fire signs, Leo women have the loftiest ego and an equally high self-respect quotient. Interestingly, six out of every ten Leo females I have met have admitted this too. The good part however is that if you are friends with a Leo girl, what you see is what you get. There are no behind the scene surprises in store for you. Although I admit that I have observed a certain amount of hypocrisy too amongst Leo females, I would hasten to add that it is largely due to immaturity. As she matures and grows with experience, a Leo woman learns to curb her double standards and ego.

Responsibility: A Leo woman wins (and I am not using this verb lightly) an eight on ten for responsibility. She is extremely responsible especially towards her relationship roles. You will generally find her a dependable daughter and sibling, one who will grow up into a responsible person, who'll put her family before her needs. Being a control freak, she finds it easy to take charge and organise stuff. But she is incapable of dealing with stress and can crumble if cornered or put under pressure.

Etiquettes: Almost 100 per cent of Leo women are either born with or later in life learn impeccable social etiquettes. Naturally they expect the same from others. Everything she does has a touch of class to it—from dressing up for casual coffee date to donning an evening gown for a high profile award function—you will never find her missing out on any point of decorum. As a mother she ensures her children have high standards of social propriety, and while with others she almost expects them to take a crash course in etiquettes before interacting with her.

What is her approach towards life?

Women belonging to this sun sign are powered by a buoyant attitude, fierce aggression, with a dash of fun and frolic thrown in. Highly ambitious, a Leo woman would indulge in using her influence and charm unabashedly to acquire what her heart desires. She knows she can attract anyone she wants and she uses this to her advantage, enjoying every bit of being in the limelight as she goes along. Often overbearing, her dominance is exhibited in the way she commands others (read 'men') to do her bidding, with them complying to her wishes with delight.

Impatient at times, especially when things aren't done her way, the lioness has a childlike quality to her. This comes to full bloom when she is engaged in activities that suit her fancy. She would readily agree to go on an expedition through the roughest of terrains or going dirt biking with her pack; she could also be the perfect woman, spending a nice, lazy day by the beachside, romancing her man.

Bright, undaunted by failures, resilient and exuding positivity, the Leo woman handles life with a true 'bring it on' attitude!.

How does she score on the following points?

Cynicism: I would say 60 per cent of Leo women are cynical and this trait arises from their stubbornness. A Leo female is obstinate to the extent of being intractable when it comes to things she wants to have or do. If her mind is set on something, (irrespective of whether it is positive or negative) she would commit herself to attaining it and yes, any interference or contrary opinions are strictly prohibited. This habit is actually a weakness and most Leo women are aware of it but it is precisely because of this awareness that they are able to stop themselves from getting into difficult situations.

Suspicion/Jealousy: Being a fire sign, she is extremely passionate and possessive of the people she loves. The same extends to her immediate family as well as her material possessions. Given the minutest reason to doubt, she can get extremely suspicious too.

This lady scores full marks on jealousy. Be it personal relationships or professional success, she can go crazy with envy. She can't stand her man getting friendly with another woman, can't stand her colleague getting a promotion at work, would find it difficult to see her best friend tying the knot before her; jealousy can turn this lioness into an alley cat (she can purr and claw like one too), so much so that she is likely to give you a tit-for-tat reply. For instance, when jealous she will try to make you also as jealous as possible.

Dishonesty/Infidelity: Honesty is dear to a Leo woman's heart. She is never dishonest herself and therefore finds it difficult, nay almost impossible to accept deceit from others. That is almost non-bailable offence for her. Any kind of lies, fraud or deception can turn things nasty. If you have ever lied to your Leo girlfriend or wife and got caught, you would know what I am talking about!

Like I stated before, a Leo woman is steadfast in her emotions. She is not casual about her relationships hence if she is promiscuous, there has to be a good, solid reason for it. She is high on energy and usually possesses an outgoing, extrovert nature and this makes her compatible with most people around her, especially men. And it is this compatibility that can lead her astray at times. But for a Leo girl this attention only reassures her confidence; it does nothing to budge her love for you. Once she has surrendered herself, she will consider it below her dignity to cheat on you.

An odd observation that I have made about Leo women (and their Taurean counterpart) is that as they grow older, they fancy younger men.

Success and failure: Success for a Leo woman is something to be flaunted. Apart from the 20 per cent passive kind of Leo females, the rest would exhibit their success stories in every possible way.

Monetary success means a lot to a Leo woman. This goes back to her love for materialistic pleasures. She knows that to fulfil her desires, she needs money (given her taste, it's loads of money).

In most cases, failure equals to challenge for any fire sign and the Leo is no exception. It becomes a matter of pride and integrity for Leo women to prove to themselves and others that they can't fail. But if they do, they can sulk and spend days being miserable.

Host: A Leo woman is passionate about most things, including being a host. No matter what her monetary status, she would make all efforts in laying out a grand spread, (I am not saying she would spend hours in the kitchen as she is quite capable of ordering in but a Leo woman enjoys creating the right ambience for her guests).

Let me tell you a little bit about a Leo woman as a homemaker and it will give you a better idea of her as a host. Since she is a control freak, she likes to rule her house like a kingdom. She has great taste (sometimes an expensive one!) and knows how to enliven her home. Also, given her interest in the minutest detail about her house, she is likely to put in extra efforts to make her social do an affair to remember. She will be as charming as a host as she is efficient as a homemaker.

Guest: As a guest she will observe everything—from crockery to cutlery and from ambience to hospitality. She can also get terribly critical once she leaves the venue. However, this doesn't mean she lacks compassion towards someone whose monetary status does not permit him to be flamboyant. It is not her arrogance or ego, but her superior taste that makes it difficult for her to step down from her high horse.

How does she handle difficult situations?

It takes a lot for a Leo woman to accept her fault in any given situation. She will make every effort to argue or convince others of her innocence. Post-quarrels you will find her sulking and waiting for you to apologise and mend things. Some Leo women are known to have temper issues (and only in rare cases would rationalise that, that too when in a calmer state of mind). Mostly they would be on their own trip, brooding and wondering what's taking you so long to mend things!

What is her characteristic weakness?

I'd say being over blunt and overly critical. Very few Leo women know how to control their tongues or know when to shut up. This is something most of them realise from an early age as this peculiarity in their nature often makes them lose out on friends.

But since a Leo woman is aware of this flaw, she makes a constant endeavour to overcome it as she matures. The outspoken attitude will remain her chief fault lifelong, but she will eventually learn to limit its disastrous consequences.

Is there more to this diva's persona?

Here is one lady who is emotional, and ego sensitive too and given all this knows the shortcomings of her nature. Dreamy and idealistic, Leo girls are not very realistic or very practical. But they sure know how to lead and have an innate talent of forging ahead and making way for others to follow.

In her craze to grab a spot in the limelight, a Leo girl might miss out on many teeny-weeny details of life. She might tread ruthlessly upon the sensitive feelings of her loved ones and often overlook the fact that her forthrightness might be hurting someone. Although this is not intentional, it is an important aspect of her self-centred nature.

This one loves to be pampered! Next to flattery and admiration, the one thing a Leo girl adores is being petted. The lioness will purr contentedly at your side if you pamper her with love, gifts (expensive ones!) and attention. Be it her parents, friends or husband, she likes to be the top most priority for everyone. But that doesn't mean she is emotionally needy. Far from that...the Leo girl is fiercely independent. She is quite capable of taking care of herself in any given situation, but she needs to bask in the glory of everyone's attention.

How should one deal effectively with a Leo woman?

What she looks for is a 'gentleman'. A Leo woman lays great stress on social etiquettes, graceful manners and a caring attitude. Naturally she wants her man to have all these attributes. Further, she also wants someone who is aggressive enough to dominate her...although not overtly. To effectively deal with a Leo woman, one needs to have a good idea of social decorum, an outspoken and honest nature and the right dose of flattery. I repeat: flattery, my dear friends, is the key to this lady's heart!

One of the most distinguishing characteristics that a Leo woman possesses is a certain amount of humility. Due to this she is able to understand and accept healthy criticism, making it easier for people to handle her. This stems for her ability to distinguish between a well-wisher and a casual friend.

Another important aspect to be kept in mind while interacting with a Leo female is respect. She appreciates people who respect her for her intelligence and persona. Also she likes to have lot of space for herself and possesses an inherent need to be independent. She is extremely compatible with people who understand these basic needs of her personality.

How does she handle money matters?

A Leo female is quite casual with her money. Although nobody's fool, her compassion often makes her an easy victim to people who want to borrow as she gets easily moved by tales of sorrow, But one thing that a Leo woman knows very well about money is that it can buy material things and sometimes, also happiness.

With her extravagant taste and love for material things, it would be quite a task to restrain her, especially when she is on one of her innumerable shopping sprees. Although everything about her—her home, car, her appearance—will look stunning, she will often shell out more money than called for to get the desired look. What she needs is a restraining hand that lets her spend on stuff she wants but also teaches her the importance of saving.

While Leo women are usually in a hurry to make money, they know how to maintain grace and tact in the process.

How is she on the professional front?

The Leo's innate ability to lead and motivate makes people born under this sign perfect candidates for managerial roles. Since they don't appreciate being dominated or told what to do, Leo women often experience a bit of a problem when working in teams. However, if taken into confidence, the mature Leo woman would understand her role in being an efficient team member and contribute towards achieving set goals.

The desire to be in the spotlight propels them towards professions that offer them space to exhibit their ability in full view. Not ones to be content with working behind the scenes, one would often find Leo women drawn to the performing arts, especially singing and acting (which comes naturally to them). Vyjayanthimala, Sridevi, Melanie Griffith, Madonna, Whitney Houston...these are just a handful of names in the long list of Leo women who've created a niche for themselves in this field.

With their friendly approach and ability to convince others, an inherent confidence and offering full information in support of their cause, Leo women also score in sales and marketing jobs.

How is she in various relationship roles?

I have already expounded on her ability to take initiative as a homemaker and bring about a complete overhaul of her home to suit her taste (and home is one place where she gets to exercise her absolute authority). When it comes to her roles as a wife and mother, the Leo woman lives by two golden rules—high standards and complete control and when I say high I mean really high! As mentioned earlier, she wants her man to be a gentleman and this is evident in her attitude towards her husband. In return, she will be loyal, loving and caring towards her life partner. Moreover, she is not a hypocrite so she will ensure that the standards she seeks in others are present in her too. She also has the ability to be self-denying and unselfish if need be for her husband and family.

If you ever come across over pampered kids with a beautiful mother, chances are that she is a Leo. Leo women love to indulge their children. They will shower love and care on them with unmitigated generosity, at the same time expecting respect and obedience. A Leo woman will not accept any indiscipline in her children and manners and etiquettes will be first lessons she gives them.

How is she when alone?

Unless she is spiritually inclined, a Leo woman will not prefer to be by herself. When left to her own devices, she would ponder over trivial issues and accumulate negative thoughts and energy. Only with a spiritual bent of mind can she direct her thoughts to higher things in life. Being attention seekers, Leo women like to be surrounded by people and nothing pleases them more than being the topic of discussion or centre of attraction in a crowd. The only time a Leo girl would like to be alone is when she has to recharge her powers. 'Me time' signifies a renewal of energy for the lioness but her sabbatical is short-lived and she's usually back with a roar!

How is she when in love?

For a Leo woman, love can also be a ticket to success. She may scout for the most successful man to 'fall in love with'. Details like being financially secure or high-up on the social ladder, matter to her and her attitude towards love can be governed by these considerations, but in a bid to be monetarily secure, she will never go for the regular 'bird-brained brawny boys'. To her intellectual capability is as important. To sum it up, the Leo girl wants her partner to have everything if not in goodly amounts, then at least proportionately proper.

When in love with a Leo girl, you would also need to learn to manage her fragile ego. Although she is not forcefully dominating, the lioness can take matters in her hands, if she finds that the man she is in love with, is not 'manly' enough.

Whatever her shortcomings, a Leo woman is generally aware of them and therefore appreciates it if her partner manages her with patience and understanding.

What does she look for in her partner?

The Leo woman's fierce bid for independence is somewhat diluted when in love. You would see a much mellower version of her feline powers when courting her. Of course, she has the tendency to become impatient at times, and loses her composure now and then (and therefore needs a partner who knows how to deal with her tantrums and her constant need for attention).

This woman is possessive and likes her man to exhibit the same trait, but only in terms of being passionate without being overbearing...nah! That's her department! With a very high sexual quotient, the lioness seeks a partner who is capable of satisfying her physical needs, while providing her with the emotional support, praise and commitment she so desires.

With a terribly covetous approach towards life, she would hunt for a partner who can make her special through open display of his emotions for her, showering her with gifts and compliments all throughout their relationship. With a Leo woman, the passion never ebbs out and (God forbid!) if her partner lacks romance, she would soon end up feeling dejected, neglected and unwanted.

While dating her, you should…

…match her standards for starters! She expects gentlemanly behaviour from you, so don't think she will be impressed with your cowboy acts and rugged looks.

A Leo woman will come across as polished, stately and gracious and she is all that without doubt. But that doesn't mean she lacks depth. Her stateliness is not skin deep, it penetrates her mind and thought process as well. She is an intelligent woman and needs a man who understands her.

She is always high on passion and energy (another typical fire sign trait) therefore she needs a 'cool' person to balance her. More than dominating she wants her partner who knows how to restrain her.

There is something truly original about her so if you are wooing her make everything you do as original as you can, be it with gifts, compliments or surprises. Trust me your efforts will not go in vain.

A Leo woman is also witty and loves to have a good laugh. Once you get to know her and she is in the desired 'comfort zone' with you, she will floor you with her charm and wit. And eventually when she falls in love, she will also be generous with her affections and love, for this lioness has a warm and loving heart.

With a Leo girl, the maxim 'first impression is the last impression' holds true. She won't bother you with a second date, if the first one doesn't satisfy her. Remember her fan following! If you are serious about seeing her a second time, make sure you hit the bull's eye in your first date itself. Try and do something that would appeal to her aesthetic sense—take her to a cultural event or a classic romantic movie. Add that extra touch of glamour to a usual date affair, such as taking her to a fine dine restaurant rather than a Chinese hangout, or give a personalised scarf as a gift rather than the ever-present perfumed candles. Trust me she would love these tiny details and with that adoration in your eyes, it will be enough to land you a second date with this amazing lady.

Getting intimate with a Leo woman can be quite a task. For all her forthrightness and extrovert nature, the Leo girl is quite unsure about physical intimacy. This may be because she either prizes her beauty a bit too much and is afraid she might lose it, or because she thinks getting intimate may end her chances of getting out of the relationship, whatever her reasons, she would prefer extending the dating sessions. You may have to eat quite a few dinners and luncheons with her before she invites you over for that special cup of coffee at home.

But at the end of the day when she turns to you for a relaxing hug, make sure you tell her how much you appreciate her love...your appreciation will forever keep the fire of romance glowing within your Leo girl.

Compatibility quotient:

How to be compatible with a Leo woman? Be the ringmaster or play into her hands? You've got to have the passion to match her fervour and the mental stability to be her anchor. While a relationship with her might start off on a fun note, it would take a lot more to make it last in the long-term. Let's see how compatible the Leo girl is with men on the zodiac.

Leo woman and...

Aries man: 6/10. These two can set the house on fire (maybe) literally too. So much has been talked about a Leo and Aries being a great combo etc but I beg to differ! Both are passionate, fiery and adventurous. While their mutual interests can strike the right chord, too much of similarity can be a hindrance, more so because both have an unruly tongue and can be extremely stubborn, landing into stalemate situations often. If she finds a passive Aries man she can dominate or if the passive Leo woman finds the aggressive Aries man, things could work out well. I strongly feel in the long run for fire signs opposites attract and stick.

Taurus man: 7/10. This combination can work wonders only if both are able to tweak their personality traits a bit. He will have to be more understanding of her extrovert nature and she will have to be patient with his dominating attitude, but more often than not Leo women get drawn towards Taurus men for their charm.

Gemini man: 8/10. The Gemini is knowledgeable and good at conversation, while the Leo girl is beautiful, intelligent and witty, something that he would appreciate. Once he learns to concentrate all his attention on her, rather than other women, this would be a great relationship.

Cancer man: 8/10. The Leo girl can give the Cancerian love, care and loyalty but she would need to understand his hypersensitive nature and control her tongue accordingly. As long as the Cancer man knows how to give her the space she needs, this can be a rocking relationship.

Leo man: 6/10. This combination can go either ways. Both will have to understand that there is only one spotlight and at a time it can be turned on only one of them. If one of them learns to take the backseat, this relationship between the lions can work well.

Virgo man: 4/10. What might kick-start well, may not last in the long run. The Virgo man doesn't have the answer to the Leo girl's constant need for attention. Moreover, she is not submissive enough to suit his needs.

Libra man: 8/10. Again a wonderful match! There will be romance, dance and much more in this relationship. The Leo girl will appreciate the Libran creativity and consistency, while in return the Libran would shower her with attention and care. As an add on, both are expressive about their emotions something that would keep both quite satisfied.

Scorpio man: 5/10. Here the passions can go astray. This relationship would require anger management on a large scale. Moreover, the Leo woman can get frivolous at times and the Scorpio guy can leave her dissatisfied with his constrained love. Bossiness and impatience in both can also lead to strife. But the right amount of adjustments could make this work really well.

Sagittarius man: 7/10. Fun-loving, cheerful and adventurous is the best way to describe this relationship. The Sagittarian however will have to learn to curb his flirtatiousness otherwise the lioness can get hurt. Romance and chemistry between these two is likely to last in the long run.

Capricorn man: 6/10. If they learn to make their disparity work for them, this can be a good combination. He should get used to her socialising and outgoing nature and she should get along with his sedentary lifestyle. But on the bright side, he would appreciate her determination and will-power, while she would love his dependability.

Aquarius man: 6/10. With a few tactful moves this relationship can be made to work wonderfully. The Leo girl will have to make the Aquarian feel committed yet not tied down. On the other hand, he should give her ample warmth and care. With more understanding this combination can go places and there will never be a dull moment in this relationship.

Pisces man: 7/10. This relationship can work on the basis of 'opposites attract'. He is bound to his self and lives in his own world, while she is a worldly person and loves to socialise. With true love and diligence, they can make this relationship work and they definitely have romance and passion to help them.

Famous Leo women personalities:

Madonna
Jennifer Lopez
Sridevi
Manisha Koirala
Kajol Devgan

Virgo

24 August-23 September

Virgo man

Practicality rules the mind of a typical Virgo male. He thinks, acts and sometimes even dreams logically. The best way to be around him is to 'cut the fuss'. He has a dislike for flowery language or unnecessary emotional gestures. With a Virgo man, no emotional baggage please! Although emotional himself, he is not likely to understand the state of emotions of others around him. And when in love, he needs ample room to be himself, to do his thing and to take-off, if required.

Behind his serious expression is a mind that loves to laugh. I say 'mind', because he likes intelligent humour and not slapstick comedy. He is knowledgeable, opinionated and shrewd enough not to let others, especially strangers, see the hand that is being dealt to him. A man who knows his mind and understands his needs—a man who frequently asks himself 'what's in it for me?'—that's a typical Virgo guy.

How would you identify a Virgo man in a crowd?

A Virgo man is quiet and reserved, not much into initiating conversations unless spoken to. He is the type of person who would take initiative only if he has a motive, (only if you have a hobby like mine of observing people and their behaviour will you be able to spot a Virgo man).

While in a conversation, he might display interest in keeping it interactive and spend time getting his point across. He is also very opinionated. Here again I am at a loss on how to classify Virgo men into aggressive and passive categories because I have observed that Virgo men behave aggressively only when provoked or pushed.

This might sound funny but most Virgo men are fond of speed, racing fast cars or jet skis. I once visited an apartment in Bandra in Mumbai where the owner's son, around twenty-two years of age, had posters of racing cars all over the walls in his room. After speaking with him for a few minutes and observing his love for sports cars, I asked him if he was a Virgo. The poor guy almost jumped out of his wits! But he regained composure in a split second and showed neither excitement nor interest beyond mere politeness. This too was typically Virgo behaviour. Virgo men like to be in control of situations and don't like anyone else reading them or sizing them up, especially strangers.

Most (not all) of the Virgo males I have known are fitness freaks and are infrequent drinkers. This again comes from their need to be in control, which can be dislodged with one drink too many.

What are the key features of his personality?

Virgo represents the sign of the problem solver. Given his analytical bent of mind and rational and logical thinking, a Virgo male is good at solving problems. He regards every crisis like a mechanical device, which can be taken apart and then put together again. On a scale of ten, he scores an eight as a solution provider.

He is also a creative person and with a mind that is constantly ticking with ideas, he is likely to come up with some bright ones every now and then. Because of his creative streak, a Virgo man often excels in any given task, be it his job or business.

He can be temperamental at times. Although he is not prone to mood swings, his temper can make him a difficult man to handle. Due to this he can be unpredictable at times. He is also very sensitive and can get touchy about subjects close to his heart, like his accomplishments and his persona.

Sometimes he displays flashes of inconsistency in his nature. This can be attributed to his muted emotions and lack of communication. However, when in his true element, he can be a true diplomat. He has the natural gift of dealing with people with tact and discretion. I would give him a nine on ten for diplomacy.

How is a Virgo man on the following aspects?

Appearance: It is difficult to describe a Virgo man by his looks. I would take the best way out and give you an example—one would be Hindi film star Akshay Kumar, another would be the British actor Hugh Grant.

Ambition: Ambition rules the game for Virgo men. Seven out of every ten Virgo men are overly ambitious...for them 'the sky is limitless' (this isn't malapropism, I mean it!). They like to set targets for themselves and spend a lot of time and effort in achieving the same. During their struggle days, they are capable of spending fourteen to sixteen hours at work, thereby compromising on family and social life. They are very shrewd and calculative and have a great ability to save and spend sensibly in case of a windfall. They also have the ability of negotiating well.

Ego/Self-respect: While a Virgo man may never show his true self to many people, he does possess a great amount of ego and self-respect. He would very rarely take favours and would try to create his own mark and identity in the career path of his choice.

But, his ego can make him self-centred too. Because of this, he is not very good at maintaining relationships and friendships and is usually found befriending people he can dominate and have his way with. He is rarely the one to take initiative to build and enhance relationship with a friend/lover unless there is a motive.

Responsibility: To a Virgo man it is usually about 'me, my and myself. His responsibilities are limited to himself and somehow he never finds time for others. Only when he has achieved great success and is able to manage his time well will he look at fulfilling his responsibilities towards his parents, siblings, girlfriend, wife or children.

Etiquettes: A Virgo man, although assumed to be meticulous and detailed, is sometimes found lacking in etiquettes, but that largely depends on his upbringing and monetary status. However, he does seem to be adaptive and learns from his mistakes (and being image-conscious, he will not hesitate in taking these pains). But Virgo men, who are born with a silver spoon in their mouth or have achieved good amount of success, will pay appropriate attention towards their etiquettes.

What is his approach towards life?

A Virgo man is not very realistic, but he is practical enough to know that life is full of highs and lows. Since he likes new challenges, his pragmatism is of great use to him. On an emotional level he is rather partial; not so emotional about others and quite emotional about himself. He is also sentimental.

Given his ambitious drive, a Virgo man is quite a dreamer. He believes in dreaming big and achieving big. He is fine with someone else taking the lead, but only till he learns the tricks of the trade; from there on he would prefer being the ultimate leader.

A Virgo man's list of desires is virtually endless. Not only does he want everything from life, he also wants to be good at everything he does...the best in the industry or field as they say. Though not one to be satisfied with an ordinary life, he has the perceptive to make do with low standards while he is struggling. Later his grit and determination to achieve his targets, with a quality life being one of his prime targets, help him.

How does he score on the following points?

Cynicism: I have observed that 70 per cent of Virgo men are cynical. Sometimes, being cynical can be good because it can bring forth the zing required to achieve success. If used correctly, cynicism can bring out the best in you. Somehow, most Virgo men have the tact to use it positively. The flipside is that given a situation of dispute/disagreement their cynical side gets them into awkward situations.

Criticism: Is it true that the Virgo man is a born critic? This is the most common complaint I have heard against Virgo men. A Virgo man's criticism comes from his belief that he can do things better than anyone else. This would apply to any role in life. For instance, as an architect he would say he could make the best structure, as a developer he could say he can develop the most futuristic and modern skyscraper, and as an actor he would believe he can act better than the rest.

However, the positive aspect of his criticism is that he could put sincere effort and conviction in what he claims he can do better than others, if given the opportunity; this however may not apply to all walks of life.

Suspicion/Jealousy: Is a Virgo man of suspicious disposition? Yes and no. 'Yes' because he is suspicious when it comes to his career and achievements and 'no' because he isn't suspicious about his relationships. He is possessive about his achievements and personal belongings. With his work and people related to work, he is forever on guard, especially where money matters are concerned. But regarding his relationships, he displays a secure and non-caring attitude. He is not likely to be suspicious except when given a reason to doubt.

A definite YES when it comes to jealousy! A Virgo man can be jealous and very easily so. If at work or business his direct competition scores over him or is successful, our man can go green with envy. The reason for this is that he thinks he deserves it more than the next man. On the relationship front, he can be extremely jealous if his girlfriend or wife displays interest in another man.

As for his partner's jealousy, he would be no different from other men by going on a defensive mode (but if you look closely and if you are a keen observer, no matter how good an actor he is, you might just be able to tell if he is lying). Also, since he is driven by his moods, he could react differently each time he encounters his partner being jealous of him or his doings.

Dishonesty/Infidelity: A Virgo man expects his woman to be completely loyal and manages to convince her of his loyalty too. However, a good percentage of Virgo men find themselves attracted to other women quite often. While some of them might not pursue such temptation (mostly due to lack of time), most of them manage to take time off to please their fancy. And usually they are successful in their efforts at two-timing as they have fierce determination and don't stop till they have achieved their goals. No matter how much self-control a Virgo man claims he possesses, being occasionally promiscuous remains his core weakness. However (and not to be diplomatic), there are exceptions here too.

Hardships: A Virgo man displays enormous patience during hardships. This usually comes from the immense confidence he possesses to achieve his targets. When faced with hardships he might at times hit a low. This is the only time you will catch him displaying his emotions and I say this because Virgo men are not good at displaying emotions.

Success and failure: Now here is one man who likes to keep it very low. When successful he would prefer to be in his own company. Only when he is overly successful would he celebrate it with family and friends.

Most Virgo men I have met are poor losers. They would spend time in analysing and moping over the why's and how's of their failure... be it a game of sport, a business deal or a fight.

Host: Unless you are very close to him, he would be a very casual host to you. This is chiefly because home is not his domain and organising events involving catering, entertaining and the like is not his forte. A Virgo man defines home as someplace you go to eat and sleep. It has to be handled either by a woman or hired help...he should have no share in the running of a house.

Guest: Usually very picky in accepting invitations, especially when invited to somebody's home, a Virgo man can be either casual or demanding as a guest depending on his mood and the level of interaction at the party.

How does he handle difficult situations?

A Virgo male would very rarely admit his mistakes and would make every possible attempt to cover them up. He tries to portray an image of perfection that of an ideal man who is incapable of doing wrong. More often than not, this is not the case. I have time and again found Virgo men involved in discussions trying to convince others of their innocence rather than finding a solution. Only if things seem to get out of hands will they bend their stance and apologise.

What is his characteristic weakness?

Although I have mentioned his characteristic weakness earlier, I would like to elaborate on it here. His chief shortcoming is his disability to create and maintain relationships. He avoids people generally and is not particular about keeping up with friends and acquaintances. Yet he is dependent on them for one thing or the other; this habit makes him come across as selfish and self-centred. And who isn't sensitive to such behaviour?

Is there something more to his persona?

Another interesting aspect that I have noticed in some Virgo men is the difficulty they face in believing in the supernatural or the power of the Almighty. I would like to clarify that this is my observation and not a judgment on Virgo men, who can be as spiritually inclined as any other enlightened being.

Given his analytical and logical mind, a Virgo man can find it difficult to accept something that has no rational explanation. But this trait may vary across cultures. Sometimes one starts believing in God as a response to fear. To a Virgo man, it is usually the fear of failure and the need to be successful that make him a believer.

How should one deal effectively with a Virgo male?

Typically, one needs to gauge what a Virgo man is after. I say this because of his tendency to have myriad ulterior motives behind that quiet demeanour. If he approaches you it is because he wants something and if you approach him he assumes you want something of him. Virgo men can make good politicians and bureaucrats as they spend most of their time thinking, planning and strategising.

The only tip I can give you on how to deal with a Virgo man is; don't ever (and I mean EVER) open all your cards before him under any circumstance—else he would exploit the situation to the fullest, needless to say to his complete advantage.

How does he handle money matters?

A Virgo man is only into earning and saving. He knows all good things in life come at a price and wants to be prepared for all price tags. With his usual shrewdness he also knows the value of money and therefore believes in saving for future and difficult times. While he is not stingy to the core, he is not extravagant either. But of course, once his position in life changes for the better, he starts using money as a tool and not as an end. This also comes from the fact that he has an image to uphold.

How is he on the professional front?

The fact that he is great at planning, ideating and organising, makes a Virgo man good at work. He is the one with bright ideas and solutions. A thinker and a practical man…or let's say a 'practical thinker', a Virgo male is efficient at any given job. As an employee, he will excel in any given task and will outdo his co-workers—firstly, as he is ambitious and secondly, because he is competitive. He also makes for a good colleague as he understands rather too well the maths of dependability.

However, his analytical mind and criticising nature can sometimes be a hindrance. Since he sets standards that are too high for himself, as well as for others, it is difficult to please him.

Given all their faults (who hasn't got faults anyways!) Virgo men are intelligent and shrewd. Combined with an excellent memory and a sharp mind, it arms them with all the attributes of being good entrepreneurs.

Most of them have innate business acumen and the necessary drive to succeed. Above all, they are quite rational in their thinking and astute in money matters—those being the all important ingredients of a good businessman.

How is he in various relationship roles?

A Virgo man has immense respect and regard for his parents. But often, due to his various commitments and disability to communicate emotions, his true feelings don't get conveyed.

With someone he loves, like his girlfriend or wife, his work and ambition can lead to a strained relationship. Here is one man who is clear about his dreams and drives and will always give priority to his work, be it a job or business. So ladies in love with Virgo men, prepare yourself for playing second fiddle to his professional involvements.

He is most comfortable with his children and is able to relate to them. I am not trying to hammer down Virgo men here, but having observed display of emotion to be a major shortcoming with them, I have realised that they are at ease only with children.

As a father the Virgo man also scores on another point. He likes to teach discipline, good manners and proper way of living to his children. When around children, a Virgo man is able to communicate well, as children are less demanding of emotions and attention.

How is he when alone?

You may often catch a Virgo man alone but you will rarely find him idle. He gets restless when left with nothing to do. Even when unoccupied, he will think of ways to fill in time—calling up close friends for a social do, sorting his stack of CDs, downloading new games on his laptop and what not. But on the whole, a Virgo man is so submerged in his work or a sport or some other activity that he rarely finds time to be alone.

How is he when in love?

Just the same as he is on any regular day. There is no difference between a Virgo man in love and a Virgo man not in love. Like I said before, he finds it difficult to emote and even when in love, you will not find anything lover-like in his behaviour. If you are expecting scented love letters and sweet nothings from your lover, you are clearly with the wrong man! Also, he is a hardcore practical man, the proverbial 'man of the world', so nothing he does is for the sake of sentiments and emotions.

Maintaining a love relationship with a Virgo man is like being in a chemistry lab—everything has to be mixed in the right way in the right amount. Else, fireworks are in order! To get the best out of your Virgo man you have to maintain the right amount of closeness and the right amount of distance with him. He wants to be loved but not overburdened with it. Overt display of emotions can turn him off, so keep everything subtle.

Being extremely cautious by nature, he is selective about whom he meets, befriends and courts. No love at first sight for this man! He will try and test your love before displaying his. And when in love and ready for commitment, he requires just one thing...a genuine relationship.

What does he look for in his life partner?

Inclined towards women who can hold an intelligent conversation, a Virgo man's choice of a life partner would be someone who's his version of a 'complete package'. What he actually looks for in a woman is someone who knows and understands 'who' and 'how' he is before getting into a commitment like marriage.

Once you are in a steady relationship with him it would be quite an uphill task to get him to propose marriage. Although he likes to be seen with the best faces in town, he would prefer a homely girl for a wife—someone with good looks, who is a good homemaker, an excellent cook, a terrific mother and a responsible wife (a complete package remember!).

Also make sure you know how to create the right ambience at home. A Virgo man wants to come back to a home that is clean (spotlessly!), neat, warm and welcoming. And he firmly believes that it is a woman's job to do so or to get it managed through help.

While dating him, you should...

...make the first move. And if you think it sounds un-ladylike or needy, you can steer clear of the Virgo guy. If you are waiting for him to ask you out, chances are it won't happen for a long, long time.

Before dating a Virgo man you need to learn certain lessons about this guy and his nature. While he is a funny and an intelligent friend and a wonderful companion, when it comes to dating, he sort of breaks all the rules. Romantic in his own peculiar way, he can redefine the role of a Romeo, if not the term 'love' itself. In a word, expect the unexpected while dating a Virgo guy.

Lesson one: He won't chase you no matter how beautiful, intelligent or rich you are. Although he appreciates these qualities in a woman, he always thinks there are plenty of girls out there for him and he won't make much of an effort at convincing you to date him. So when he asks you out, if interested, just get ready. Don't waste time in throwing airs about it.

Lesson two: His serious expression and unemotional stance is a façade. He is basically insecure about getting hurt and therefore limits the amount of true emotions on display. But deep down, he is sensitive and loveable. Don't get fooled with his unenthusiastic response to your advances.

Lesson three: Be smart...in every respect. From your clothes to your home décor, keep things neat and tidy. And remember, he hates wastefulness—be it an expensive gift or that extra layer of make-up on your face. If you are dining out with him, make sure you are not being extravagant.

Lesson four: Don't try to impress him by showing off your list of admirers. If he finds out that other men are interested in you, he would back off gracefully. He thinks jealousy is a wasted emotion and would detach himself from a girl who has admirers, rather than fight it out with them.

Lesson five: Put-up with his critical eye (besides knack for cleanliness and secrecy). Learn to take his criticisms. If you can adjust with these prominent traits of the Virgo guy, you can be a good candidate as a life partner for him.

Lesson six: Don't rush. Date a Virgo man only if you have enough patience at your command. Firstly, he won't go for a second date unless he is sure he likes you. Secondly, he won't show any emotional attachment even after months of dating. He may even consider physical intimacy improper while dating. This is not to be mistaken as 'pure-mindedness'—it's only a security measure against emotional harm.

Lesson seven: Remember there is a pot of gold at the end of the rainbow. He might take you out on endless dates, give you good practical gifts and show his true romantic self, but the decisive proposal might take a really long time to come. But when it does, it would/could be forever. A Virgo man won't waste much time once he is convinced you are the one for him.

Compatibility quotient

Who can best deal with the secretive and cautious nature of the Virgo man? Which woman amongst the zodiac is perceptive enough to understand the true depth of his emotions? While a lot would depend on individual circumstances, there are certain personality traits that can help us predict the compatibility quotient of a Virgo man with women from different signs. Let's find out how.

Virgo man and…

Aries woman: 7/10. This combination can work effectively if the Arien learns to keep her adventurous streak in check. She would also need to put-up with the Virgo man's secrecy and emotional detachment, but she has the verve and spirit to earn the respect and love of the Virgo man.

Taurus woman: 8/10. The Taurean practicality would appeal to the pragmatic Virgo male. Since both are dependable, they would get along well. Moreover, the Taurean passion would help the Virgo guy be more romantic and vocal about his love.

Gemini woman: 7/10. The Gemini woman has many qualities, like intelligence and good conversational skills, which the Virgo would admire. But it would be important to make this mutual admiration last in the long run.

Cancer woman: 9/10. A 'well-baked' relationship this one! The Cancerian has apt culinary and housekeeping skills to have a beautiful home and a delicious spread for the Virgo man. Moreover, both are sincere and romantic enough to keep the fire going for a long time.

Leo woman: 4/10. Too many compromises can suck the charm out of this relationship. While her passion can attract the Virgo guy initially, the Leo girl's constant need for attention is too much for him to take. Also she is not adjusting enough to get along with him in a long-term relationship.

Virgo woman: 5/10. This relationship can go either way. While both are practical and sincere, they are very demanding of each other. The relationship can also get quite monotonous. But with proper efforts, it can be made to last.

Libra woman: 5/10. A difficult match! A lot of hard work will be required to make this combination a success, mostly from the Libran. She will have to counter his cynicism with her optimism, his detachment with her affection and his critical nature with her patience.

Scorpio woman: 9/10. An excellent combination! Both are smart, intelligent and very often good-looking. They would admire each other for these qualities. The Virgo man will let the Scorpion take the lead on the home front, while he would impress her with his perfectionism.

Sagittarius woman: 6/10. This relationship can be a strain due to the basic difference between the temperaments of these two. She is an extrovert while he is a reserved person. Her wild nature can go against the conservative thinking of the Virgo guy.

Capricorn woman: 8/10. This combination has all the qualities of a successful relationship. The Capricorn woman has warmth and affection which will help the Virgo man open up to express his emotions, while he is dependable enough to give her the security she needs. But he would have to curb his roving eyes to make her feel secure and gain her trust. Also, the reassurance of love that a Capricorn woman needs is something this man may not be able to provide.

Aquarius woman: 6/10. With the right amount of adjustments, this relationship can work fantastically. She can counter his pessimism with her optimism and take his emotional needs in her stride. They would also please each other on the intellectual level.

Pisces woman: 6/10. The Virgo man would be quite at sea about handling the sensitive Piscean. While the Pisces woman will not comprehend his emotional detachment, the Virgo male will find her too needy and pushy for comfort. But if he provides her with the comforts of life and display love (emotion) once in a while, it might just work out well for both.

Famous Virgo men personalities:

Akshay Kumar	Hugh Grant
Keanu Reeves	Michael Jackson
Rishi Kapoor	Sean Connery

Virgo woman

Do you know that reserved, polite, politically correct and emotionally disciplined Virgo woman? Well, look again. You see...still waters run deep. She appears reserved, but she can be quite a chatter box, she is polite but if you hurt her ego, she can sting like a bee. And emotionally disciplined? That's a mere masquerade. She is as emotional as the next girl, but believes in hiding her emotions.

With a hint of lethargy and shades of being a Nosey Parker, the Virgo woman's personality has almost all shades of the spectrum. Practical to the extent of being selfish, a Virgo woman is too emotionally restrained and her lack of emotional expression makes her appear frigid.

In the long run, two personality traits completely govern the Virgo woman. The first—emotional detachment—if she does not learn to be expressive at a young age, chances are she would remain emotionally latent all her life. And secondly, given her critical nature, a Virgo woman is in grave danger of turning into a nag as she matures.

But overall, the Virgo lady is full of charm, femininity and good humour. Good at the art of keeping a clean home, a Virgo girl is as homely and conservative as they come.

How would you identify a Virgo woman in a crowd?

My estimate says that 60 per cent of Virgo women are aggressive and 40 per cent are passive. It is not difficult to identify them in a crowd. Almost all of them like to talk a lot and speak at the speed of lightening. When it comes to fitting maximum words in one breath, a Virgo woman can give Aquarian female a run for her money. I have also noticed that Virgo women like to gossip and sometimes they seem to mind other people's business more than their own.

In comparison to their male counterpart, they are quick at making friends and are usually very social. The aggressive Virgo woman is expressive and is capable of emoting and smiling with her eyes. Her eyes have a distinct quality of catching your attention with the multitude of emotions in there. The passive Virgo woman is extremely warm and friendly and is also very caring about her friends and loved ones. However, I would say about 15 per cent of Virgo women are reserved and introvert.

During my interactions with various Virgo women, I realised that they are extremely sharp and very quick on the uptake. Depending on their mood they can be quite witty and funny too. They seem to have an uncanny way of matching the wavelength and thought process of a man, which makes them more compatible with men. Ergo, Virgo women have a lot of male friends.

What are the key features of her personality?

A Virgo woman is a strange mix of shyness and boldness. Since she is opinionated and loves to talk, you will find her voicing her thoughts most of the time, but she can simultaneously be reserved and keep to herself. She is the kind of woman who thinks it is better to remain quiet unless she has something startling to say. Relevant or not, whatever she says has to be startling. But once you get her into arguing or discussing, she is a verbal express and then there's no stopping her.

She is also wary of people. Although appearing friendly and approachable from a distance, she is capable of building a fortress around her and blocking people out. This appears to be a contrast from her usual talkative and chirpy self. Such behaviour might lead a man to think she is playing games, when actually she is not. You can best describe such behaviour as the interplay of lights and shadows, with the Virgo woman exhibiting an entire gamut of emotions at different times. And of course there are also her mood swings to contend with!

Once again exhibiting traits akin to the male of the Virgo clan, there is a small percentage of Virgo women who like to make the move and call the shots. If you are pursuing a Virgo woman in love, don't overwhelm her with your interest. She knows exactly what she wants, or rather, who she wants and the less attention you pay to her, the more she is likely to approve of you.

A Virgo woman goes through various levels of growing up. With maturity comes self-realisation but no matter how 'grown up' she may act, she can never stop being self-indulgent, nor can she control her talking sprees.

Another prominent quality of hers is her knack of worrying... about herself and everybody else in the vicinity. Usually her worries are exaggerated and needless. In her intricate maze of worrying, she ends up driving herself and other people up the wall. This irritating quality is coupled with another more irritating one...her being repetitive.

I have found Virgo women to be unforgiving and at times vengeful. They often fall into the habit of making a mountain out of a molehill. It is difficult to reason with them as during quarrels or disagreements they don't stick to the core topic and keep jumping from one thing to another and very often, irrelevant things.

I have observed Virgo women to be low on immunity and prone to falling ill quite often.

How is she on the following aspects?

Appearance: Having keenly observed Virgo women, I have found that a very small percentage of them almost walk, talk and dress like men, but the majority of them are of course feminine and even ultra feminine in some cases. However, both kinds have a subtle dressing sense and nothing loud works for them. You will usually find them dressed as occasion demands. They seem to be obsessed with shoes and handbags (now I know how so many stores survive).

Ambition: There is a wide chasm between the ambitious and non-ambitious Virgo women. About 80 per cent of them are ambitious while the remaining 20 per cent are sheer lazy.

Since we are discussing ambition here, I would like to elaborate about the majority. Independent minded and determined, the average Virgo woman is often seen having a preference for print or television media or the hospitality/airline industry. She is equally detailed and meticulous about her work and home chores.

Ego/Self-respect: I would say that Virgo women have more self-respect (nine on ten) than ego (seven on ten). Given their ambitiousness, they sometimes tend to be self-centred and even selfish, which makes them appear egoistic too. However, their self-centredness springs from their desire to achieve their targets. I don't think it is wrong to be self-oriented in order to achieve your set goals in life, provided you don't hurt anyone in the process.

Also, you cannot please all the people all the time. It is important for you to be happy in order to make people around you happy. I believe this concept is mastered by most women on this planet and a Virgo woman is no exception.

Responsibility: A Virgo woman is extremely responsible and dependable. Unless you have a casual relationship with her, you will hardly ever find her unresponsive. This actually applies to all the people in her life. Depending upon the kind of relationship she shares with you, her level of responsibility towards you will vary.

She has the ability to think ahead and estimate the responsibilities coming her way. Because of this uncanny sense of speculation, she is able to match up easily with what is expected of her.

Etiquettes: I would give an 8.5 on 10 to a Virgo woman for etiquettes. She is quite particular about how she behaves in public and she also demands similar behaviour from her partner and even children. She has high standards of social decorum, both for herself and others, and you will have a lot of tight rope walking to do if you want to please her on this front.

What is her approach towards life?

A Virgo woman can undoubtedly be both realistic and practical but she is governed by her moods and the extent of her practicality largely depends on that. She is less emotional and sentimental but more sensitive. She is also dreamy and idealistic.

Although she has a strong opinion about everything, a Virgo woman finds it easier to follow than to lead. This could also be because of fear of failure, in which case she wouldn't want to take responsibility for the task at hand.

I think the passive Virgo woman can remain content with what life has offered her, but the aggressive kind, in her own subtle way, has an endless wish list. She is rarely satisfied with ordinary living and always aspires for a better lifestyle. This is purely my observation that she needs support in everything she does—at work, with emotions and in almost every walk of life. So in most cases she becomes dependent on others for her performance in whatever character she plays in life.

How does she score on the following aspects?

Cynicism: From amongst all Virgo women, 65 per cent are cynical. Sometimes they can come across like a pre-recorded track where they allow no room for other people to speak or bring in their point of view, rattling away their woes and miseries in a never ending tirade. And this also happens to be their characteristic weakness.

Suspicion/ Jealousy: When it comes to these green demons, a Virgo woman draws a lot from her male counterpart. Much like a Virgo man, she is suspicious of everybody in her professional circles. She likes to remain on her guard when anyone at work approaches her for anything (even if it is a goodwill gesture), but when it comes to relationships, she is quite complacent and will rarely be suspicious about her partner unless he gives her reasons to be.

Being possessive of her accomplishments, she can get jealous of her more successful colleagues or competitors. But this only eggs her into doing better herself. A Virgo woman can also feel pangs of jealousy if her boyfriend or husband shows interest in other women.

Dishonesty/Infidelity: A Virgo woman is mostly sincere about her relationships, but she sometimes can get swayed by charm, flattery and power of other men. This could partly be because she gets bored easily and prefers moving on. If her situation does not permit moving on, she would at least think of some diversions.

But she is extremely possessive of her partner and unforgiving by nature and stepping over the line will not be tolerated.

Hardships: Here again, a Virgo woman takes after a Virgo man. She is extremely resilient and can emerge triumphant in times of hardships. With patience and hard work, she is capable of making her way out of difficult times. However, the ups and downs of life can take their toll on her emotions and she might come across as emotionally weak at times during her days of struggle. But with the right kind of moral support from family and friends, she will find it possible to overcome her difficulties.

Success and failure: Success is a private affair. She would prefer being by herself in the glory of her success. But if she goes past the ordinary achievements in life, she will include family and close friends in her celebrations.

With failure, she can hit a real low. With her logical turn of mind, she will endlessly go over the nuances of her failure and analyse it from every aspect. In short, she is a poor loser.

Host: From culinary to cutlery, this woman wants to oversee everything if she is throwing a party. Nothing misses her detailed eye and everything at her social do is done with perfection. She is also careful about the likes and dislikes of her guests, especially regarding cuisines, unless you have encountered a young tomboyish Virgo girl who believes that home delivery and eating out of paper plates rock!

Guest: Being a careful and particular host, she expects the same standards of any other hosts. So if you have invited a Virgo woman over and plan to be hospitable or please her make sure everything is in the right place and the dinner table has the best food your cook or you can manage.

How does she handle difficult situations?

A Virgo woman is not very diplomatic (the passive kind being the exception). Although I may have (so far) made her sound sensible and practical (which she is!) in situations like quarrels, fights or arguments she comes across as one possessed. With her ability to talk non-stop, her arguments too seem never ending. I sometimes wonder if she looks back at unpleasant situations in her life in a calmer state of mind and regrets not having drawn a line at a certain point. Or in other words...shut her mouth when the time was right.

Moreover, if she is at fault, she usually ends up blaming circumstances or people involved. Very rarely will you find her giving in and owning up her mistakes, (a great percentage of Virgo women are poor listeners and stubborn in their attitude—it is from there that they draw the tenacity of being unbending in their stance). But if she is madly in love and a quarrel with her lover ensues, she will put in all efforts to mend things.

During difficult times it is best to leave her alone and give her time to cool off. There would be no point in arguing with her as she just won't listen to you.

What is her characteristic weakness?

That has got to be her unique ability of talking herself into trouble. A Virgo woman's tongue works faster than her brain, which results in endless and often meaningless arguments, where she is the chief talker. She (most, not all) cannot keep a secret to save her life and being a habitual gossip monger, she often finds herself in awkward situations with friends and family members.

A narrow margin of 20-25 per cent of Virgo women can keep secrets. If you ever come across such a Virgo woman, you can confide in her. Apart from that I would be circumspect about what I say in a Virgo female's presence.

Is there something more to this lady's persona?

A Virgo woman is a stickler for punctuality. She cannot tolerate late comers and her patience runs low when she is waiting for someone. According to me, she would score a nine on ten for punctuality. Although not short-tempered, she can let her lid fly when her expectations are not met with... especially about things she cares.

Her ambitious drive is well backed with a hard-working spirit. Given her analytical mind, she knows that nothing can be achieved without sincere efforts. However, when it comes to work or relationship, she is quite conservative in her attitude and you may have a difficult time to get her to accept new ideas.

And now, I would like to bring in another of her prominent characteristics...namely, fault finding. About 50 per cent of Virgo women are critical and good at finding faults in others, be it behaviour, work or table manners. As she tends to over analyse and is meticulous to the core herself, she finds it difficult to accept any shortcomings in others. Another reason for this is her opinionated nature. With a strong opinion about everything, she usually has the last word when opining about people's faults.

However, the remaining 50 per cent of Virgo women refrain from such criticism. They are more carefree, practical and easy-going. Though they too may find faults in others, they are able to live and let live.

But for Virgo women criticism is a one way street...they cannot tolerate being criticised.

How should one deal effectively with a Virgo woman?

As much as a Virgo woman may appear to be clear and straight forward, she is inexplicably confused in her head. At the risk of being hounded by all the Virgo women reading this, I would like to add that very often a Virgo female may say something, mean something else and end up doing something totally different. She belongs to that category of women who are described by the character of Professor Higgins in the musical *My Fair*

Lady as, 'She will beg you for advice. Your reply will be concise. She will listen very nicely and then go out and do exactly what she wants.'

So before making a deal of any kind with Virgo women make sure you are clear about what she is saying and meaning (if possible get it in writing), since they have a memory of convenience, (and this is applicable to both Virgo males and females).

How does she handle money matters?

How a Virgo woman handles money depends on how much money she has. If she is not so successful in life and is living through strained times, she can be conservative in her spending and stress on saving. But if she is monetarily successful or has a goodly inheritance, she would show a free hand at spending.

Not withstanding this, generally she is good at finances, neither too stingy, nor too extravagant.

How is she on the professional front?

Diligent in her approach, with a keen understanding for matters related to finance, the Virgo woman can hold the fort beautifully well when it comes to her professional life. A thinker, she is also a good mediator who readily provides counsel to her peers and subordinates.

Owing to her in-depth perception of money and money matters and also her ability to critically assess situations, Virgo women excel in the fields of finance, banking, marketing, accountancy and even law enforcement.

How is she in various relationship roles?

Provided she has had a happy childhood, a Virgo woman can be extremely dependable and responsible as a daughter, she will remain devoted to her parents if she has been properly raised and looked after.

As a wife, she will excel in her duties as she takes her responsibilities very seriously. With a Virgo woman for a wife you will have no complaints about love and devotion. Moreover, she is also an excellent homemaker. Since she likes to be in control she regards her home as her castle and does everything in her power to protect it. Also, being in charge at home she gets to do what she pleases. I have also found many Virgo women enjoying housekeeping duties and other related chores like cleaning, cooking, gardening, etc.

Being dedicated in every sense of the word, Virgo women prove to be genuine friends. They usually wouldn't have a huge circle of friends, but the ones that they do befriend, they'd hold them very close to their heart.

A Virgo woman can be a good mother too. She knows how to befriend her children. While being gentle with them, she also wields an iron hand with them as she is a strict disciplinarian.

How is she when alone?

Since they have a perpetual need to talk, 80 per cent of Virgo women prefer being in people's company. If not actually, then even virtually would do. A Virgo woman does not like to be idle and she can take-up various activities like yoga, spirituality or fitness training to fill in her free time.

How is she when in love?

Hmm...before I answer that one let me tell you what love is for a Virgo woman. There is only one definition of love for her...true, pure and exclusive. She will not tolerate passing affairs or insincere feelings. Once her heart is set on something, she will move with a determined gait to achieve it.

While courting her you will have to keep a lot of things in mind. Firstly, etiquettes...this lady is a classic nit-picker when it comes to mannerisms and social behaviour. She will watch you with a hawk's eye and will be satisfied only if you match up to her rather high standards of decorum. Secondly, underplay. She dislikes loud and brash behaviour, especially if it is about love. Public display of love is a big no-no with her. So keep it simple and subtle and of course, genuine. And throw in plenty of charm and before long you will be humming *The girl is mine* a la MJ!

What does she look for in her partner?

A perfect gentleman, with a strong financial backing, someone who would pledge his unerring love for her till time eternal! This is one lady who would scrutinise each and every aspect of a man's personality, critically examining every minute detail of his mannerisms and also, his financial status before deciding to take the plunge.

Pragmatic to the extent of being cold, the Virgo woman wants a man who can provide her emotional support, while at the same time offer her the financial freedom to splurge on materialistic pursuits. Obsessed with what the world thinks about her, she would desire a partner who is presentable, one who knows how to carry himself and make intelligent conversation.

While dating her, you should...

...be her friend first! Getting a Virgo woman to date you isn't an easy task. She seems hard to get as she lacks emotional expression. But if you are friends with her, it would be easy to break her self-imposed barricade.

A Virgo girl is conservative. She is a straightforward, traditional-minded girl and loves routine. Even if you take her to her favourite restaurant every day, she would be as pleased as punch.

She is a stickler for cleanliness. She likes people and things around her to be neat and tidy. Make sure you are well groomed while dating her. You may not be wearing the clothes that are in vogue, but as long as they are clean and well-ironed, she would be impressed. And here's a tip—don't wear a strong perfume. Virgo girls are sensitive to strong smells.

Be careful with your spending. The Virgo girl will appreciate that. She also loves Nature and nothing can win her heart like a serene Nature walk. But make sure you have a cozy armchair ready for her at the end of it all... she will welcome your gesture. Her satisfaction will be evident from the glow on her cheeks and the spark in her eyes.

The Virgo girl is feminine in every sense. But you won't find her indulging in the usual feminine activities like dressing up and/or applying make-up that often. She prefers keeping herself as well as her life easy and simple.

The Virgo woman is ruled by the sign of the virgin. But don't you be fooled by that! Under all her intensity, lies a frail heart. As you enter the second zone of dating, you should get your timing right before making advances. Get her into the right mood and emotional state and you can easily step into the realm of physical intimacy with her. But if you fail to read her body language and make an untoward move, she will spurn you instantly and recoil into her shell. She is mature enough to know what is coming, so somewhere in her mind she has prepared herself for that...to the extent of expecting a healthy physical relationship before long. While dating her, you would need to impress her totally and win her exclusive loyalty. If you are unable to do so, she is likely to look elsewhere for pleasure.

Compatibility quotient

With the emotionally latent Virgo woman, compatibility can mean much more than mere getting along; it could mean interpreting untold feelings and unseen sentiments. It involves understanding her nature and needs as well. Let's find out more!

Virgo woman and...

Aries man: 4/10. While contrasts may work well on canvas, it is not the case with this combination. The Arien will find the 'preaching' Virgo woman a little hard to deal with, while the dominating trait of the Arien might make her further repress her feelings.

Taurus man: 8/10. The Virgo girl is as feminine as the Taurean wants his partner to be. Both are well suited on an emotional level too. She will feel secure in his company and he would take delight in looking after her womanly needs.

Gemini man: 7/10. If both learn to adjust, this relationship can work beautifully. The Gemini man must take care not to provoke the green demon in the Virgo girl, while she should limit her criticising streak as he won't appreciate it at all.

Cancer man: 9/10. A perfect romantic combination! The Virgo girl has the tact to draw the Cancerian out of his emotional shell. In return, he would give her the security and affection that she needs in a relationship.

Leo man: 6/10. This relationship demands too many compromises on both sides. While the homely Virgo woman would keep her kitchen and home sparkling clean, the Leo man would hardly notice it, let alone appreciate her effort. On the other hand, known for his love for compliments, he won't take criticism from her sportingly.

Virgo man: 5/10. This relationship can go completely right or completely wrong. With both Virgos being overly practical, there are chances of monotony setting in. Moreover, both can get too demanding of each other's attention.

Libra man: 4/10. Not a very promising combination! The Libra man's indecisive nature might make her go crazy, while the Virgo woman's constant fault finding and pessimism can frustrate him to the extreme.

Scorpio man: 8/10. The Scorpio man's emotional quotient can be well balanced with the Virgo woman's pragmatism. He will be enthralled with her femininity, while she will be impressed with his ability to take the lead.

Sagittarius man: 4/10. Both are worlds apart! The Sagittarian is outgoing, adventurous and quite untamed, while the Virgo girl is homely and serious. Each may not be able to answer the other's need for companionship. He would get bored of her predictable way of living, while she would find his adventurous enterprise too much to digest.

Capricorn man: 8/10. With effective communication, this relationship can go places. The Virgo woman would have to rein her critical nature and possessiveness, while he would have to control his flirtatious endeavours. But overall, both are compatible to a great extent.

Aquarius man: 6/10. After the initial attraction, both might find it difficult to manage this relationship. The vivacious Aquarian will be bored of the sedate Virgo girl. To make this relationship work, both will have to learn to count their blessings instead of finding faults with each other.

Pisces man: 6/10. Both have disparate yet not necessarily conflicting traits. This relationship can work if they make efforts to understand each other.

Famous Virgo women personalities:

Asha Bhonsle	Cameron Diaz
Claudia Schiffer	Gloria Estefan
Kareena Kapoor	Salma Hayek

Libra

24 September-22 October

Libra man

A Libra man is a man of the world. He has infinite charm and a friendly demeanour. Once you meet him, you are not likely to forget the casual chat you had with him for a long time. And chat with him you will, for he has an irresistible attraction factor and you will be instantly drawn into his circle of influence.

But no amount of charm can help the Libran in making decisions. The scales of his sun sign will keep tipping every time he is caught in a decision-making situation. It is the urge to get the best in life and do 'a thousand things in one go' that propels him ahead.

Romantic and carefree, a Libran can as easily shrug off responsibility as a cat shakes water off its fur. His ability to connect with people on a social level makes him befriend many but he shares true friendship with a very few but no matter what relationship role he plays, he is fun to be with and extremely entertaining.

How can you identify a Libra man in a crowd?

In a group, gathering or party, it is easy to identify a Libra man. He is usually the one with a warm and friendly expression on his face and is popular with everyone. From an early age he develops a calm and composed expression on his face but one which belies the restless dynamo beneath. You will never be able to spot hurry or restlessness in his behaviour or conversations. He would show deep interest in a conversation but upon seeing other friends may include them in the same. He has a natural way of networking, which very few sun signs possess.

There is no particular face type to describe a Libra man but it is the calmness of face and sharpness of eyes, combined with sincerity in speech and attitude that makes him friendly. Melting smile, hovering eyes constantly darting from one place to another—that's a Libran man for you!

Libran males are extremely adaptable and adventurous by nature. Whatever they do, they do with full intensity, whether it is partying, exercising or practicing spirituality. Usually there is no half-way for them and they see it through, but at the same time they are practical enough to know when to let go.

What are the key features of his personality?

A Libra male is a romantic at heart and discovers romance at an early age. He likes the idea of falling in love and being in love, hence his mind is in a perpetual state of romance. His source of inspiration lies not in romantic novels or movies but in his own nature. Charming and friendly, he connects easily with people. His impressive looks and good humour match his skills, but the strong practical side of him ensures that his romantic ideas are not baseless or in the air.

Another peculiar trait in a Libran is his concept of fair play. Although he is capable of playing practical jokes and doing crazy things that boys do when young, as he matures he understands the difference between fair and unfair. He can become a strong believer in justice and fair play (but somehow when it comes to his own cause, he would try and swing things his way).

A Libra male is not much of a risk-taker and at the most he can only take a calculated risk. He always needs to be sure when it comes to decision-making, until then he will keep weighing the pros and cons of a situation at hand. But once if dead sure of what he is getting into, he can be extremely impulsive and get into the action mode quickly.

Generally, Libra men are good-looking, ranging from possessing a sophisticated clean shaven appearance to rugged looks. Added to that is a certain boyish charm, which makes them appealing. No wonder women are drawn to their enchanting persona! This veritable charm is coupled with an irresistible smile and a slick tongue which makes quarrelling or getting angry with a Libran man a difficult task. If you know a Libra man intimately you would understand what a task it is to be and stay angry with him for long. And the worst part is the rogue knows the exact force of his powers!

Even when it comes to his own self, a Libran tallies really low on anger. The Libran male is not one who loses his cool easily, unless provoked. I guess that is one of the reasons why he is generally liked by his peers.

A Libran male's polished manner and smooth tongue makes him extremely persuasive and diplomatic. I would give a Libra man an eight on ten for his ability to convince others and be suave at the same time. He also has an excellent sense of humour, which can get whacky at times. But behind all this smooth exterior is an iron will. Here is a man of grit and determination for you.

How is he on the following aspects?

Appearance: Being adaptive and adventurous by nature, a Libra man is capable of switching from classic to casual and even funky, just to please his moods. For him it is important to have a wardrobe for all occasions, be it golf, tennis, mountain climbing, river rafting...of course that's besides his regular office and party wear.

He enjoys following fashion and trends but prefers to develop his own style in dressing, which distinguishes him from others.

Ambition: Nothing but the best will do for our man. A Libran male is ambitious and will work resolutely till he accomplishes what he sets his heart on. And to fulfil his dreams he is capable of working fourteen to sixteen hours a day too. But all his efforts must yield results and rewards. He hates it when his efforts go in vain.

All this doesn't mean he is not capable of having fun. If given a choice, he would put in four-five hours of work everyday and spend the rest of his time goofing around. This is chiefly because he wants to do so much in so little time. My Libran friends often laugh with me when I tell them that one lifetime is just not enough for them.

The wish list of a Libra male surpasses all other wish lists on this planet. His wish list comprises of things to do, places to travel, stuff to buy and what not. Obviously there is no credible way of including all this in one life span. But the catch here is...most of them manage to do it too!

I have noticed a peculiar quality in Libra men—they like to calculate their desires in terms of money. For instance, a Libran will think to himself how much money would be required to fulfil his and his family's survival needs and desires. And then that X amount of money will become his target. This calculation lets him decide on other things in life.

Librans are focused and ambitious yet at the same time they can be quite content with what they have. If it is not a great inconvenience, status quo doesn't bother them much.

Ego/Self-respect: I would say Libra men are more self-respecting than egotistic. For example, if a credit at a restaurant was not accepted or rejected at the time of payment his self respect would take a beating and not his ego. In case of an Aries or Leo man in the same situation it would become a matter of ego. Their ego only shows when they are unable to win situations or battles (that's when the switch from respect to ego takes place).

Responsibility: Let me begin with the statement—Libra men are better at managing and delegating responsibilities than executing them. And now for the explanation.

A Libra man is quite responsible and would take-up his roles rather seriously. But since he likes to remain carefree, he finds it difficult to complete his responsibilities end to end. He would prefer someone else doing the actual duty on his behalf. However, this doesn't mean he is irresponsible; it merely means that if there is no one to execute a job, only then will he move himself to fill in. Unless he approaches such a roadblock, he would like to merely manage and delegate work to others.

Etiquettes: Libran men are extremely casual regarding etiquettes. They can adapt themselves to any situation at hand, but are way too practical to follow what they call the 'dramas' of etiquettes.

What is his approach towards life?

A Libra male is realistic and practical in his approach to life. But he is also highly emotional and sentimental, which sometimes clouds his ability to think clearly. There is something of a dreamer in him but he is also idealistic about life. Like I said before, he wants to do everything, be everywhere, learn everything...and more. I have nicknamed a few of my Libran (and Sagittarian male friends who show the same traits) as walking-talking encyclopedias because of this quality of theirs. Libra males are capable of being both followers and leaders.

How does he score on the following points?

Cynicism: Of the Librans that have crossed my path, I haven't met any who exhibited overt signs of cynicism. In fact, their positive approach towards life and innate ability to see both sides of the coin makes them excellent arbitrators. The only (and might I add rare) circumstance where this man might take a stubborn stance and exhibit a mild amount of cynicism, is when he has vested interests in the argument at hand.

Suspicion/Jealousy: For some reason most of them are suspicious about everything. In spite of being carefree and easy-going, they have this need to be or show that they are in control. They are doubtful and want to question reasons and motives of everybody around them.

Librans are not jealous by nature, neither in relationships nor in professional life. They are definitely possessive and protective but not necessarily jealous. Let's say they get as low as a four on ten for jealousy.

Dishonesty/Infidelity: Most Libran men ensure that they have all possible fun in the early days of adulthood so that when they settle down, they are actually ready to commit sincerely.

Although most women would say Librans are big flirts, I am not very sure about that statement. Librans are a case of being 'more sinned against than sinning'. It's just that because they are generally likeable and usually different from other men, women start developing an interest in them. Can you blame a Libran man if women fall like nine pins to his charm? Later when he turns around and tells them 'we are just good friends' (with the same disarming smile that got these women in the first place) they complain of heartbreak and brand him as a flirt.

Hardships: When it comes to hardships, a Libra male's initial reaction is of discomfort. It takes him a while to accept his situation and settle with it. But once he totally accepts that, he will actually get down to the business of overcoming the hardships and that too with hard work and sincerity.

Success and failure: Libra men are quite hushed about their success. They would share the joys of their success with immediate family only.

For some reason they are also quite secretive and superstitious about publicly displaying their success stories or pipeline plans.

They may seldom declare it, but Libra men are extremely competitive, however, they are not poor losers. Not one to lose heart at the sight of a setback, a Libran will accept failure as a challenge to improvise and make a spirited rebound.

Host: Going back to what I had said about responsibility and a Libran man, he is on a similar track when it comes to playing host. Since he likes to delegate work, you will find him giving instructions and ordering people around (sometimes even yelling!) rather than doing anything himself. He is quite satisfied with other people's work and with himself in the role of a manager.

Although he likes to have the best of stuff on his table, it need not necessarily come from his kitchen. He is absolutely at ease with 'ordering in'. He is not an overbearing host either, but he likes his guests to be at ease and enjoy the party.

Guest: Good food, good company and with entertainment thrown in for good measure—that's all that you'll need to please your Libran guest. He would appreciate your culinary skills by eating well and enthrall other people on your guest list by talking well, but I must add here that your house décor, crockery and other nuances might be wasted on him. Not that he won't enjoy any of it; but to him all your extra effort would just be part of the big picture. Least expecting as a guest, a Libra male just needs the right cuisine to tease his palate and the right conversation to stimulate his intellect.

How does a Libra man handle difficult situations?

A Libran male in a quarrel…quite bad! As bad as his female counterpart! He would become extremely stubborn and would always expect the other person to apologise. I think this is one trait that any woman dating a Libran should be aware of. He is capable of tolerating his woman's tantrums and her feminist views, but during quarrels he is tenacious in his stand and will not bow down no matter what. Apparently this is the only cynical quality in a Libran man, other than that he is a fun guy to be with.

What is his characteristic weakness?

The Libra male's 'eager to please everyone' nature prevents him from saying 'no' to those around him. He thus finds himself incapable of refusing to help out someone who asks for his aid. This makes him commit to much more than he could possibly deliver, making him as well as those around him a tad frustrated.

The most prominent of his shortcoming is inconsistency in nature. His behaviour is often based on mood swings rather than strength of character. He is also unreliable at times. I have often noticed most Libran males shirking responsibilities.

Though known for his adventurous nature and vitality, the Libran male is often seen to be lazy. You'll often find him lounging around, cribbing about a hard day at work. Yet, give him time to recharge, and he'll be soon offering to take you out for an outing even past midnight.

Is there more to his persona?

Libra is represented by the sign of the scales and you will notice the balancing act becomes an important factor of a Libra male's personality. He spends a good deal of time (a great deal actually!) in thinking, working out details and deciding about every minutest aspect of life. He finds it difficult to make-up his mind but the only person he would consult in times of confusion is himself. You will rarely find him being impulsive about anything and even if he is…it's a calculated impulse. Ironic, isn't it?

The funny part is his mental act of weighing the pros and cons of people and situations. This is quite evident in his unvarying eye movements that offers him the opportunity to scan the entire perimeter constantly.

He prefers having a balance in things around him—relationships, work, career, household et al and any imbalance can throw him out of sync. As I had pointed out earlier, he is also great at negotiating and his diplomatic nature is best seen in the role of an arbitrator.

His inclination towards fair play (however biased that might get at times) makes him take active interest in social issues. You will find Libran males getting involved in charitable acts and championing the cause of the underdog.

Having an attractive personality, a Libra guy likes his surroundings to be aesthetically engaging too. Even if he has limited resources, he will see to it that his home and office are pleasant places to be in. In short, he cannot abide by ugliness and muddle.

For a Libra man emotions are of two kinds; one—his emotions and two—other people's emotions. Obviously his priority lies in his emotions, but strangely he is not very good at tackling his own emotions. In moving situations, he can lose command of his emotions. Once the scales start tipping, it is not easy to get them into balance again.

However, let me clarify that a Libra man is not over-sensitive and he is definitely not touchy. He can take practical jokes from friends in good spirit. And he is sentimental more in terms of treasuring his relationships rather than preserving gifts and greeting cards.

And now about other people's emotions...this is something which touches him only superficially. I am not implying that he is not compassionate or lacks understanding, it's just that he is so absorbed in his own emotional processes that he fails to realise the depth of others' emotions. For instance, he would be kind and supportive towards you if you are depressed, would even go to the extent of entertaining you to change your dark or down mood. But he will not be bothered about the reasons behind your emotions. To put it precisely, a Libra man will look for immediate relief rather than the root cause of any emotional disturbance in his near and dear ones.

However the brightest aspect of a Libra man is that he doesn't hold grudges...and if he does, they are not for long. He believes in the maxim of forgive and forget, even in matters of the heart.

How should one deal effectively with a Libra man?

The easiest way to deal with him is to be honest and straightforward. If you have too much to say that can get you in trouble, so make sure you play your cards a little tactfully. As much as he is patient, there are certain things that he might not be able to take that well. Moreover, he is a very demanding person—be it for your time, attention or physical presence. So be prepared to be a good listener and also be attentive in the company of a Libran male.

How does he handle money matters?

In the stingiest of ways! A Libra man and his money are not easily parted. Although he likes to spend on himself and can be impulsive while buying stuff for his personal use but, when it comes to spending extra bucks, he is quite selective. He likes to be in control of his money, be it ready cash, credit cards or his bank account. A Libran man will never let anyone else manage his finances for him.

He is firmly into savings too but in spite of his penchant for saving and being miserly at times, when a Libra man sets his heart on something, he goes all out to make it his. His aim could be anything from some expensive thing he wants to helping out someone in need.

How is he on the professional front?

The Libra male's 'lazy boy' image displays itself in full regalia on the work front. As I stated earlier, he is prone to delegating work rather than getting down to doing it himself. This by no way means that he isn't a good worker. In fact, Librans make excellent workers. They are rather innovative and are often seen suggesting inventive methods of carrying out mundane tasks and if deadlines demand it, they can turn into workaholics too.

Going back to their being notable mediators (and their gift of the gab)...they can do really well as salesmen, lawyers, bankers, event managers and welfare workers or in any other profession involving advocacy.

How is he in various relationship roles?

As a son, a Libra boy is extremely affectionate. He will always remain by the side of his parents and be around for them. With siblings, he believes in co-existing in harmony and is also adjusting, unless pushed over the edge.

Now about a Libra man as a boyfriend...even in a committed relationship he would come across as a friend—someone to hang around with. Unless he is very sure of going ahead, conversations with him will never be intense or about commitment or love especially in the early stages of a relationship. You will find it difficult to make a Libra male commit to a long-term relationship as he is engrossed in fulfilling his desire list (which won't even be 25 per cent complete till he reaches adulthood). Obviously he wants no roadblocks in the same.

Like I had mentioned earlier since he is popular amongst friends, he is usually wanted and dragged to many places and events. He may be able to handle a woman being possessive out of love but he will definitely run away from her if she is controlling and obsessive. Amongst all zodiac signs a Libra man demands maximum space in a relationship and this is applicable even if he is married and has children.

But this man knows how to respect a woman and understands the need to give her space too and all this while with the romantic fires burning brightly! A Libra man also knows how to make-up for lost time with his beloved...with impromptu drinks, dinner and movies.

As a father, he would teach his children discipline and the art of thinking independently. Doting on them, he would expect love and respect in return.

How is he when alone?

A Libra man is quite content when alone. He likes his 'me time' and will usually devote it to personal activities like playing video games, messaging his friends, or on devices such as his cell phone and computer. I have noticed that his activities are kind of mechanical; things that allow his mind to unwind and do what it is best at...thinking.

'Me time' for a Libran also means rest. You will find him sprawled across the sofa and watching TV or listening to his favourite tracks endlessly. Give him a task to do and he will procrastinate for hours, but it's best not to disturb him as after the long ideating sessions, his rest is truly well-deserved.

This rest is also the calm before the storm. While resting, the Libra man is only gathering his resources for another outburst of ideas and activities.

How is he when in love?

If a Libra man is a micro-chip, then the only language he understands is love.

Love brings the best out in a Libra man, but the first step towards love has to be friendship. His natural flair to connect with people enables him to forge genuine friendship bonds (with men and women alike). With women, friendships can lead to love, but not necessarily marriage. Given his knack for weighing the plus and minus of everything, he will not commit to anyone easily.

But once you have his love, it is for keeps. Not one to back out on his commitment, he will put in every bit of effort to make a relationship work. And it is up to you to keep the romance alive in your relationship... for this guy is a real sucker for it!

Romance or no romance, a Libra man finds it difficult to let go. Even if the relationship is heading for the rocks he will hold on. 'Splitsville' is one place he dreads! One reason that I can think of, for this is his need to be with someone...he just can't be alone.

When in a relationship with a Libran guy, you will have to deal with another thing—the admiring glances that he gets from other women. As I have explained earlier, your Libran may not be flirtatious intentionally, but he can't help being nice to people, especially ladies.

What does he look for in his partner?

A Libran's first step in building a relationship is friendship and he would first test the waters and only then take the plunge. If you can be his best friend, he'll know you can fit into his life plan.

One important criterion that women who want to reach to his heart should have, is their ability to be a perfect homemaker. Our man likes the idea of coming home to a smiling wife, a neat and tidy setup and a well-stocked refrigerator. If you can give him all that, you have all the ingredients for a happy marital bake!

Even though he isn't too picky and choosy about looks, most Libran males end up settling for partners who are attractive, with a little bit of spunk.

The men of this zodiac know how to make their women feel special and your Libran man would want someone who reciprocates at least once in a while in a similar fashion or acknowledges his efforts with genuine appreciation.

While dating him, you should...

...learn to balance. A Libran seeks balance in everything around him. Show him a painting and he would instantly tell you which colour should be added to have an even distribution; throwing the painter's muse out of the window. Likewise, when it comes to dating, he would appreciate it if you take pains at balancing things with him—his work, your work, his schedule, your schedule, and your dates together.

The typical Libran is incredibly romantic. He will shower you with affection and love and you will be the recipient of his undivided attention and friendliness, but when I say love it is not to be mistaken for long lasting love. Not that this man is incapable of that, far from it, but love while dating is different for him...it is tinged with friendship, a sort of mutual attachment and flirtation.

The Libra guy loves to flirt with his date and will appreciate it if you do the same. Keep everything lighthearted and be uber cool, but don't go brash or show him unseemly behaviour. He would want his date to behave in the most ladylike fashion and do everything with finesse. Although he likes to be the one in charge of the relationship, he secretly yearns for his girl to take the lead. So go on and make the first move, but do so in style and your Libra date will love you forever for it.

He has a strong aesthetic sense. Therefore, dressing up well, having the right touches of make-up and general grooming means a lot to him (he would himself spend as much effort on these aspects to impress you). Your endeavours to make an impact on him won't go unnoticed or unappreciated. He likes to be in the company of good-looking people amidst genial surroundings. You can trust him to take you to the best fine dine restaurant and if you are the one selecting the venue, make sure it is something as elegant and chic.

Apart from your appearance, the way you conduct yourself and express your thoughts will be minutely observed by your Libran date. The Libran guy needs to see 'good breeding' in every aspect of your personality. He enjoys stimulating and witty conversations. Mere good looks won't take you a long way with him—you need to have a good amount of intelligence too. You would need to maintain a fine balance in all these aspects to get the best out of your date with him.

He has charm by the loads. He can fill you with mirth, make you sentimental with his voice, make you blush with his compliments and arouse your sensuality with his melting smile in the span of few minutes. His charm however is not limited to his date, as other people (especially females) will be pulled by it too: accept that.

And lastly, once he has committed himself, the Libra man will be patience personified. A thorough gentleman, he will wait till you share a certain comfort level with him before attempting physical intimacy. He won't ever force you into accepting his sensual advances nor will he allow you to do the same. Don't rush into things, simply go with the flow and enjoy your Libran date's wonderful company.

Compatibility quotient:

Being compatible with the charming Libran is a fine balancing act. Getting along with him on friendly terms is easy but eking out a long-term relationship with him is a totally different ball game. If you succeed in understanding the pros and cons of his personality, it would be fairly easy to gel with him. And there is always his irresistible charm to egg you on.

Libra man and...

Aries woman: 7/10. These two can hit off pretty well. Once the Arien learns to deal patiently with the Libran indecisiveness, this relationship will be full of passion and of course romance.

Taurus woman: 7/10. With the right amount of hard work and understanding, this combination can work in the long run. The Libran will have to be more conscious of the Taurean's need for security, while she will have to be less emotionally needy.

Gemini woman: 9.5/10. Ah! Looks like we got a perfect balance for our Libran man! The Libran wit and the Gemini liveliness make a wonderful match. They suit each other perfectly and their passionate nature and love for socialising only adds to their compatibility.

Cancer woman: 6/10. This relationship can work only if both stress on understanding each other. The Cancerian's high emotional needs might go unfulfilled if the Libran takes off on his intellectual trips. Hence both need to meet each other on common ground.

Leo woman: 8/10. Since both are expressive and outspoken this relationship will work wonderfully in the long run. There will be enough romance and excitement to keep the passion alive for long.

Virgo woman: 4/10. Opposite forces are at work here. The Virgo woman's pessimism might frustrate the Libran while his indecisiveness will make her run out of patience.

Libra woman: 7/10. Love for finer things in life will form the grounds for initial attraction between them. Being romantics and intellectuals, there would be enough camaraderie and conversation between the two, but their understanding should go beyond their innate charm to make this relationship a successful one.

Scorpio woman: 6/10. Compatibility will come only with compromise. The Scorpio woman will have to curb her possessiveness and understand the Libran's need for freedom.

Sagittarius woman: 8/10. Her spontaneity and extrovert nature will surely attract a typical Libran. Whatever differences they have can be cleared with communication and understanding. This relationship will also have lot of chemistry, thanks to Libran romance and Sagittarian passion.

Capricorn woman: 6/10. This one can go either way. His flirtatious nature and the constant feminine attention that he gets won't go down well with her. She will also find it hard to comprehend his disorganised nature. Both will have to make adjustments in order to build a successful relationship.

Aquarius woman: 9/10. A real bonanza for both! He will appreciate her spontaneity while she will be impressed with his intellectual bent of mind. It is likely to be a comfortable and fulfilling relationship for both.

Pisces woman: 6/10. Both will need to look beyond themselves to succeed in this relationship. Once the initial attraction wears out, they would need to have something more to hold them together. The Libran has to come to terms with the Piscean sensitivity while the Piscean has to realise and accept the fact that he has a life beyond home.

Famous Libra men personalities:

Amitabh Bachchan	Akon
Bruce Springsteen	Jean-Claude Van Damme

Libra woman

Have you ever come across girls who look you in the eye every time you talk and constantly interrupt your flow of words or thoughts with their 'come to the point' interjections? Well, those are the ones governed by the sign of scales—Libra. Libran girls are brisk, business-like and precise. They dislike dilly-dallying and are rarely found to mince words, but they are not brash. In fact Libran ladies are graceful and well poised to the point of perfection...as crisp as newly minted bank notes.

As much as she is intense, the Libra woman is also emotional and sensitive. If you are friends with a typical Libran, you would know what a fantastic sense of humour she's got. And it is a sight to watch her do the balancing act with her constantly tipping scales. All in all, she's a wonderful person to be with.

How can you identify a Libra woman in a crowd?

To identify her in a crowd you would need to watch her behaviour very closely. If you are a stranger to her you will notice that her interaction with you will be limited to an exchange of pleasantries, but sitting in the same gallery, she would be totally in the spirit of having fun.

What is interesting to observe in a Libran woman is the way her facial expressions change, from intense to absolute fun and back to intense, within a few minutes, depending on her mood. A typical Libran woman is a mix of emotions, feelings and thoughts—all visible on her face, if you can read it well.

Another giveaway of her identity is the prankster in her. You may not detect the mischief monger in her (this lady sure can keep a poker face!) but she is quite prone to playing pranks. If you are the butt of a practical joke among your friends, chances are that the mind behind it is of your Libran female buddy. With her great sense of humour she is excellent company. But a Libra girl is also self-obsessed to some extent, which is why she is misunderstood by people around her.

She has a unique ability of appreciating and wanting the good things in life. She is extremely intellectual and finds herself attracted to scholarly and philosophical conversations. When it comes to making new friends and alliances, she is quite selective (a trait she shares with her male counterpart). But when with her friends she can be spontaneous and fun-loving and with her loved ones (especially her boyfriend or husband) she can be involved to the extent that the world outside would cease to exist for her. A horse with blinkers, I say!

What are the key features of her personality?

Libran women deal with people in a peculiar way. For starters they don't want to emotionally hurt people because of which they find it difficult to say 'no' to anyone (just like the typical Libran male). Having given their word, they find it difficult to back out or fulfil their commitments, and then to get out of this tricky situation, they start re-negotiating. Because of this habit though they may not hurt anybody, they fail to make them happy.

A Libran girl is very charming (I would give her an eight on ten for that). Like her male counterpart she has a smooth tongue and therefore is very convincing and persuasive.

Being conservative in thought and action is another of her features, not that she lacks confidence but she prefers toeing the traditional line rather than doing something out of the box. She prefers stunning people with her success and not with her untoward actions.

She also gets angry easily. She is the kind who is ready to flip her lid at a moment's notice, but then again being a thinker and a rational one at that, she is quite capable of reasoning and managing her anger.

When in love a Libran is a true woman but under crisis she is as strong as a man. This statement best describes her femininity and will-power. She has an unbreakable spirit; be it financial problems or emotional issues, she is indefatigable in her endeavour to overcome it. The feminine side that love can bring out in her, is all about emotions, care and devotion, and that is what her partner will usually see. He will get to see her dominant spirit only in a crisis situation.

Another characteristic of a Libra woman which I would like to mention here is her unpredictable nature. With her it is difficult to predict what is in store for the onlooker.

As a homemaker, a Libran female is par excellence. With her exceptional taste and ability to manage things, you will find her keeping a sparkling clean and neatly arranged home. And then there is this grandma-like quality about her. At times she can go a bit far with her rationality, so much so that it can be overwhelming and make her come across as too 'preachy' (of course this trait also helps her in striking a balance with her partner).

Libran women are keen on justice (again much like their male counterpart). But with fair play they can take the deviant road and use their charm and femininity to get things done...very tactfully of course! But whatever said and done, this woman is not conniving or manipulative. Usually if she finds the situation or people around her uncomfortable, she will quietly move out of it without creating too much of a fuss.

How is she on the following aspects?

Appearance: Libra women are extremely fashionable. They are also very adaptive of trends—from shorts and tees at home to evening gowns at cocktail events, a Libra girl can carry it all off with panache. She is also quite detailed about all aspects of grooming, right down to her manicured fingers, trimmed and polished nails, well set hair, etc.

Ambition: Amongst all women, Librans are the most ambitious. A Libran woman wants to grow and climb to top positions and titles. She has the innate talent of knowing how to get things done and perceiving where she needs to be, at any given point in time and she will meticulously plan things out when it comes to getting what she wants.

Ego/Self-respect: This makes for a curious case for Libra women. I have observed that they possess a great amount of self-respect and a greater amount of ego. Many times in life their ego is what gets them in trouble, sometimes even to a point of no return. And then again it is their ego that stops them from mending matters.

Responsibility: Unlike the male Libran, a Libra female is able to take-up responsibilities and fulfil them too. At times she might find responsibilities a burden but mostly she can conduct her duties with ease and grace. She is dependable too.

But a Libran woman is not always 'duty-bound' as they say. Given her desire to have the very best of everything (including materialistic pleasures) she tends to be selfish at times, thereby sidelining her responsibilities.

Etiquettes: I would give a Libra girl a nine on ten for etiquettes…and similar points for her expectation of high standards in etiquettes from others. She is refined and sophisticated in every sense and expects the same from others. She believes in the ideal behaviour of ladies and gentlemen, be it a social tête-à-tête or a business brunch.

What is her approach towards life?

She has the vision of a dreamer and the idealism of a philosopher. Sure of her abilities and confident of her talent, a Libra woman prefers to be a leader in every sphere of life.

Not very realistic, a Libra female however is quite practical towards life. Like I mentioned earlier she is also very emotional, but the sentimental side of her nature is well under control (however, that doesn't stop her from being hypersensitive and this lady can get quite touchy about issues close to her heart).

How does she score on the following points?

Cynicism: Libran girls are sweet natured and as they mature this trait gets further transformed into genuine friendliness. Their even-tempered nature hardly leaves room for cynicism. But yes, once in love their outlook changes and they can get skeptical in their quest to achieve their love.

Suspicion/Jealousy: In a relationship, a Libra woman is able to give a lot of space to her partner and also expects the same from him. Even though she's a complete romantic at heart she finds it difficult to have someone around her 24x7. She'll get suspicious only if given substantial reason for it. But if she has a doubt she is quite capable of cross checking (it is in her nature to follow through whatever she feels). She can go to great extents to discover the truth, including following her man and prying his personal papers (a trait common to Pisces and Sagittarius women too). But she'll do these things only to satisfy her doubts and not otherwise.

Usually known to be level headed, if pushed a Libran woman can get jealous too. For example, if a promotion due to her at work is given to another or after taking pains getting decked up for a party, her boyfriend compliments another woman, our Libran woman will be none too pleased as she fights the pangs of jealousy.

Dishonesty/Infidelity: Neither will she tolerate nor does she have these vices in her nature. A relationship for Libran woman is for keeps. She can be extremely devoted in a relationship and expect the same in return. When it comes to infidelity, it's a big no-no for her... and I mean both ways. She will not even encourage flirting and will cling to her ideals of love, no matter what. Naturally, she expects her partner to follow suit.

A Libra woman will be dishonest only when pushed to the extreme. Since she has ample confidence to own up to her acts, you will rarely find her being untruthful about anything, (so much so that getting her to tell a white lie can be quite a task!).

Hardships: When you probe deep into how a Libra woman thinks, you can actually hear her say 'hardships are meant for others', but when faced with hardship she's quite capable of handling the same. Being an achiever and a go-getter (which she most often is), she'll plan for days how to overcome those obstacles.

Success and failure: Success is what she yearns for...you can almost say she lives like her life depends on it. What she enjoys the most is the adulation that accompanies success.

A Libra woman is somewhere in-between being a good loser and a poor loser. When faced with failure she is prone to cribbing and snivelling about it, even trying to pass the buck at times. If nothing works, she will offer excuses to appease herself and others, but she also has the common sense to pull herself out of them.

Host: As hosts, Libra women are extremely detailed and meticulous (she gets a nine out of ten from me for playing the perfect host). The best part about her, as a host, is her sporting spirit. She'll take any critical remark from her guests as a part of a learning process.

Guest: Highly opinionated, a Libra girl as a guest is hard to please. Depending on her mood, her reactions will range from critical to hypercritical. She can be both picky and relaxed or fussy and adjusting. Her behaviour as a guest depends a lot on her social status too.

How does she handle difficult situations?

I have observed a range of Libran women in difficult situations and based on my observations I have three points to make. First; I have concluded that a Libra woman in a complex circumstance tends to blow things out of proportions, thinks way too much and puts her foot where her mouth is!

And then comes her ego, because of which she cannot apologise and end quarrels. She will hold a grudge (not in her heart but in her head which makes it all the more unforgettable) and sulk for days. And thirdly but thankfully she is not vengeful, neither is she wicked enough to do mean things even when deeply hurt or wounded.

What is her characteristic weakness?

Although she comes across as a strong personality, a Libra woman is extremely emotional, especially around her loved ones—her boyfriend, husband, children or immediate family. She is extremely devoted to people she loves and finds it difficult to manage her emotions when with them. Every emotion that she feels like pain, disappointment and sorrow are taken to intense levels, which not everyone is able to comprehend.

She can also worry herself silly over the social behaviour of her husband and children. Given the high standards she has for etiquettes, she cannot abide by any deviations in decorum. This might be irksome if her partner has a casual attitude.

Is there more to her persona?

Well, I guess there is! Her nature has an uncanny resemblance to the symbol of her zodiac sign—the scales. A Libra woman enjoys all good things in life but she also knows that these things come with a tag (a rather expensive one at that) and so she has to do a fine balancing act between fulfilling her desires and saving for a rainy day.

Another reason why her scales tip to and fro is her need to conform to the likes and dislikes of her loved ones while having her way. She also has a leaning towards fair play and you will find her playing arbiter or mediator amongst friends and family.

A Libra woman is a true lady in every sense. She likes everything around her to be appealing, people around her to be graceful and the man of her life to be gentlemanly. She intensely dislikes violence so make sure all your Arnold Schwarzenegger, Jean-Claude Van Damme and Jackie Chan DVDs are stowed away when she comes visiting.

She is also quite opinionated but is open to other people's views too. Like her male counterpart, she likes to weigh the pros and cons of every situation before forming an opinion. Although this habit is a healthy one when it comes to business or life in general, she takes it rather too seriously in matters of heart. You will have to spend much quality time with her before getting the classic 'yes' from her.

This woman also has a lot of tact, which is evident from the way she orates and behaves. Add to that her intelligence and she gets along well with most people. Her natural friendliness, with good measures of humour thrown in, makes her all the more charming.

Most Libra women I have met have a touch of spirituality and that is why they have high ideals regarding long-term relationships. They look for a certain depth of character in their life partners and an understanding that is suffused with sincere love.

A Libra girl is also quite materialistic and therefore making money is quite important to her. She is not the one who will be satisfied with mediocre living; she yearns for a quality life. And with her go-getter spirit she often succeeds in achieving what she wants. She is also resilient and will keep going, irrespective of setbacks.

How should one deal effectively with her?

When dealing with a Libra woman as a friend you should know that she likes to be known as a leader, and respected as the lady with brains, with plans and ideas. She would give in only to someone whom she considers more intelligent or shrewd than her.

She likes to dominate so she likes to be with easy-going, submissive people. But if provoked, a Libra woman can turn fiery and aggressive. So you can't classify them into aggressive and passive. They are the kinds who are aggressive at work and passive after office hours.

The best way to deal with a Libra female is to be straightforward and honest. Flattery works on her, but she is smart enough to know if it's appreciation or plain sucking up.

When it comes to work, you need to have a balance between giving her independence to do her own thing and guiding her to the right path. If pushed she can launch off on an emotional spree and get negative ideas (and that certainly won't work in your favour).

How does she handle money matters?

Usually very careful with her money, a Libra woman likes saving her funds. In the early stages of a relationship you will find her buying gifts for her boyfriend or any person she gets along well with, as she likes spending on her loved ones. But other than that she is quite calculative when it comes to dishing out the moolah!

On the other hand, she can sometimes be very impulsive about spending. You may catch her returning with full bags and an empty purse after a shopping spree and you are also likely to catch her repenting the latter. She is the kind who will spend when she gets in the mood and tighten her belt later.

How is she on the professional front?

With their innate ability to gel easily with people, Libran females make charming co-workers. They are extremely supportive team mates who believe in giving credit where due. However, being ambitious, with a million dreams in her kitty, the Libran woman would be none too pleased to see others around her being given too much attention, especially if she feels she's better than the lot.

Akin to her male counterpart, she is attracted to professions related to law, teaching, advocacy, banking, public relations, news anchor and even artistic ventures. Here too, she'll prefer working as part of a team rather than going solo.

With her penchant for keeping everything 'proper', her working area would be free of clutter, probably done-up with plants, decoration pieces or some other artefacts.

How is she in various relationship roles?

A Libran girl is quite focused and determined and therefore prefers least interference but with the right amount of guidance from her parents. As a daughter she could be a devoted, caring and compassionate child to both her parents. She would expect her mother to be her friend and her father to be a source of strength. But, she can turn stubborn and rebellious in order to achieve her needs and wants.

Once you have cleared her check-list or minimum criteria and gained her confidence, she can be extremely dependable as a friend.

In a long-term love relationship, she is devoted and sincere and expects the same in return. She is rarely found around men who are powerful. When she looks for power it's not in the physical sense, but more in an achiever and provider sense. I guess what she actually wants is long-term security.

As a mother, she is to her children what she wants her mother to be for her...a friend and a guide.

How is she when alone?

As much as she likes company, a Libra woman can be very much at ease with herself. Maybe this comes from her need for space. When she does have space or time, she can be quite comfortable browsing through a book or watching a movie. This proves she is restless only about ambition, work and career. Otherwise she is quite content with herself, which I guess is natural.

How is she when in love?

Love can completely floor her. A Libra woman is very romantic and gets totally involved with her man. When in love she can be extremely submissive and adjusting.

Her kind of love is also full on understanding. A Libra girl is extremely understanding of the feelings and situations of her husband, children, family and friends. She is ever ready to help those she loves. But with people with whom she doesn't share such a bond, her understanding can be had only with a good amount of reasoning.

Although a Libra woman has a balanced outlook towards life she finds it difficult to implement this in her relationships. Once she has found her true love, her family is likely to become second priority for her. She will be totally devoted to her husband and her love is long-term in every sense.

What does she look for in her partner?

It isn't easy to win the heart of a Libra girl as she has high ideals for the man in her life. She seeks refinement, grace and intelligence (a major dose of all these qualities actually!) as well as understanding, sincerity and a balanced outlook towards life in the man of her dreams. She wants her man to be strong enough to give her the security she needs and tolerant enough to give her the freedom she wants. And above all she wants her man to respect her for what she is.

While dating her, you should...

...be on time! Yes, and that's just for starters. The Libra woman is a stickler for etiquettes, so make sure that you memorise the social code of conduct before meeting her.

Let me simplify things here and take you one step at a time. *Step one*: Be careful while selecting the venue. Remember the Libra girl appreciates beauty and has a strong aesthetic sense, therefore make sure the restaurant that you choose has an appealing ambience.

Step two: She is ultra feminine. You can carry a bunch of flowers with you on your date and sending her a touching text message just before you arrive would be perfect to get things started.

Step three: Close shave, gelled hair, good clothes (immaculate is the word here) and fabulous cologne can help you go a long way with the Libra girl.

Step four: Be prepared for some stimulating conversation. Nothing will floor a Libran more than an intellectual companion. Once she is convinced you are not just adept at conversation but are also intelligent and well-informed, asking her out the second time won't be a problem at all.

Step five: Show her you care. If you are meeting her on a windy day, carry a warm shawl for her. She will try and assess how loving or caring you are with all your gestures. And being a romantic at heart none of your sincere efforts will ever be wasted on her.

A Libra woman is subtle. If she likes you, she will drop delicate hints to let you know this. If you are sharp enough to understand her body language, you stand a chance to win. Don't ever expect her to ask you out. She is too womanly for that!

Compatibility quotient:

The Libra woman is governed by the sign of scales. She will swing to and fro with indecision and doubt. Confident and intelligent in her own right, she is nevertheless quite laid-back. Known to be extremely feminine and charming, how much can she connect with the men on the zodiac? Let's find out.

Libra woman and…

Aries man: 7/10. With the right amount of adjustments at both ends, this can be a good relationship. The Arien might have to curb his aggressive nature, while the Libran woman should learn to take fast decisions. Both are emotionally charged beings possessing the ability to interact with people and that will work in their favour.

Taurus man: 6/10. Although there are similar qualities, a long-term relationship is a difficult bargain for both. He is too possessive for the freedom-loving Libran and she is too outgoing for the homely Taurean.

Gemini man: 8/10. Wonderful chemistry! Both are outgoing and adventurous as well as adept at sharing a good conversation. The Gemini man will be able to meet the balancing needs of the Libra woman perfectly.

Cancer man: 6/10. A deeper understanding of each other's traits can help this relationship. Since a Cancer man is not good at voicing his feelings, the Libra woman might feel frustrated. Problems can also arise over money matters, since the Cancer guy loves to save every penny, whereas the Libra girl loves to splurge occasionally.

Leo man: 9.5/10. A match made in heaven! Both share qualities that they take pride in. Outgoing, affectionate and fun-loving, a relationship between the Leo man and Libra woman is likely to rock.

Virgo man: 5/10. This combination can work, but with a lot of effort. These two are poles apart as far as their attitude in life is concerned. They would need to come to terms with the disparities in their nature to make this relationship successful.

Libra man: 7/10. This one can swing either way. Since both have similar traits, if they don't keep their negatives in check, their relationship cannot stand the test of time. However, both will infuse each other with innate charm and their love for finer things in life can make their relationship last long.

Scorpio man: 6/10. In a Libra woman-Scorpio man combination, the path is strewn with potholes. Although she may find his passion attractive to begin with, she won't be able to take his headstrong way easily. Likewise, he will find it difficult to give her as much freedom as she craves for.

Sagittarius man: 8/10. Once they get the relationship started, it would be a ball. But the catch here is to get it started. Both are hesitant to commit and would need lot of convincing to agree for a long-term relationship. They have plenty of creativity and good humour to make their relationship an affair to remember.

Capricorn man: 4/10. This might be a case of attraction at first and repulsion later. She will like his 'feet on the ground' nature at first, but later get tired of it, while her gregariousness will fire his imagination initially, only to be burnt out later. This relationship can only work with continuous doses of understanding and unlimited compromises.

Aquarius man: 9.5/10. The relationship between these two will be based on mutual satisfaction. Since both would value each other's freedom, there would be enough space for the relationship to mature beautifully. Both will enjoy each other's adventurous streak, intelligent conversation and good humour.

Pisces man: 6/10. Again a relationship that can swing either way. If she learns to handle his idealistic and emotional nature and he learns to manage her intellectual mind and independent attitude, this relationship can be pulled off.

Famous Libra women personalities:

Catherine Zeta-Jones	Gwyneth Paltrow
Hema Malini	Kate Winslet
Margaret Thatcher	Rekha

Scorpio

23 October-22 November

Scorpio man

Boundless energy is the term that comes to my mind when I think of Scorpio men. They are so full of life and vitality that it's no wonder they manage to do umpteen tasks in a day. But the catch is that with the Scorpio men, their passion borders dangerously on obsession.

Extremely fond of good clothes and good food, you might find them indulging in either of these quite often. But being extremely attached to their money, they can balance their indulgences well. Infact so deep is their love for the moolah, that they are frequently seen taking measures to double it!

While this man is fun to be with, he can become possessive of his relationships, especially with his girlfriends. Life with him will undoubtedly be a passionate affair but like every passion, it has its fallouts. Living life in excess, being with a Scorpio man is a Catch-22 situation...if he loves you God help you, if he hates you God help you double quick!

The Scorpio guy can go around like a whirlwind, carrying everyone along in his frenzy and fantasy. If you are with a Scorpio man, gear up for one helluva ride!

How can you identify a Scorpio man in a crowd?

A Scorpio man displays the right mix of passion and composure. He is passionate about work, help, conversations, dressing, food and just about everything else. Around 70 per cent Scorpio men come across as passive in nature but can get aggressive if provoked. The 30 per cent who are actually aggressive can behave passively and diplomatically when needed.

It is quite easy to identify a Scorpio man in a crowd. He's the one smooth talking everyone, especially women. If not that, you will find him in intense conversation involving money, work and investments, generally about stuff related to economics.

Known to be extremely enterprising, he has 'growth' on his mind, always. It's not surprising to find a Scorpio man getting maximum promotions in an office environment. This could be one reason for Scorpio man's arrogance.

What are the key features of his personality?

If there is a goddess of passion then Scorpio men are her true devotees. So much is this man taken in by whatever he does, that it leaves no other words for him but 'passionate'. And his passion often makes him go into excesses with everything he does. Believing in living a larger than life existence, a Scorpio man will let his hair down in any enterprise that catches his fancy, from working in the wee hours of the night to partying till morning.

In spite of the burning ardour he has within, it gets rarely displayed on his face. He has a 'cool dude' image, which at times is carried to the extremes of coldness. But it should not be mistaken for indifference as he is concerned about all and sundry that touches his life.

A Scorpio man is shrewd. In a work or a business scenario he likes to deal from a position of power and prefers to be the dominant player. But he won't be your typical action hero delivering the kicks and punches on screen; rather he would be the man behind the scenes—the director calling the shots. That's where his shrewdness comes into the picture. Unlike his female counterpart, this man is not interested in hogging the limelight—all he wants is to have his way and achieve his goals.

Coming back to his core characteristic 'passion'—there are many consequential traits that appear in a Scorpio man due to his passionate nature. His passion can make him extremely obsessive. Once he gets obsessed with an idea or thought he is like one possessed and then there's no stopping him!

But his passion is what gives him high energy levels and good sportsmanship. He is always buzzing with unabated energy and therefore leads a very active life. You will seldom find him lazing around and even when he is resting, his mental wheels are on the move, churning out new ideas and strategies.

And with his passion comes daring, a rare courage to do and act as he deems right. Not one to conform to rules laid down by others, the Scorpio man likes to be a trailblazer in everything. But if he encounters someone superior than himself, he has the humility to respect and admire that person.

He also scores high on sincerity but this quality varies in different circles of life. For instance, while he would put in sincere efforts at work (getting a nine on ten for it), his earnestness towards his love life might take a dip (to seven on ten). Again, his innate shrewdness tells him where and when and how much he needs to be sincere. This could probably be because of his personal mantra (a la the Virgo male) 'what's in it for me?'

Another quality he shares with his Virgo counterpart is that of being a critic. But unlike Virgo men who's sole intent is finding faults with others, Scorpio males are more refined in their criticism, using a good deal of diplomacy and tact. Some might even consider their criticism as constructive.

Scorpio men also score highly on creativity (nine on ten). Known to have a fertile imagination and a razor sharp mind, they are very good at creative jobs and are often found excelling in the performing arts, media related work and fine arts.

They make excellent speakers courtesy their good communication skills, especially when it comes to their emotions. Don't be surprised if you catch your Scorpio friend begin a monologue (filled with dramatic punch lines) in the midst of an emotional situation.

On the flipside, the Scorpio male is manipulative. He is capable of scheming and plotting to achieve his ends. Like the female Scorpio, he can manipulate people and situations to get his way. But his worst trait is his unforgiving nature. Those who have erred or hurt a Scorpio man better get ready to pay up, for this man is full of vengeance and venom if hurt. Apparently he doesn't believe in the saying 'revenge will be mine sayeth the Lord'. To him revenge has to be his!

How is he on the following aspects?

Appearance: He is extremely stylish and fashionable. He is amongst the first few (like the Aries man) to adopt and adapt to new trends and fashions. His looks and appearance matter a lot to him and he is very conscious of the same. Both Scorpio men and women have fiery eyes.

A Scorpio man likes to be well groomed (to the extent of carrying a comb in his pocket). His need to always be immaculate is so intense that he won't even shy from shaving his chest to go swimming. That's grooming to a tee, I'd say!

Ambition: Scorpio men are very enterprising and have tremendous risk-taking ability. No matter what field he is in, for a Scorpion the sky's the limit. If he likes you he will not hesitate to share his ideas with you but yes, he can get superstitious about his plans. But on the whole, be it his own venture or someone else's, a Scorpio man is a great motivator, with a warm and affectionate nature. This makes him extremely popular.

Ego/Self-respect: Unless you get to know him well, you will never know what a big ego he has. His tactfully humble and diplomatic nature usually shields the egocentric man that he could be...or is. He is extremely sensitive and emotional and possesses great amount of self-respect too and this gets reflected in his attitude. I have noticed that a Scorpio male for most part is extremely quiet and subtle. Unless completely cornered or provoked he is not the one to create scenes by walking out or away from someone.

Responsibility: Here is one man who wants to have everything...have his cake and eat it too. While through his behaviour and speech he would come across as responsible, a Scorpio man is essentially accountable only for the things he desires or wants to get done. Apart from that he is not so dependable.

Moreover, since he wants to squeeze out so much from life and the material world, he is often seen biting-off more than he can chew. This makes him less reliable and slightly irresponsible. But let me add a word here in his defence: It is largely because he is overcommitted.

Etiquettes: This is one area wherein our man scores a low six on ten. Carefree and casual in his stance, a Scorpio man is too relaxed to follow the rules of social decorum. Also, you will never find him complaining if others around him are as casual as him.

What is his approach towards life?

Where a Scorpio man is concerned, it's all about acquisition. His life, his wife, his children, his home, his profession, each and every aspect is an extension of his personality. Anything and everything that matters, has to be done in style. This attribute leads him to working dedicatedly and shrewdly towards creating ways to fund his dreams and projects.

With a bearish approach towards all and sundry, he would try to exercise his dominance in all spheres of life, especially on the work front. His desire to always be in control of things makes him a good leader and initiator. At the same time, his tendency to go green whenever anyone scores over him or cuts him off, can sometimes make him terribly aggressive and negative in his attitude towards others.

How does he score on the following points?

Cynicism: A Scorpio man can be very cynical, though you will rarely know or notice it. He is an achiever and would go to great lengths to achieve success and this tinge of cynicism in his attitude helps him forge ahead.

Suspicion/Jealousy: This is one man who wouldn't stop till he confirms or does away with his suspicions if given a reason. He is the worst person to be with when he is in an apprehensive mood. He is generally suspicious about everything—people around him, competitors, colleagues, etc. Perhaps this characteristic of his makes him a good entrepreneur too, being always watchful and on his guard. In a competitive scenario he is always alert lest his rivals get ahead of him. Scorpio men are as jealous as...shall we say Leo men...or more. The slightest glance or change in attitude can make them go the deepest shade of green. This arises from an extremely possessive nature.

Dishonesty/Infidelity: A Scorpio male is incapable of accepting dishonesty or infidelity on his partner's part. But he is quite likely to commit either or both. Can't blame him, the guy is charming and has so much love to give!

Hardships: Because he is an ace risk-taker, hardships become a part of a Scorpio man's life. But thankfully, he knows that any kind of difficulty is never forever and he has the courage to overcome life's setbacks.

Success and failure: Success to a Scorpio man is a benchmark that he has set and every milestone he plans is on a higher level than the last.

He can be very vocal and display his success in public, but will be genuinely humbled on receiving compliments for his success.

Scorpio men are definitely not very graceful losers. Given that they are achievers and like winning, they find it difficult to accept failures in life. But there is this huge reservoir of energy that they bank upon. Energy from this reservoir never lets them be down for long. With guts to fight and vigour to bounce back into the arena, Scorpions will never accept complete defeat.

Host: With his casual approach towards etiquettes, a Scorpio host can be very laid-back and relaxed in his attitude. For him home delivery rocks! His bit in making his party a success will be his social skills. He will be at his entertaining best with his guests, and they will never feel the dearth of intelligent and amusing conversations with their Scorpion host.

Guest: As a guest, he is not too picky but can get critical about the ambience, food and other guests. But generally he will remain well pleased if his host is attentive and takes care of his comforts. He is comfortable mingling around if in a bigger party or be very involved and intimate in conversation, if in a small group.

How does he handle difficult situations?

Passion is the governing factor in everything a Scorpion does including quarrels. Arguments, debates, cross-fires and even informal discussions can set him off and being opinionated, he participates wholeheartedly.

In case of a quarrel he will rarely be passive or submissive. Moreover, he likes winning and you will find him talking his way into convincing others that it is actually not his fault, the diplomat that he is, he would of course not openly say that the fault lies with his opponent! I have often found myself opining to my Scorpion friends about how they'd make brilliant politicians.

What is his characteristic weakness?

That has got to be his tendency to overcommit. Like I had mentioned before, in his urge to do too many things at the same time, he is always falling short of fulfilling his commitments. This obviously makes him unreliable. Because of his habit of saying yes to anyone and everyone he is seen running pillar to post to meet deadlines.

Is there more to his persona?

Yes there is a dark side to the passionate Scorpio man's personality. There are certain aspects to him that I have found unique only to Scorpions.

Apart from wealth, prosperity and happiness, the one thing that preoccupies a Scorpion man's mind is death, the inevitable stop to all his enterprises. A Scorpio man is afraid of death and disaster. He is therefore an easy victim to superstitions and the knick-knacks that accompany it. He is curious to know what his future holds and is likely to take the aid of astrology, tarot reading and numerology for it.

Another factor that keeps him in check is 'public'. He knows his image depends a lot on what the general public thinks about him and so is very conscious about creating a positive public image and opinion. For this he will focus on his dress, grooming, the car he travels in, the restaurants he eats at, etc. He is forever striving to make good impression on people around him.

A Scorpio is not satisfied with anything and is always in constant need to do more and get more. He believes in living life king size and has the courage and vision to achieve it. The word 'mediocre' does not figure in a Scorpio man's dictionary. But sometimes he can go overboard with it and wants everything in excess. Be it food and drink or work and entertainment, a Scorpio man will want to do too much of all this. Not all his excesses however go unpunished. For instance, he would lose out on his private life as he drowns himself in work.

A Scorpio is not very realistic but his nature is an unconventional balance with practicality. He is also highly emotional and sentimental, but finds it difficult to forgive and forget.

How should one deal effectively with a Scorpio man?

It is wisest to hold on to your cards when you are with a Scorpio male. You will have to use tact and diplomacy while dealing with him. Any untoward word or action can be detrimental to his ego and then you would see the worst of him.

While in love you will have to indulge in a game of cat and mouse with him. Play hard to get and see if he retracts; if he does, tease him a little and make him come back. Believe me he will enjoy this as much as you.

Also remember not to arouse his anger. He is not the best person to be with when angry. If you rub him the wrong way, you will get a lashing you'll never forget. Boy, this man knows how to get back at you!

Since he tends to be vindictive, it is best to play it straight with him. If you hurt or betray him, that could very well be the end of the story for you and your relationship with him.

A Scorpio man will do anything for his loved ones. But don't expect him to change. He will improve himself as per his calculations but not for anyone else. So it is best to let him be. He is also prone to emotional outbursts and during such moments don't try to bully him. Like everything else he likes to manage his emotions himself.

How does he handle money matters?

A Scorpio man likes to earn, spend and save. He is unquestionably one of the smartest and shrewdest of men when it comes to money. He can also be a gambler because of his risk-taking ability and an innate urge to make money. His compassionate side makes him available to friends and family, when in need.

The funny part about Scorpio man and money is that he is very good with other people's money. He knows, whether intuitively or with experience, exactly how to make others put their money on him and utilise it to make profits for himself.

How is he on the professional front?

The Scorpio male is the most determined and focused of men that I have ever met. So intense is his desire to win, to achieve and to succeed that nothing he does will ever be enough for him. He has very high standards regarding achievements and will put in 100 per cent efforts to attain his goals. Many a time his personal life and love interest are sacrificed in the bargain.

At work a Scorpio man is very much like an eagle circling the skies—on a lookout for a prey. Like the predatory bird, he will watch his target with unflinching eyes, work towards it and scoop in to grab his prize in a flash. And win he must at any cost.

How is he in various relationship roles?

As a son, the Scorpio boy yearns for his independence but at the same time has no qualms in being dependent on his parents for small luxuries like fuel for his bike. If he has been respected and loved as a child, he would reciprocate the same to his parents.

With friends he is extremely adjusting and easy-going. Although devoted towards them, he is often committed at multiple places because of his popularity.

The most dominant emotion that he would display towards his girlfriend or his spouse is passion. Therefore, it is of utmost importance for his woman to know how to keep his interest; keep his passion alive in order to keep him for herself.

As a father he is a disciplinarian and expects his kids to be well mannered. Some Scorpio men I have met are extremely attached to their children, while some because of their overcommitted nature and love for work and money have their priorities sorted another way.

How is he when alone?

If there is any man who shouldn't be left alone, it's him—the incorrigible Scorpio man. He needs constant company to talk, to argue, to entertain and be entertained and to prove again and yet again that he's the best. While alone he is prone to think like the devil—a harmful repercussion for him and those around him!

How is he when in love?

I think he can go completely blind when in love. Since he is obsessive by nature he gets obsessive about his relationship and expects the same from his partner too.

You need to have a lot of energy to keep up with him. He is entertaining, adventurous, fun-loving and passionate, but the slightest casual attitude from you can get him to lose interest and focus his attention elsewhere. He can be unforgiving in situations like these.

He has a magnetic personality and women often find themselves gravitating into his field of influence, but he is selective about the women he dates. No matter how many females fall for him, he will pick only the one who fits in his image of a perfect woman.

An important aspect of a Scorpio man's love is his concept of the ideal. To him the woman in his life should conform to the ideal female he has in his mind, and no she need not be like his mother! Moreover, don't try to entice him for fun because once he is on your trail it will be impossible to shake him off. If you seriously have feelings for him, then only go for it, otherwise it is advisable to stay away. And don't even think of giving him any heartbreak...he will give you one in return and you will never be able to forget it in your lifetime.

What does he look for in his partner?

As I said earlier, to the Scorpio man, his partner is an extension of his personality, of who he is. With most Scorpio males desiring trophy wives, they usually seek someone who is good-looking, has as appetite for satisfying his emotional and physical needs, and is sensible and capable enough to maintain his empire on the home front.

It is of utmost importance to a Scorpio man that his woman has a spotless reputation. Since he gives a lot of significance to public opinion, he cannot abide by the fact that his girl has a tainted past.

While dating him you should...

...never be mushy. Although this guy is as emotional as any other, he hates the flow of sentiments and heart-rending emotions. He likes to keep it simple and straightforward with emotions. Keep your feelings in check and be ready to have a blast.

It would be repetitive to mention how passionate his approach towards dating can be. He looks at every aspect of life with verve and dating is quite a prominent factor here. Expect him to come dressed to kill. If you spy on him before meeting up, you can catch him checking out his profile in the restaurant glass.

On your first date, let him talk. Remember he is opinionated about everything and is likely to make his feelings heard. Give him a patient hearing and you will find yourself getting involved in his ardent repartee.

You will have to be a complete woman, from grooming to behaviour, as he is the epitome of masculinity. He would expect you to do all things womanly and do them with finesse. Don't try to dominate him in any way. He won't like it at all. And let him make the first move. Patience can get you a long way with the Scorpio man and it would be totally worth it.

Dating a Scorpio guy can be a fabulous experience as he is daring, adventurous and also extravagant to a great extent. He will date you in style and do everything that he thinks can impress you. But that's the catch here; he would prefer doing things his way and if you resist, he can manipulate you to liking his way.

A last word...if you have managed to turn him off then yours is a lost cause for sure. No matter what you do, he is not likely to come back to you. He doesn't believe in wasting his 'precious' emotions on someone who won't reciprocate in a similar fashion. With emotions, as with everything else in life, he swings to the extremes. He either loves or hates, there is no in-between for him. While dating a Scorpio guy, make the most of it...or forget it.

Compatibility quotient:

Should one match passion with passion or balance it out with patience and forbearance? Should one submit to possessive or aggressive behaviour or hold one's stand? Answers to these questions can lead to a better understanding of what is compatible with a Scorpio man. How easy or difficult is it to get along with a Scorpio guy? Here are some answers.

Scorpio man and...

Aries woman: 7/10. She has the vivacity to match his passionate nature and he has the intensity to keep her interested. But she should learn to curb her controlling nature while he should rest his possessive mind a bit. With a good amount of understanding this relationship can work out pretty well.

Taurus woman: 5/10. A difficult match! Both can try each other's patience to the limits. He will find it hard to cope with her stubbornness while she will be perturbed by his secretiveness.

Gemini woman: 4/10. This combination might result in clashes as the Scorpio man is too possessive to suit a Gemini woman. She is also too impatient and wild to be able to adjust with his dominating nature.

Cancer woman: 9/10. These two can, between themselves, redefine perfection. The passion in him will be complemented by the romantic in her. He will be able to draw her out and she will find it easy to communicate her feelings in his presence. He can give her the security she wants while she will put him on a pedestal...something that would please him infinitely.

Leo woman: 4/10. A good deal of anger management will be required at both ends to make this relationship work. Both are bossy and impatient. She can get frivolous at times while he will find it difficult to fulfil her desires for affection and warmth.

Virgo woman: 8/10. This relationship can go a long way. The Scorpio man's passion will be matched by the Virgo woman's romance. Further, they will balance each other well especially with his emotions and her pragmatism. Her femininity will be an add-on.

Libra woman: 6/10. Not a very good match, but it can work if both learn to adjust. His bossiness will irk her while her love for freedom might keep the mercury of his suspicions always on the rise.

Scorpio woman: 8/10. Once the Scorpio man learns to take the admiring glances thrown at his female counterpart in a sporting way, this relationship can work admirably well. Both share a lot in common and are therefore likely to understand each other better. However, both will have to rein in their egos.

Sagittarius woman: 4/10. This union lacks the basic essentials of a good match—romance and depth. She is too playful for his passionate disposition, while he is too forceful to suit her outgoing nature.

Capricorn woman: 9.5/10. A fantastic combination that works for both. The Scorpio man has the tact of bringing the Capricorn woman out of her shell. She on the other hand will offer the loyalty and dependability he looks for in a woman.

Aquarius woman: 6/10. The success of this union depends on compromises. The Scorpio man can be stumped by the Aquarian's constant demand for attention. The Aquarius woman would find his sarcastic sense of humour a complete turn-off.

Pisces woman: 9.5/10. Jackpot! The Scorpio man and Pisces woman get along really well with each other as they understand each other's emotional needs. Both have the indispensable elements of loyalty and dependability that the other requires.

Famous Scorpio men personalities:

Bill Gates
Jawaharlal Nehru
Leonardo DiCaprio
Bryan Adams
Kamal Hassan
Shah Rukh Khan

Scorpio woman

There is only one word that befits a Scorpio woman…captivating! There is something of a hypnotist in her and she knows how to make men fall in love with her and do her bidding. Although this may sound vamp-like, the Scorpio woman indulges in these arts with such grace and polish that it is impossible to resist her charms. She is good-looking, (more often than not downright beautiful) and knows very well how to use her beauty to make way into other people's hearts.

But her ingenuity does not end with her looks. She has brains to match her beauty. The typical Scorpion female has loads of intelligence, a fantastic sense of humour and an innate sense of leading a sophisticated lifestyle. She is high on passion, style and a certain oomph factor that sets her a cut above the rest! Not one to settle for the common fare, she would always aspire for the skies. But there is a lot more to her persona; let's take a peek into the shades of this striking personality.

How can you identify a Scorpio woman in a crowd?

Scorpio is the only zodiac sign where the passive and the aggressive can be classified date wise. I have observed that the majority of the aggressive ones are born between October 23 and 31, while the passive kind are born between November 1 and 22. When I say 'aggressive', in the case of a Scorpion, it's not the regular 'in your face' assertive type but the kind which is prone to responding in an aggressive manner when provoked or given the slightest reason to react.

Scorpio women can easily be identified by certain facial features and behavioural traits that are peculiar to them. A strong jawline and ever-wandering eyes exchanging flirtatious glances…a Scorpio female's mannerisms are a dead giveaway.

Scorpio women are unabashed about befriending people, especially males, if they take a fancy to someone. Once again, the October born Scorpio women differ from those born in November in being naughtier and more adventurous. While both yearn for love and emotional security, the October born seem more dominating and overly possessive, which usually causes anxiety and discomfort to their prospective partners (not that the November born are less possessive...but they somehow seem more secure).

What are the key features of her personality?

I feel that the very essence of most Scorpio women is beauty. I would give them an 8.5 on 10 for beauty. Their looks can range from 'drop dead gorgeous' to 'raving red hot' to 'a summery calm glow', but whatever look they sport there is a radiance of beauty on their face. This, together with their magnetic and appealing persona, makes them quite irresistible. These qualities are accompanied by boldness (ten on ten for this one!), femininity (nine on ten) and sociability (nine on ten again). These features make a Scorpio woman a femme fatale to watch out for!

You can implicitly trust your Scorpio friend with your secrets for this lady is highly secretive. But don't bother sharing casual information with her as it will spread like wildfire. When it comes to gossip she is a total windbag! A Scorpio woman is secretive in another sense too. She will never allow anyone to read her innermost thoughts, which could be a maze of ideas. She guards her ideas with an iron hand and has a strange way of executing them. You will find her making plans to spend an evening with you at a coffee shop and at the same time arrange for another more interesting do with her girlfriends. The best part is, she will manage to do both without giving you the least reason to be suspicious. Now this is how eager she is to fit in as many things as she can in the time at hand.

When it comes to expecting things from life, much like a Scorpio man, the Scorpio female wants to over-achieve. She wants to be in tens of places and do scores of stuff at the same time. She yearns for everything 'big' and anything mediocre is not her cup of tea.

However she scores a low five on ten for will-power, which renders her ineffective in adopting self-control. But she ranges on the same levels as a Scorpio man for passion (eight on ten; both Scorpio males and females are passionate to the extremes, about everything that touches their lives... more so with love), power (seven on ten) and anger (eight on ten). Of course the way they manage these three traits is completely different.

A Scorpio girl is also adventurous and knows how to use her boldness effectively. However, she will never take a foolish risk in the name of adventure to jeopardise either her marriage or other relationships.

Since she scores pretty high on anger, it is interesting to note that much of this is exhibited sarcastically. A Scorpio woman is armed with a good stash of sarcasm and is capable of putting it across either through her acerbic humour or caustic words. I think her sarcasm is seen at its best when the proverbial love turns into hatred. 'Hell hath no fury like a woman scorned'...well you don't need to scorn her really, an emotional wound is enough to ruffle her feathers. She will strike back with vengeance—something you are not likely to forget in a long time. With friends and loved ones, a Scorpio woman is devoted, sweet and affectionate but once the tide of her love turns to hatred, you will find a most formidable enemy in the otherwise lovely Scorpio lass.

How is she on the following aspects?

Appearance: I guess a Scorpio woman gets maximum points for appearance. She's one woman who is not afraid to try out new styles and trends which quite often are her own innovations. She can be seen sunbathing in a bold bikini in the morning and stepping out of a car clad in a sari in the afternoon, and partying away in a hot number at night...it's all a day's work for her.

I sometimes feel there is something of an aspiring actress in a Scorpio girl, because of her experiments with her dressing and her ability to emote. Added to that there is something uniquely sexy about her face, which distinguishes her from women of other sun signs.

Ambition: A Scorpio woman will compromise only if her monetary situation is average. Once again, purely based on my observations, I have found that the October born are usually more ambitious and focused on their goals than the November born, who are more laid-back and lazy. But both are equally creative, innovative and ever ready to take on challenges. A lot of them take on responsibility and work at an early age.

Let me illustrate this with a fitting example: A friend of mine born on October 24, a single mother, had to take-up a job to support herself. Having never worked before, she started off with a marketing job in a dot com company for a measly ₹10,000. Her need to earn for herself and her family made her work for nearly fourteen hours a day. I've yet to meet someone more committed to her work.

Not only did she successfully complete all the targets and goals set before her, but she stuck it out in conditions where others would've easily chickened out.

Almost after a year of such toil, she got an offer from another firm, which she accepted. The jump in her package was from a monthly of ₹10,000 to ₹60,000. After about four months of working (with a radio station) she was drawing up to ₹1,00,000 (that's her salary plus incentives). Two years later she joined as a senior official in the marketing department of a TV channel. I was extremely proud and happy to see her covering the ground from ₹10,000 to ₹2,00,000 a month, in a span of three-four years. With sincere effort and hard work, she bravely fought every adversity in sight to achieve a sustainable lifestyle, living up to her Scorpio image!

With sheer grit and determination, that makes up the core of a Scorpio woman, she can achieve great heights.

Ego/Self-respect: As far as ego goes, the self-respecting Scorpio woman takes after her male counterpart. Most women I have known have the right balance of retaining self respect and grace. In a few exceptional cases, I have noticed that she can lower her self respect to achieve what she wants, for example, if she is a struggling model or actress she is capable of taking short cuts (read: compromise). She will never display her ego openly and until you see her at close quarters, you'll never know just how ego-centric she really is. This quality of hers is well hidden behind her diplomatic attitude. But being the touchy person that she is, any sensitive subject is likely to brush her the wrong way.

Responsibility: Here she treads a completely opposite path to her male counterpart. A Scorpio woman is extremely responsible (okay, some are not). Although she can be extremely selfish at times with regard to her want of time and space, she is not one to shy away from her duties. She is very dependable but you may need a few follow-ups to get her to fulfil her obligations to you. But she has a better sense of responsibility than the Scorpio male. So, though she wants to be everywhere and do everything at the same time, she will rarely give you reason to complain for she is excellent at multitasking.

Etiquettes: Social decorum is one area where the Scorpio woman walks way ahead of a Scorpio man, scoring an eight on ten, according to my observations. She has goodly standard of etiquettes for her own self and an equally high expectation of those around her. She is usually very conscious of chivalry, mannerisms and courteous behaviour in people, especially men and more so the ones she is interested in. She really appreciates people who display correct etiquettes and manners when she is around.

What is her approach towards life?

She is not very realistic and certainly not practical. Although she is a dreamer, she isn't a 'head in clouds' kind of person and is shrewd enough to understand which ones of her dreams are workable. However, her chief characteristic remains her emotional and sentimental nature.

A Scorpio woman is quite capable of being a follower as well as a leader. She has what it takes to be a leader. She is also ready to give respect where it's due and accept the leadership of a superior person.

How does she score on the following aspects?

Cynicism: A Scorpio woman is generally not cynical, but the achiever in her can turn the tables. In order to attain her targets, be it at work, in business or simply to prove herself, her thinking can turn towards cynicism. Another thing that can make a Scorpio woman see red is when she is emotionally hurt.

Suspicion/Jealousy: She is as suspicious as her corresponding male, (it is curious how both display a similar way of being suspicious as well). Although she may not doubt someone's intentions routinely, she will get suspicious the moment anyone behaves out of character. There is no stopping her once she is suspicious. She will investigate to the extremes to satisfy or clear her doubts, with none being spared from the scrutiny, be it family or friend.

If you have ever dared to flirt with another woman while your Scorpio girlfriend is looking, you will know what jealousy is! Given her possessive nature, she treasures her love relationship rather too much and can go green at the drop of a hat and this emotion can further ascend to anger and then extreme anger. Trust me, you really don't want to go down that path and invite her wrath!

Dishonesty/Infidelity: If a Scorpio woman is completely in love and in a committed relationship, she is incapable of indulging even in casual flirting with anyone else, let alone think of an adulterous alliance. And if she ever indulges in a promiscuous escapade, she would have valid reasons to support her act—the duration of her current relationship, an inactive sex life or just plain boredom. She usually has a long list of needs and desires and craves for the fulfilment of all of them.

Hardships: Scorpio women are capable of taking hardships in their stride. They have the vision and courage to deal with difficult times and spring back with renewed energy. They are also aware that hardships are a passing phase in life and it is best to live them out rather than moaning and groaning about them. In my opinion there are only two kinds of women who can bounce back in life with such vigour—Scorpio and Gemini. I am not saying that others can't, but yes, Scorpio and Gemini women can do it better

Success and failure: Nothing can stop the vivacious Scorpio from displaying her success. She is quite vocal about her accomplishments and likes the whole world to acknowledge her efforts. This is more so because after all the hard work, she feels she deserves to be in the limelight and enjoy every moment of her success…especially since it involves public adulation. However, 20 odd per cent of them might keep such things limited to family and close friends.

Failure too brings to the fore the disparity between Scorpio women born in October and November. I have observed that October born Scorpions are mostly (not all) poor losers while those born in November are usually (not all here too) able to put-up a brave face and handle failure with grace.

Host: How a Scorpio woman conducts herself as a host largely depends on her guest. If it is someone she cares for or likes, she will be extremely detailed and meticulous in her party planning. Otherwise she can be quite casual and is likely to take the easy way out and have maids or caterers manage the food. But if she has invited you home, she'll be warm and affectionate.

Guest: As a guest she is very moody. Although not fussy, she can be choosy about the kind of party to attend and the type of people to mingle with. If not in her best of moods she can also criticise stuff around her, especially food and ambience. But on the whole she is quite adaptable and 'cool'.

How does she handle difficult situations?

A Scorpio woman is extremely sensitive and a quarrel-like situation is likely to stir her up emotionally. She turns into an emotional live wire and will display a range of sensations from anger to tears (and that includes everything from sobbing to wailing). While a certain percentage of Scorpio women will avoid putting up an exhibit of their emotions, a considerable number of them will go overboard by making a mountain out of a molehill. I have noticed that this holds true especially of those Scorpions born in October.

What is her characteristic weakness?

A Scorpio woman is emotional in any common place scenario...and she is extremely emotional in any intense situation. And with her, the intense moments are rather too many. She is not very good at hiding her emotions and therefore her over-emotional display makes her vulnerable to others. She is also compassionate and sensitive and you will have to meet a Scorpio woman to know how lethal that combination is...more for her than others.

Is there more to her persona?

Just like her male counterpart the Scorpio woman is diplomatic and tactful too. The one thing I have noticed in almost 50 per cent Scorpion women is that they are low on will-power and self-control. Let me illustrate this point. If I resolve not to drink during weekdays and find myself at a party where friends urge me to share a drink I am faced with two choices, either to give in and enjoy a drink or to deliver a firm 'no' and continue sipping my orange juice. In case of the former, I would display lack of self-control and with the latter I would exhibit rigid adherence to rules. In a similar situation, a Scorpio woman is likely to choose the first option and show signs of low self-control. A Scorpio girl will go with the flow and will be sporting enough to join her friends. I sometimes think these kinds of impulsive things should be allowed to oneself.

Sometimes her intelligence (which she has in abundance) can take on a negative shade and make a Scorpio woman play manipulative games, (remember she has a long list of desires which are to be fulfilled completely and most of them are under the heading 'priority'). Obviously, she finds it easier to twist and turn people and situations in her favour to achieve her end. But given her emotional nature she is not likely to get manipulative to hurt anyone intentionally.

How should one deal effectively with a Scorpio woman?

This lady likes direct talk, so don't twist your words and come straight to the point. Very rarely will you see her falling for flattery, so drop all thoughts of making way into her heart with smooth talk. This makes life simple for straightforward men who don't like being pretentious (especially those belonging to the Aries, Sagittarius and Aquarius signs).

Most Scorpio women are smart from an early age and are well able to tell fake from real. The only place they find themselves fooled is with fake emotions shown by men.

A Scorpio woman enjoys chasing more than being chased, but at the same time she is not one to make the first move. She is likely to fall for men with husky voices (a trait I have noticed in Gemini and Capricorn women too) so much so that cupid will strike them even over the phone, even if they've never met the men. Once in love she will be very vocal about her feelings and will expect her man to be the perfect gentleman.

If you are dating a Scorpio girl, the most effective way of dealing with her is to be sincere, honest and even critical wherever necessary. A word of caution here...don't overdo the criticism part. Remember...this Scorpion can sting!

How does she handle money matters?

A Scorpio woman is quite adept with her money be it earning, spending or saving. With her strong ambitious drive and achiever streak, she knows how to earn money the right way. And with her shrewd and calculative brains she knows how to spend and save it. Let me clarify another point here. When I said a Scorpio woman is compassionate, I meant it in terms of time, energy and advice. When it comes to loosening her purse strings to show compassion, our lady is never in a hurry to share. Having said that...if she has plenty stacked away, she will not be stingy with her money while aiding others.

On the flipside, some (very few) Scorpio women are likely to fall in the habit of borrowing money, without being prompt in repayments.

So be on your guard while lending cash to your Scorpion friend. With her it's mostly the case of 'borrow from Peter to pay Tom'.

How is she on the professional front?

At work, the female of the species likes to exercise complete power play. Not ones to appreciate being dominated by others, Scorpio women make for excellent leaders, though they have a tendency to become overbearing and nasty if rubbed the wrong way.

The most important streak she displays while at work is competitiveness. Be it work, sport or a business deal, a Scorpio will be at her competitive best always. The Scorpio woman is extremely critical of others (if she finds them lacking) and strives to maintain high standards herself. She fares well in almost any profession, especially where she feels it can 'make a difference to the world'.

How is she in various relationship roles?

Scorpio girls tend to be very independent and understand their responsibilities from early childhood. Till they reach teenage they are not much of trouble. Come teen age, and that's where the worrisome period begins for their parents, with the young ladies discovering men!

Given a choice, the Scorpio woman will choose her home over career and makes an excellent homemaker. As a mother, she is a good mix of a disciplinarian and a friend. But being the control freak that she is, she would want to know what's happening in her kid's life...including school, play, as well as thoughts. With a Scorpio mother, a child will have to answer a lot of questions to satisfy her curiosity.

In her role as a wife or a girlfriend, if in a serious relationship, she is totally committed and devoted.

A Scorpio woman makes a reliable friend, who'd stick it out with you through thick and thin. But like I mentioned earlier, she'll blabber details about anything you say to any third person, but if you take her into confidentiality, she'll guard your secrets with her life.

How is she when alone?

A Scorpio woman is much like her male counterpart when alone—she shouldn't be left alone. The devil's workshop would be in full swing in her head the minute she is alone. Moreover, she is a people's person and therefore likes constant company.

How is she when in love?

'Blind, blind, blind' wrote Charles Dickens in *David Copperfield* while describing his hero's love. Ditto for a Scorpio woman! In addition to this, she loses all her other senses too. If any man is looking for the classic Juliet, his search will stop with a Scorpio woman.

It seems the saying 'behind every successful man there is a woman' was coined for a Scorpio female. She understands the role and importance a woman plays in a man's life and knows how to make a winner of her man. So deep is her love that she goes all out to support her man in any venture and he will never feel a dearth of emotions. However, in spite of her assertiveness, she cannot be with a weak man as she loves being dominated and controlled. No, she's not crazy, she's simply smart. It is her way of knowing that her man is as madly in love with her as she is with him.

When in love a Scorpio woman can show two distinct reactions. Either she will take a lot of time to settle down or will be double quick to get into the domestic mode...but that's only when she is dead sure that you are indeed *the* man for her.

What does she look for in her partner?

A Scorpio woman wants a custom made man, one who is tailored to meet her demands. The essential qualities that her love interest must possess are simplicity, the right amount of authoritativeness and arrogance, along with spiritual awareness and philosophical bent of mind. But above all he should be expressive and be able to communicate his emotions well, very much like her. A Scorpio woman also appreciates a man with high family values.

Although I have explained how emotional she is, I must add here that when in love she is quite methodical with her emotions. Being suspicious and on her guard, she won't display her emotions readily at the beginning of a relationship. Don't be surprised if your Scorpio date comes across as an ice queen in the first few meetings. Until she is completely sure of you and of her feelings for you, she will not display her true feelings. But once she is truly in love, be ready for an overflow of passionate display of emotions.

No matter how wary she is, she is not totally invincible. With her high emotional quotient, she can be easily misled or misguided or taken for an emotional joyride. She can also fall prey to devious men who play the part of a loving and caring partner only to turn otherwise after marriage. And the fact that she is blindly in love (as well as deficient in other senses) only aids her emotional downfall.

Strength of character will win you praises from your Scorpio girl but any show of weakness will get you negative points. When you are with her you have to be a 'real' man. With her good looks and attractive personality she is likely to have many admirers but she will choose only the one who has true feelings for her. And don't even think about working on a casual fling with her...it won't help your case at all. She detests anyone who trifles with her feelings and you might see her worst vindictive face if you rub her the wrong way.

It is also not advisable to make her jealous or give her reason to be suspicious. She is extremely possessive of her loved ones and emotions like jealousy make her behave quite like the devil...not what the lovely Scorpio lady actually is!

While dating her, you should...

...search and research, delve and dig, try and pry to understand the term 'demanding'. A Scorpio girl on a date can be extremely demanding, and I don't mean in terms of money only. She would demand your undivided attention, your time, your thoughts and the last drop of admiration that you hold for womankind. In short she will rule your heart!

This is not to be mistaken for dominance. A Scorpio woman will never date a spineless man but at the same time she would expect her date to give her everything she demands.

If there is one thing that the Scorpio girl prizes on the dating scene, it is privacy. She is not loud or brash and hates to put-up with general public when she could be sharing a private moment with you. So that gives you a cue to make the right selections while booking your dinner table.

It is needless to repeat here that while dating a Scorpio girl you should be careful with the way you dress and behave. Given the high grace quotient she possesses, she would expect you to play the quintessential gentleman and treat her like a true lady.

Once she is through with making demands on every facet of your life, she would touch the subject of money. Herein she does a fine balancing act between her love for good things in life and her spirit of self-reliance. She would be thrilled every time you buy her a gift, but would be conscious of your effort and reciprocate your gesture. A word of caution here...be very careful about what you promise to buy her as the lady in question can make all kinds of demands from a black rose to go with her dinner outfit to a blue emerald to match her evening gown.

Dating a Scorpio woman will get you the closest to the affectionate side of her personality. Her love and warmth will envelope you with a restful cocoon, which can only be disturbed if you incite her wrath, possessiveness or vengeance. Once she is secure in the knowledge of your love for her, she will remain by your side forever.

Sensuality is another thing you should get accustomed to. While she may appear to be cold and distant initially, the Scorpio girl is smouldering with sensuality inside. Unless she has had a break up recently or is plagued by her past failures, she will reveal her sensuous charms quite early in a relationship.

Adventurous, passionate, beautiful and sensuous...dating a Scorpio woman is one romantic adventure that would leave you wanting for more.

Compatibility quotient:

Each zodiac sign brings along a different lesson on compatibility. While sensitivity might be the highlight of a relationship, it might be a bone of contention for another. Since the Scorpio woman is high on passion and adventure, it would be interesting to see who amongst all the males on the zodiac is able to match up to her verve.

Scorpio woman and...

Aries man: 9/10. If both can summon enough amount of respect for each other, this relationship can rock from the word go. He would appeal to her for his assertiveness, while she would floor him with her womanly charms. Passion, which they both possess, becomes the key to their long-term relationship.

Taurus man: 5/10. Both share a lot of negative traits in common. Their innate stubbornness, domineering nature and possessiveness might come in the way of a successful relationship. Lots of hard work would be required to make this one work. Yet, I must say that I have also seen a few couples sail through comfortably with romance and harmony.

Gemini man: 6/10. Once the Gemini man learns to curb his flirtatious nature and give her the security she needs, this relationship can work wonders. Both are extremely passionate, which works in their favour. She will be taken in by his cool attitude but will need him to keep the romance alive to keep it going.

Cancer man: 9.5/10. This alliance would be full of romance and understanding. Both have the inbred quality to understand the other's emotional needs. The Scorpio will be full of warmth for the Cancerian's sensitivity, while he would give her the commitment and security she needs.

Leo man: 5/10. Not a very happening combination! The Scorpio woman's need for privacy will be spurned by the Leo man's constant yearning for the limelight. Although both are sensual, there is marked difference between their sensuality, which can stick out like a sore thumb in this relationship.

Virgo man: 8/10. Good combination! Both will be compatible with each other due to their intelligence, smartness and good looks. The Virgo man will make her happy by giving her the lead on the home front, while keeping her suitably impressed with his charm. But here too, the Virgo man would have to be expressive in order to keep the fire burning.

Libra man: 6/10. The Scorpio woman will have to show restraint and understanding to make this relationship work. She would need to learn to curb her possessiveness in order to give him space. On the other hand, the Libra guy will have to understand her passionate nature and fulfil her demands accordingly.

Scorpio man: 8/10. Here's a jackpot! Both share a lot in common in terms of adventurous nature, passion and love for good things. But both will have to keep their egos under check for this relationship to work.

Sagittarius man: 4/10. His easy-going nature might be too much to take in for the intense Scorpion. She will find it difficult to find security and undivided attention in a Sagittarian male. It is likely that he would find her passion too monotonous in the long run.

Capricorn man: 9/10. The Scorpio girl is the Capricorn guy's dream come true. She has the right amount of liveliness to get the best out of him while he would be devoted and loyal towards her. He is capable of understanding her emotional needs and giving her the security she wants.

Aquarius man: 6/10. A relationship based on good conversation may not last long and that's what this is all about. These two are basically disparate in nature and their personality traits can come to loggerheads every now and then. A lot of compromise is required to make this work.

Pisces man: 8/10. If both are mature individuals, this relationship can work wonderfully in the long run as both have a compatible dose of similarities and dissimilarities to add different colours to a fulfilling relationship.

Famous Scorpio women personalities:

Aishwarya Rai
Indira Gandhi
Meg Ryan
Demi Moore
Julia Roberts
Sushmita Sen

Sagittarius

23 November-21 December

Sagittarius man

He will age but never grow old; he will flirt with many but never break a heart; he will laugh with you but never at you: he is the quintessential Sagittarian man. Easy to talk to and easy to be with, he can take mere social small talk to new levels of stimulating conversation. Not only is he blessed with eloquence but he is also knowledgeable enough to converse on a range of topics. With a Sagittarius guy for company, there would never be a dreary moment to crib about.

His penchant for knowledge and eagerness to know more is touched with a childlike innocence, although this does not mean that he lacks worldly wisdom. He is street smart, and his easy-going nature belies a rare spiritual consciousness.

The Sagittarian guy has patience but just enough patience to get along smoothly in life. You can't make undue demands on his time and generosity as that might make him lose his patience. The best way to get friendly with him is to share his sense of humour. But that's not all; there is a lot more to this Sagittarian male persona.

How can you identify a Sagittarius man in a crowd?

Sagittarius men are seen and known to be more assertive than aggressive. There might be some 15 odd per cent of Sagittarius men who would have an aggressive body language but the majority come across as extremely composed, patient, and sure about what they want or where they wish to get without showing the least amount of apprehension or urgency.

You can identify a Sagittarius man through his speech. He is usually very knowledgeable and when he speaks you will notice certain authority on the subject of his conversation. He is great at playing with words but likes to blend everything with logic. He can get very animated during conversations with men and women alike (charming the latter). Although practical, he is also extremely adventurous and not one to dread trying untested waters.

In his commitments (as well as words) he is extremely straightforward and blunt yet he possesses a unique quality of being a diplomat too.

He is so systematic in his mind about what he does and says that if you were to interrupt his flow of words in the thick of conversation, he will hit the 'pause' button in his mind and the minute he gets a chance to start again, he would 'play' from where he had left.

A Sagittarius man remains restless till he has put his point across or has spoken his mind. This guy is extremely detailed and meticulous and does not believe in short cuts or cutting corners. Amongst the three fire signs, the Sagittarius man is the only one blessed with patience.

What are the key features of his personality?

The Sagittarius male is much like his female counterpart in various aspects. He is adventurous by nature, often boisterous, loves the outdoors, gets easily frustrated by the mundane, and is quick to fall in love and is passionate in expressing the same.

For a Sagittarius man two and two make four. Life's as simple as that and he will be quite direct about it too. He doesn't waste time mincing words (although he is pretty good with them). While expressing his opinions he is forthright and sometimes even blunt, but has the ability to balance it out with charm and diplomacy, ensuring that his sharp tongue makes no difference to his popularity.

This attribute makes him an ace at maintaining relationships. He always prefers being on good terms with everybody and dislikes unpleasantness of any kind. He will therefore patch up any dispute he may have with them. Because of this quality Sagittarius men tend to be friendly and at ease with ex-girlfriends and ex-wives too.

In fact charm, diplomacy and optimism are the most prominent features of his personality. He is also trustworthy, and easily trusting of others (I would give him an eight on ten for that) and impulsive to some extent (eight on ten here too). He is quite sensitive too, which often makes him short-tempered.

The fun-loving Sagittarius man, with his commonplace but pleasant humour, and carefree charm, is known as the perfect jester. Not one to fret over trivial issues, here is one man who knows how to have a good time. The Sagittarius male loves to hang out with the boys over a beer or two, angling all day, into the sunset. His temperament won't allow him to be alone for too long and he would almost always be surrounded by people, enjoying himself to the hilt. A total social creature, he'll find his way to the most happening do in town, get himself invited to the neighbourhood barbecue and provide respite to any boring party, much like the female of the species.

He scores well at work too, getting along fabulously with others who share his passion for life, working and enjoying at the same time.

With their penchant for exploring new things, Sagittarius males are avid travellers who enjoy checking out new places and people. They also have a knack of collecting the finer things of life during their journeys that are amply manifested in their homes and offices.

Their ability to smoothly adapt to situations makes them pleasant in their approach allowing them to forge amicable relationships with new acquaintances. However, Sagittarians are not usually known for befriending people just for the heck of it. They wouldn't indulge in unnecessary chit-chat either.

Passionate in every sense of the word, he is a loyal friend and lover. Though flirtatious by disposition, you'd rarely ever find a Sagittarius man cheating on his mate.

Optimism personified, a Sagittarius will make it through stormy weather and seldom give in to cribbing. Even if he feels down and out, he'll bounce back in no time. Yet, this social creature would choose to 'cool off' on his own terms and you'd rather not cross his path when he's working on getting his head back on straight.

How is he on the following aspects?

Appearance: When it comes to clothing and accessories, he believes in style and fashion. He might not admit it but he is conscious about his looks, literally from head (hair) to toe. Just like his fire sign counterparts, he appreciates everything that comes with a luxury tag and regal air. He is usually metrosexual and belongs to that category of men who subscribe to men's magazines in order to keep up with trends, fashions and what not. He has deep-pocket, sunken eyes and sports a mature look on his face from an early age itself.

Ambition: If you ever come across a Sagittarius man who is not ambitious, let me know. Sagittarius men have an instinct to have the very best of everything. Coupled with their desire to excel at everything and an in-built mechanism to succeed, they manage to achieve their goals. But with a Sagittarius man, ambition is not a mere drive to earn money or create wealth. It is a manifestation of his creativity. I have seen excellent examples of two well known Sagittarius men (friends of mine) who have not just excelled in the construction industry but have created landmark properties in Mumbai. For them, ambition is not about name, fame or money only; it is also about putting one's creativity to test and turning a concept into reality.

Very often a Sagittarius man is led into ambitious plans due to his passion and he can be quite intuitive at that too. For example his passion for good food can get so overbearing that he will be propelled into starting a restaurant, (interestingly, 30 per cent of the Sagittarius men that I have met either run/own a restaurant or plan to open one).

Ego/Self-respect: Being a diplomat he might not show his ego, fooling you into thinking it's his self-respect, but actually it is a mix of both. He also has a good amount of humility in him, which balances out the rare displays of his ego. But for some reason, I think I can grant him the right to gloat in his ego because he has his feet firmly grounded.

Responsibility: A Sagittarius man is and wants to be responsible and takes his duties very seriously. However, due to his controlling nature and an ardent desire to oversee everything, he usually has his hands full. As he matures, he understands how to delegate responsibility and share work with other members of his family and social group.

Etiquettes: He likes a lot of discipline, which explains his fondness for right etiquettes. On very rare occasions and quite often due to simple laziness, you will see him compromising on his set view of decorum.

What is his approach towards life?

A Sagittarian man's approach to life is practical and realistic. Though the average Sagittarius (especially in his youth) may display streaks of recklessness from time to time, he never loses sight of the pragmatic path in life and all his decisions are based on it. However, that is not to say he lacks emotions; this man is quite emotional although he scores low on the sentimental front. He is also dreamy and idealistic and prefers to be a leader.

How does he score on the following points?

Cynicism: I would say he is cynical only to the extent of being detailed and passionate about getting things done exactly the way he wants; other than that I am yet to meet a Sagittarius man who is cynical by nature for no apparent reason, unless of course he is completely derailed or into drugs.

Suspicion/Jealousy: Although he is not completely untouched by these traits, a Sagittarius man is a goodly distance away from them. He is happy in a relationship if he is given the desired amount of space and time. Neither overbearing or overpowering, a Sagittarius male understands the need to have space and grant space for a relationship to work smoothly. Although controlling, he is not dictatorial and in spite of being possessive and protective, he knows where to draw a line. If at all he ever gets suspicious or jealous, be sure he has very, very strong reasons to do so.

Dishonesty/Infidelity: A Sagittarius man is charm personified and the proverbial 'ladies man', but this is not to be construed as flirtatious. He has a magnetic personality, peppered with strong doses of charm that attracts people (read women). His charm is flavoured with etiquettes, knowledge and power and I assume that works greatly in his favour. He is usually very quiet about his liaisons and relationships and once he commits himself he is known to be trustworthy and loyal. Having said that let me add here, if his woman doesn't know how to hold his interest, he is liable to give in to 'temptation'—after all he is always in demand.

Hardships: The pragmatic aspect of his personality comes to the fore with greater force in times of adversity. His logical mind and positive attitude urge him to accept that life is full of ups and downs. To him, difficult times are just a passing phase and herald the good times to come.

Success and failure: Sagittarius men can be divided into two kinds over their display of success. The first kind would host parties and announce his success to the world. The second kind will prefer sharing success with friends and family, over a quiet glass of beverage, wine or cognac. But one way or the other, both kinds know how to attain success and bask in its glory.

Failure is something that would disturb the archer. He will conduct a full autopsy of any failed activity to try and understand the reasons behind it. And once he knows why he failed, he will accept his mistakes as part of a learning process.

Host: Although known to be sociable, a Sagittarius man is selective about whom he invites over to his place. But once he decides to, he can be extremely gracious and warm with his hospitality. If he has brought you to his abode he will take into account every practical consideration to make you comfortable and at ease.

Guest: I have found him to be somewhat peculiar as a guest. I don't know whether it's his ego or something else but he likes to get a lot of attention. His host should welcome him properly and look after his comforts adequately. Don't mistake this behaviour for the usual 'centre of attraction' device; it's not that. It's just that he believes that since he has been invited over it is the host's duty to take care of all his needs and you might notice an unmistakable 'I'm here because you invited me' kind of look on his face. He will require frequent interactions with other people, especially the host, to make him comfortable at a party. This is how he is and I am yet to arrive at an explanation for this typical behaviour.

How does he handle difficult situations?

Although he is patient and practical, the archer can be short-tempered too. In a quarrel-like situation, his first attempt would be to keep his volume under control, but his tone assertive. Since he is not fond of being the cause of anything unpleasant he would look for ways to resolve a quarrel or fight. But if he finds himself up against people who are unbending or ungraceful (and especially if they are at fault) he can get into an uncompromising mode. If you are ever at loggerheads with a Sagittarius man (and more so if you are in the wrong), it's best to make a graceful exit.

Remember his bow is always arched…it's just a matter of seconds before he lets go of the arrow!

What is his characteristic weakness?

A Sagittarius man tends to take his meticulous attitude overboard. He can get extremely detailed at times, which hinders the speedy working of things. Also he can get overly logical and analytical. Although he possesses risk-taking ability and is capable of taking decisions (though rarely with his heart but his mind), these qualities tend to get the best of him.

Is there something more to his persona?

A Sagittarian male has the gift of the gab. With his persuasive skills, he is very good at convincing others. That's what makes him excel at marketing and sales. Want to sell snow to Eskimos? He's the man for you!

People say Sagittarians have a strong luck factor working for them, but the truth is if you believe in your dreams and back them up with sincerity, hard work and self-confidence you can achieve all your goals. And this, the self-confidence quotient of saying and believing in 'I can', is the secret Sagittarian mantra.

A Sagittarius male is quite independent in his thinking and I have observed that his thoughts are laced with creativity. But this is no ordinary creativity. There's something unique in his thinking process, so much so that you will find him arriving at conclusions different from most other men.

And it is this unique thought process that makes him lead a life away from home. He needs space for himself and may find the sentimental atmosphere at home a bit stifling. But that is not to say he is bereft of emotions; he values his relationships but also recognises the potency of his own needs.

He is also very secretive about his personal life, especially his love interests. Nosey Parkers can get a cold shoulder from him and any gossip about his private life can send him into a flying rage. He guards his personal life like a sentinel and it is best to let him be on that account.

A Sagittarius man likes to learn and no amount of knowledge is ever enough for him. He never outgrows the toddler age of asking questions. But his quest for knowledge is not limited to people or books; he also uses travel as an instrument to acquire more knowledge.

A conversation with a Sagittarian will never be boring (thanks to his knowledge) or one-sided (thanks to his patience) or dry (courtesy his sense of humour) or importantly unappealing (courtesy in no small measure to his gentlemanly behaviour and charisma).

When it comes to work, the regular nine to five run is a big no-no for him. He enjoys work that is intellectually stimulating and exciting. His love for adventure will never get him tied to a work bench. Give him a job that demands out-of-the-box thinking and he will be happy as a lark doing it.

He is also an incorrigible optimistic, always looking at the brighter side of things. This optimism makes him believe implicitly in his dreams, which are rather high, and aim at achieving them too.

How should one deal effectively with a Sagittarius man?

A Sagittarius male finds it difficult to deal with people who are either not at par with his intellectual level or on the same mental page. So far I have made him sound intense (which he is) but at the same time he is also extremely humourous and witty. More often than not, displaying a dry sense of humour, he finds it easy to get along with people who possess the same.

Being detailed, he has a knack for asking questions (and I mean a lot of questions) that are relevant to the situation at hand and isn't satisfied till he gets the right answers. For questions left unanswered, his follow-ups are equally prompt. So to effectively deal with a Sagittarius man you have to do your homework with due diligence.

How does he handle money matters?

To some, a Sagittarius male may come across as a flamboyant person, which he actually isn't. Like I said before, he likes to have all good things in life and if his bank balance permits, he does get what he desires.

Let me share an anecdote about a Sagittarian friend. This friend of mine took a flight to New York to celebrate his eighteenth birthday with his cousins and friends. Part of the celebration included touring the streets of New York City in a rented eight door limo. This same guy, after making it big as an entrepreneur, gifted himself an expensive wristwatch as soon as he could afford it...which happened to be his twenty-seventh birthday. Some celebration this!

I am not inferring here that Sagittarius men are incapable of money management, but they believe in living for the day even if it means paying big for it.

In a nutshell, Sagittarian males are good at earning, not bad at saving, excellent at spending and are moderately generous too.

How is he on the professional front?

This fire sign is a leader. Creativity and out-of-the-box thinking are a Sagittarian's forte and the Sagittarian male uses it to get things done in the best possible manner. With a strong bent of mind for doing the unusual, he loses interest in boring activities and looks for ways and means to keep his work 'happening'. Not one to step on other people's toes, if pushed into a corner, the archer could snap back with rage (very rare), which really could hurt the poor soul at the receiving end.

However, on the whole, the Sagittarius man is a pleasant worker, an excellent leader who knows how to get things done with panache, and a great team player too. His ambitious drive would see him planning big at an early stage and living to achieve his goals in due course.

How is he in various relationship roles?

From a young age, he displays a mind of his own but at the same time he is quite malleable and easily influenced. From teenage to adulthood you would see streaks of independence in him, yet he will be extremely comfortable in being dependent on his family for most things in life. He is also quite 'cool' about not having responsibilities piled onto him. Unless the financial situation at home is demanding, he will be happy to stay away from the yoke of earning a living. He thoroughly enjoys getting pampered and being the foodie that he is, you are likely to catch him at home during meal times or eating at his favourite restaurant.

A Sagittarian husband is something to be happy and proud of, and at times to cringe about. He will be protective of you and will indulge you to the fullest. Given his sense of style and quality living, you are sure of having a home with interiors to die for and a wardrobe with stuff you can strut. He will be understanding and liberal in his thinking and you don't have to ever consider giving up your career or hobbies after marriage.

But all this only if you can treat him exactly as his mother did. He should be the apple of your eye and the core of your existence. Be an excellent homemaker and a super-excellent cook and your Sagittarian man will reward you by being the most charming husband ever!

As a father he likes to strike a balance in many areas of his life. Here again he is practical enough to know how much pampering and love should be given to a child. He also needs to have time with his wife well defined, plus he needs some more time for himself too. But all in all he manages to be a good father.

I would give him a 7.5 on 10 on his role as a friend. Trouble brews when you start expecting things of him. If he is not on your list of priorities, you are likely to lose his interest and your friendship might end up the wrong alley.

How is he when alone?

Not many men can remain contended when alone, but a Sagittarius man is an exception. He is someone who is quite comfortable with himself. Although he likes company, he knows how to utilise his 'me time' productively. Very likely, he'll take-up a hobby, work out, read a book or simply take a walk to pass his time leisurely, but while even doing all this, his mental engine would be grinding full on.

How is he when in love?

If there's one word to describe a Sagittarius man in love, it's 'crazy'. He is a true romantic and both eager and restless to experience love. He won't fall short of doing the craziest of things to simply live the romance or prove his love.

As said earlier, Sagittarius men generally have attractive personalities and women are naturally drawn to them. Most of them buckle under the pressure of such feminine attention and become flirts. A teenage Sagittarian will learn love by trial and error and therefore is likely to have a long list of girlfriends. But as he matures and understands the concept of love, he grows more comfortable in a relationship. He would then seek and strive for emotional stability.

If your love interest is a Sagittarian, then lady you have a hard time ahead of you. You will have to make yourself visible amongst the crowd of charming ladies surrounding him. The trick to catch his eyes is to put on the right kind of feminine charm and intelligence, for this man wants a complete package for himself. His woman has to be not just a 'woman' but one with an intellect to reckon with.

Once you are dating him or even married to him, remember the ground rule—give him space. This guy likes freedom and adores people who give him that. But that doesn't mean he is totally independent. When the heartstrings start tugging he'll come running into your arms.

After having committed himself, there is slim chance of his forming a wanton relationship outside or returning to his flirtatious ways. But, however slim it may be, there is still a chance. So keep his interest strong and his spirit happy and he'll never budge from your side. My point here is that this guy isn't devious or promiscuous but just don't give him any reason to be one.

When you are in a relationship with a Sagittarius man, you have to deal with another trait of his—honesty. He is honest to the point of being rude. Whatever he has on his mind will be spouting from his mouth in simple, matter-of-fact words. If he is wrong or has committed a mistake he will own up to it with the same unfaltering honesty. And honesty is a two way street; you have to be as honest with him as he is with you.

What does he look for in a partner?

Adventure is his middle name and the typical Sagittarian male would go only for a woman who possesses similar tastes. He would want someone who would be a friend to him in every sense. Not one to settle for someone mediocre, he would be choosy about his mate (though not too much).

He can be slow in getting into a relationship. The Sagittarian temperament requires an anchor, one that holds him in line, yet gives him scope for taking in the horizon, his freedom being important to him. He seeks a partner who is the perfect homemaker, knows how to add flavor to a romantic dinner date, and also be the perfect buddy for a trekking session up a dirt-laden track.

While dating him, you should…

…be spontaneous. A Sagittarian guy loves nothing more than spontaneity—plans made on the spur of the moment, impulsive dating et al. You could impress him further with the right amount of adventure spirit in you. The mundane and routine is not for him—he thrives on life's most amazing thrills and if you are able to join him in his escapades, you will carve out a place for yourself in his heart right away. Add to that an understanding for his needs and a caring attitude and you'll have him on your side firmly.

To have fine grooming and ladylike behaviour is a given when dating a Sagittarian. While he is not gullible enough to fall for good looks only, he would definitely appreciate your taste if you are dressed appropriately and conduct yourself with grace.

But for the Sagittarian guy, more than looks and appearance, attitude is of utmost importance. If you exude a certain confidence, are sure of yourself and know generally how to hold yourself up, he will instantly find you interesting. He will think of a second date only if he likes your attitude. In the absence of the right attitude, all your beauty would indeed go in vain.

As said earlier he also likes honesty. Be open and honest about your feelings towards him, if you care for him enough to want to date him for a long-term, say so and if you are in for a casual fling, say so double quick. But whether you are honest with him or no, he would always be forthcoming. You will have to bear with his many 'truths' spoken in dry, matter-of-fact and often in hurtful ways. However, once you get into a serious relationship with him you'll be thankful for this quality.

But to begin with, it is difficult to get a Sagittarian man to commit. It will be many, many dates before he decides to propose you. But don't get disheartened as there is nothing sneaky about him; it's just that he values his freedom (or should I say intellectual freedom) that makes him refrain from committing. Time and love will teach him, and you should just be willing to play along. While the final reward might take a long time to come, there would be enough perks (his sense of humour, romantic gestures, intense conversations, etc.) to keep you going. But where he may take a long while to commit himself, he will be quite fast in getting physically intimate. And you would need to think on your feet to be able to handle this aspect of the Sagittarian personality.

And now for a word of advice—whether you are dating him casually or heading for a serious relationship, treat him as a friend. With the Sagittarian guy, at the end of it, nothing endures but friendship.

Compatibility quotient:

How does one gauge the compatibility level with a man who is not ready to commit himself? Will judging compatibility with him lead to a fruitful relationship? These questions are largely situational and generally depend on individual requirements. But based on the typical Sagittarian man's personality traits, one can to a great extent determine what kind of women from the different zodiac signs can get along well with him.

Sagittarian man and…

Aries woman: 9/10. An excellent match! Both are impulsive and adventure-loving. He will keep the fire blazing with his romanticism and good humour, while she will impress him constantly with her spontaneity. But she will of course have to rein in her tongue to make this relationship work.

Taurus woman: 6/10. This relationship can work only if both are able to attune themselves to each other's needs. The Sagittarian man will love her homeliness but won't be able to take her emotional neediness. The Taurus woman will love his adventurous spirit but may not take his flirtatious nature too well.

Gemini woman: 6/10. While they both share the same intellectual wavelength, they are too disparate emotionally. With love they can iron out the differences—he would have to be a bit more demonstrative of his love, while she would need to curb her overfriendliness with other men.

Cancer woman: 4/10. The Sagittarian man's blunt tongue might shock the Cancerian's sensitivity. If they don't make compromises, he would find the relationship too binding while she would be hurt by his flirtatious ways.

Leo woman: 7/10. Great chemistry and a happy match! Both are fun-loving and adventurous and are likely to hit it off well in the long run. Of course, the Leo woman will have to be less demanding of his attention.

Virgo woman: 4/10. Not a very happy venture! The Virgo woman is homely and serious while the Sagittarian is adventurous and loves to be out in the open. Lots of hard work and compromises will be required to make this relationship work.

Libra woman: 8/10. If they are able to overcome the initial hiccups, this can be a fulfilling relationship. It would take a lot of convincing for both of them to commit as both are hesitant and the Libran is especially indecisive. But once the first few hurdles have been crossed, it would be a fruitful and delightful alliance!

Scorpio woman: 4/10. The Scorpion is too intense to take the Sagittarian's fun-loving nature in her stride. While she has passion enough to ignite the fires of romance, he has good humour to make this relationship not fall into monotony. But both will have to work doubly hard to make this combination work in the long run.

Sagittarius woman: 9/10. Since she shares a lot with her male counterpart, both the archers will make a wonderful pair. Adventurous, fun-loving and optimistic, they are likely to have a rocking time together. However, either the male or the female archer must have sense enough to hold their relationship above frivolity and fun.

Capricorn woman: 7/10. These two can hit it off rather well, but how they would fare in the long run is a matter of adjustment and getting attuned to each other's personality traits. As far as their natures go, the woman is quite intense while the male tends to get frivolous and flirtatious at times.

Aquarius woman: 9/10. A match well made! Both have qualities that the other appreciates. There will be no dearth of stimulating conversation in this relationship. Both are also capable of understanding each other beautifully.

Pisces woman: 4/10. It's rare for a Sagittarian male to get-off on a good start with the Piscean woman. And if they do, they are likely to fall apart in the long run. There is too much of gap between his realism and her dreaminess.

Famous Sagittarius men personalities:

Brad Pitt	Bruce Lee
Dilip Kumar	Frank Sinatra
Rajnikant	Raj Kapoor

Sagittarius woman

Sagittarian women can be defined with three Fs: funny, focused and fierce. They come with a terrific sense of humour that's impossible to resist. A typical Sagittarian will find and create smiles and laughter in every detail of life and will instantly spread the mirth with her powerful 'word-of-mouth'. A compulsive chatterer and impish to the core, she can dare to do the unexpected and live on her own terms, no matter how unconventional they may be. More likely she will startle you (sometimes out of your wits!) with her non-conformist statements and outrageous logic or just plain mimicry, thereby making sure you don't forget her for a long time to come.

Ever keen on expanding her wealth of knowledge, the Sagittarian girl will be bursting with questions and often poke her inquisitive nose in places where it doesn't belong. She is practical and far-sighted to the extent of keeping a larder full of goodies (she loves food) and her study table full of interesting books (remember her quest for knowledge) for those long rainy afternoons. But books are not enough to satiate this girl! She is ever ready to go on a backpacking trip for no one loves travel more than the Sagittarian. 'The world is my book and Mother Nature my teacher'...that's the quintessential Sagittarian woman!

How can you identify a Sagittarius woman in a crowd?

See that woman striving to be the centre of attraction, chatting with the most handsome man, hanging out with the prettiest girls, and being loud in her laughter and with her words? That's her...the chatty and naughty Sagittarius woman. Of course this description does not hold true for the 35 odd per cent of passive Sagittarian women, but for the rest, it is a fairly accurate account.

This reminds me of an interesting incident. My parents once came back from a party regaling me with the wonderful experiences they had there. They then went on to describe this peculiar girl who eavesdropped on their conversation and then butted in unannounced with her opinion on the subject. At first my parents ignored her but later they noticed her doing the same thing with many guests. Having asked her the sun sign she belonged to, they quizzed me on the same (knowing my hobby) and what I would have thought if I was present there. With a few more details of their conversation with her, in less than a minute I arrived at my answer...Sagittarius! My mom and dad started grinning at that...my guess was right on target!

Some Sagittarian females will talk their way into conversations where they don't even belong. For some reason they enjoy minding other people's business as much as their own. At the same time, they are great people at heart—warm, friendly and compassionate—but have no control over their tongues. I sometimes feel the saying 'putting one's foot in the mouth' was invented solely for them.

Now for the passive kind of Sagittarian who is almost the exact opposite of the aggressive kind. She is usually more graceful, speaks when spoken to and would share her opinion or suggestion only if asked, unlike her aggressive counterpart.

What are the key features of her personality?

The female Sagittarian is known to be an impressive lady who knows how to charm her way into the hearts of those who cross her path. This maybe the direct result of her ability to break into conversation at the drop of a hat. In certain scenarios, this backfires for the archer, since her tactless, friendly banter may often be misconstrued as encroachment on other people's time and thoughts. Of course, this trait is somewhat subdued in the passive kind of Sagittarian women.

Natural leaders (something that probably stems from their desire to be appreciated), women of this sun sign seem to have mastered the art of egging others to do things even when they exhibit resistance to the same. They inspire others with their consistent 'looking at the world through rose coloured glasses' attitude and act as motivators and initiators.

Outgoing by nature, a Sagittarian woman is forthright in expressing her point of view, something that doesn't always go down well with her audience. She however, never utters anything to intentionally cause harm to people around, but her blunt statements and off the cuff remarks can easily irk others. At the same time, she is extremely appreciative of others, being very liberal with compliments where due.

This woman is one possessive associate, be it a relative, a friend or a lover, she is extremely possessive and easily gets ticked-off and goes green for the smallest of reasons. Make a deliberate attempt at making her jealous...and you'll surely be sleeping on the couch for the night!

The Sagittarian woman loves indulging in various activities that suit her fancy with shopping being a major splurging area. A big spender, she is surprisingly also good at saving and stashing away some moolah to fall back on in days of adversity. If you're dating a Sagittarian woman, be prepared to be mothered and showered with gifts and other surprises from time to time.

How is she on the following aspects?

Appearance: Sagittarius women sport a prominent jawline. I have found seven out of ten Sagittarians to be extremely pretty looking with sharp features. They have a great sense of style and fashion and carry off even the most unconventional garbs with elan.

Ambition: Generally both kinds of Sagittarius women are extremely ambitious. Whether aggressive or passive, a Sagittarius woman likes new challenges and is usually happy and content when she has a meaty role or responsibility in her work profile. In a job scenario, growth and titles are important to her.

If she is an entrepreneur, she will study the competition in the market and accordingly add more value to her products or services. If unable to meet her targets, a Sagittarian woman will not shy of, using her charm and persuasiveness to achieve her targets. Moreover she has to excel at every task at hand.

Conscious of her self image, an aggressive Sagittarian can go to any extent to protect her public persona. The passive kind can be content with whichever way the tide turns and usually isn't out to prove a point to anyone but herself.

Ego/Self-respect: The aggressive Sagittarian woman has high quotient of ego, smarting at even the slightest attack on her self-respect. The passive kind would score high on self-respect and moderate on ego.

Responsibility: An undeniable quality that Sagittarius women possess is their extremely responsible and dependable nature. A Sagittarian female is also usually very organised and fairly meticulous. Since she likes challenges at the work front, if you periodically dare her, you will be pleasantly surprised to see her meet up to those challenges with renewed vigour.

Etiquettes: Regarding etiquettes, the passive Sagittarian woman seems to be more conscious and often bothered by lack of decorum in others. The aggressive kinds expect others to follow social norms while they can be casual and laid-back about them at times.

What is her approach towards life?

Both the aggressive and passive kind of Sagittarian women show distinctly different stances towards life. The passive Sagittarian appears more content with life. She has moderate expectations and tends to be more independent minded than the other. The aggressive kind is somewhat materialistic and egocentric, because of which she wants more from life and is not easily satisfied with what she has.

Both kinds are emotional and sentimental but the degree of being emotional is rather high in the passive kind. Both are also dreamers and great believers not just in their dreams but also in ideals of life. The aggressive Sagittarian girl is realistic but not very practical while the passive kind can be both.

While the passive Sagittarius woman is capable of moulding herself in the roles of a follower as well as a leader if the situation demands, the aggressive one will definitely vie for the leader's position. She will follow only if she is sure she is next in line to becoming the 'boss'.

How does she score on the following points?

Cynicism: On the whole, 30 per cent Sagittarian women are cynical. Most of their cynicism is because of their emotional needs or their ambition. They can be extremely stubborn at times thereby making regular unpleasant situations seem like their personal cynical problem, which very often borders on the unreasonable.

Suspicion/Jealousy: I have noticed that the passive Sagittarian female is more relaxed and laid-back on these counts but the aggressive kind is suspicious of most things under the sun—from a friend's motives to her spouse's moves. Don't be surprised if you find your Sagittarian girlfriend snooping around your personal things such as computer files, diaries, mobile phones, etc. That's just her! She won't stop till she has satisfied her doubts, my guess is that because she herself is quite capable of doing stuff that makes her a object of suspicion, she knows how important snooping can be!

When it comes to jealousy, this woman can get extremely jealous when provoked and provoking her is not a difficult job at all. She needs to have all the things that others have and this covetous nature makes her go green quite often. She can display equal amount of jealousy when in love but here it comes with a blazing streak of revenge too. She can get vengeful when jealous and won't rest till she has paid back in the same coin.

Dishonesty/Infidelity: The passive Sagittarian is a loyal being and will prefer sticking to one partner. While she may enjoy looking elsewhere (that too occasionally), she is not capable of committing adultery. While this is also largely true of the aggressive Sagittarian girl, it's better not to try her on this front. Like Oscar Wilde said, 'I can resist anything but temptation', so is the case with some Sagittarian ladies.

This is purely my observation, but a small percentage of Sagittarian women are either bi-sexual or lesbians and extremely adventurous on the subject.

Hardships: Hardships extract the best out of a passive Sagittarian woman. She knows how to handle it and take it 'with a pinch of salt'. You can put your money on her when it comes to emerging out of a down-and-out situation. But this is not the case with the aggressive kind. Hardship can baffle her, make her ask 'why me' and bog her down. She wouldn't take the obvious path out of trouble but will crib and whine about how bad things are and how they are heading for the worse. An aggressive Sagittarian female definitely needs an optimistic partner to get her to face hardships.

Success and failure: A passive Sagittarian will prefer celebrating her success with family and close friends. She is a private kind of a person when it comes to sharing the fruits of her efforts. The aggressive type of Sagittarian female will be out telling the whole world about her success, even going to the extent of having it published.

Just like hardships, the more assertive Sagittarian finds it difficult to take failures in the right spirit. If she fails in her endeavours, she is likely to get depressed and even blame others for it. The passive

Sagittarian has the grace to accept failures and also the practical vision to evaluate her efforts as well as the mistakes of others.

However, I would like to say something about both kinds of Sagittarius women: they are amazingly competent. When bogged down by failure, whether they take it gracefully or otherwise, they exhibit a Phoenix-like quality, managing to rise above issues and move ahead. The only difference would be the time both kinds take in getting restarted and stepping up to the plate.

Host: As a host, the passive Sagittarian girl scores higher than her assertive counterpart. The aggressive Sagittarius woman can sometimes be very casual in her approach as a host. She'll prefer hiring caterers and leaving preparations for the party to the hired help. The passive kind will take interest in every detail about her social do and see to it that everything is in place for her guests. But both are warm hosts and make sure that their guests are well taken care of. The Sagittarius woman is known for her love for a good laugh and she will keep her guests entertained with friendly banter and lively anecdotes.

Guest: As a guest the passive Sagittarian will appreciate the efforts, whether good or bad, made by her host. She will be sensitive towards other people's feelings and will not hesitate in dishing out a fake compliment to please her host. On the contrary, the aggressive Sagittarian won't praise a thing unless she is duly impressed. She will be quite observant and whether she is appreciative or critical of her host's efforts depends entirely on what has pleased or displeased her.

How does she handle difficult situations?

Quarrels or disagreements of any kind bring to fore the calculative thinking of an aggressive Sagittarian. She will patch up matters only if she is convinced of her mistake, thereafter she won't hesitate in apologising too. But what she wants or expects from the person she has quarreled with will determine her next move. But once she is calmer the aggressive Sagittarian will move forward quickly forgiving and forgetting with a swift change of thoughts.

Passive Sagittarian females will expect the other person to apologise. More often than not they are easy-going and submissive but in a quarrel-like situation they expect others to take on the onus of resolving matters. She is not likely to forget someone else's blunder for a long time, neither is she given to forgiving easily. This one will bear grudges till bones turn to dust!

What is her characteristic weakness?

Well, well, well! An aggressive Sagittarian woman and her acerbic tongue are seldom parted. And that my dear friends, is also her characteristic weakness. She just doesn't know where to pull the plug. Her sharp tongue comes with her innate talent of hitting where it hurts and creating unpleasant situations with family and friends. No wonder she is not so good at maintaining good relations. Apparently the lady hasn't heard about cracks and chinaware!

Now with the passive kind of Sagittarian it is her emotions that bring about her downfall. High strung and sensitive, she is an easy victim to emotional blackmailing, especially if it comes from someone she loves.

Is there more to her persona?

A Sagittarius woman loves to travel. She is an adventurer at heart and not averse to taking risks as well. You are likely to find her hooting for plans of treks and hikes. This spirit of adventure will be seen in other areas of life such as work. Coupled with ambition, her explorer attitude makes her take-up new ventures and set newer, more exciting goals.

But when it comes to money, this woman is not as big an adventurer as she seems. Here is one woman who is shrewd in every sense of the term and knows (both intuitively and with experience) which horse to bet on. She is an adventurer, yes, she likes to take risks, but note it! Her risks are calculated and her adventures are not life threatening.

This 'perpetual student' also possesses the ability to learn. With her never-ending quest of knowledge, the things she wants to know are boundless. She will have questions and queries about everything—from science to spiritualism and from practical life to philosophy—absorbing information like a sponge. Her out-of-the-box thinking often keeps her ahead of the rest of the pack.

With so much knowledge comes teaching. There is something of a teacher in her too as she likes to distribute the abundant knowledge she has gathered from places, people and events. She is also quite given to preaching without following.

A Sagittarian girl is equipped with lots of charming persona. She is feminine to a great extent (getting an eight on ten from me on that). With her knowledge and aptitude to talk, she is quite good at making conversation a skill that makes her a veritable candidate in the field of marketing. The only thing that mars her charisma is her need to opine about everything.

She is also clever enough to camouflage her bluntness with a good dose of tact and tongue-in-cheek humour. Very often her saucy remarks are filled with wit and one can't help but laugh at them. Her sense of humour comes laced with a heavy dose of sarcasm. Scoring a nine on ten for her ironic humour, a Sagittarian girl knows exactly how to slash with her blunt tongue.

She is also impulsive to some extent but many a time her guarded nature stops her from going off at a tangent. She is a rational thinker... an attribute that helps her to sort out things in a more practical manner. Rarely will you find her mixing emotions with the realistic stuff. Although sentimental (nine on ten) she knows the line where emotions should rest and pragmatism should take over.

One trait in her nature which she endorses rather vociferously is independence. Be it money, emotions or household chores, a Sagittarian woman seeks to be independent. Whether she succeeds in doing so and on all these fronts is a different story. But she tends to get into a controlling mode just to establish herself in her domain. Rarely will she bend her stance or give in to others...she would prefer (and make) that others dance to her tune. People who make adjustments to suit her needs easily find themselves in her good books.

How should one deal effectively with a Sagittarian woman?

Here is a one-word mantra to enthrall a Sagittarius woman—simplicity. This lady is a sucker for it. The assertive kind prefers a passive man whom she can dominate. If you look around you, within your family or set of friends, you are likely to find this to be true in eight out of ten cases. But in order to deal with her you need to have an authoritative voice and personality. In a difficult situation it would be advisable to give in just to make her feel victorious and then work things out later when she is calmer.

To deal with a Sagittarian female is to deal with her tongue, the infamous razor-like instrument that stops at nothing. And by nothing I mean decorum, respect and obedience. No amount of social rules will stop her from speaking her mind, and that too in the bluntest of terms. She is honest to the core and will keep throwing 'in your face' statements at you. But at the same time, she has an undeniable charm which flushes out any negative ideas you may conjure up about her. So to manage her it is necessary to tackle these diverse facets of her personality.

How does she handle money matters?

Money and how to manage it are the common factors binding the two types of Sagittarian women. Both are careful with their money and understand the value it holds. I am not implying here that a Sagittarian woman is stingy. She knows the advantages of saving for a rainy day, but is also prone to spending on little luxuries of life. Moreover, she is quite optimistic about her future and hence doesn't think too much before striking an expensive bargain. And this woman has self-respect not to ask for a free meal but she is shrewd enough to look for free deals and freebies.

How is she on the professional front?

At work you will find a Sagittarian woman self-motivated and quite resourceful. Although she can take and follow instructions to perfection, she prefers carving a niche for herself and devising her own way of working.

A Sagittarian woman is hard-working and extremely competent. She likes challenges and that coupled with her tendency to lose interest in things quickly (if she has something new to do every six to eight months) she will turn out to be the most productive employee in the company.

How is she in various relationship roles?

As daughters, the Sagittarian females I have met are surprisingly self-disciplined and obedient, yet independent from a young age. But when they step into their teens, they turn demanding and rebellious just like most of us. Some might harbour the idea of breaking away from home and getting out of the shell, but a majority of them find themselves emotionally dependent on their parents.

In a relationship, a Sagittarius woman can play multiple roles. She usually excels in her role as a girlfriend or wife as well as a homemaker. As a mother, a Sagittarian female is a combination of a disciplinarian and a friend, who lets her kids do whatever they want. A word of caution here about the aggressive Sagittarian—this lady can be quite a control freak especially with people who share an emotional relationship with her.

How is she when alone?

The passive Sagittarian will utilise her time well when alone. She is likely to take-up hobbies or passions—anything from art and cooking to dancing and yoga. The aggressive kind would be keen on getting out, making social plans or planning expeditions. This is a must for her otherwise her devilish mind will be up to all kinds of tricks...naughty enough to give an imp a run for his money!

How is she when in love?

One thing that is unique about fire sign women is their need to have love in their life and their hyper emotional state of being. Sagittarian women can appear to be over-friendly and casual but the truth is that's just a façade, the only thing that can move them to the core is love.

Although she may be deeply in love with you, yet she will shy away from commitments. This is because she values her freedom above everything else and naturally is doubtful of its continuance after a commitment. Secondly, she likes to be very sure of her feelings before she commits. She also needs to confirm that her boyfriend is as much in love with her as she is and that she can dominate him to some extent. Once she is satisfied on these fronts, she will go all out to prove her love.

If you are in love with a Sagittarian woman, make sure you give her ample space, space to be herself and to have a sphere to rule. With her around you will never be short of intelligent conversation or romance. She also loves to laugh and cherishes bringing a smile to her partner's face. Just make sure you know a trick or two on handling her sharp tongue and opinionated nature.

What does she look for in her partner?

The Sagittarius woman is very particular about choosing her partner. As I stated earlier, she isn't one to commit too easily. She will be on the lookout for a partner who satisfies all counts on her yardstick ranging across emotional, spiritual and physical compatibility.

Brimming with ideas yearning to be unleashed, this vivacious sun sign seeks a partner who reflects the same madness, the same thirst for knowledge, a penchant for indulging in the adventurous and a desire to explore the unknown. Nothing will delight a Sagittarian girlfriend more than having a boyfriend who makes travel plans with her.

Being an incurable optimist (a majority of them are), the Sagittarius woman knows how to stay sunny side up even under the most trying situations, finding a thing or two to laugh about and alleviate darkened moods. She would go for a man who has a funny bone and uses it in a witty display of humour rather than buffoonery.

I believe I've stressed enough on her fierce battle for freedom of space. She would thus want a mate who gives her unconditional love in the same passionate manner that she does, without cramping her space and style.

While dating her, you should...

...give her space. Try tying her down and she will scurry off like a scared deer. The Sagittarian is a free spirit. She needs physical space, emotional liberty and most importantly—freedom to do her will. This is one area where you will have to trust her. As she is prone to do whatever she pleases, it is always a good idea to have faith in her and believe that she won't do anything wrong.

Moreover, being emotionally stable herself, she dislikes hypersensitive, emotionally needy people. Since I have already mentioned her love for freedom, it would be redundant to say that she hates possessiveness too.

Dating a Sagittarian does not mean marrying her or even having an affair with her. That might take a long time to come. Dating is the first step either towards a love relationship or simple friendship. The Sagittarian will always regard you as her friend and from thereon will start the journey of your love life with her.

A Sagittarian woman looks for smartness in her date. You have to be as dashing with your conversation as you are with your appearance while dating her. If you are able to floor her with some stimulating conversation, intelligent repartee and good laughs...it's game, set and match for you!

From whacky to sophisticated she will accept all kinds of dating experiences, as long as they are fun, but you may have a hard time getting her to exit the friendship zone and enter the love arena, but believe me it's worth all the effort. She is sweet and passionate and will show the best of her feminine side once she is convinced of your love for her.

As I mentioned earlier, she has a tendency to get bored easily, so be as innovative and original as you can while dating her. A creative dating idea coupled with an extraordinary gift is enough to floor her.

Once your dating takes the right turn and your Sagittarian date is sure of your love, the next step will come like a lightening flash. The Sagittarian girl is passionate and physical intimacy is the obvious next step for her. She won't shy away from snuggling in your arms or giving you the coveted kiss as she is sure to enjoy it as much as you do. Having entered the comfort zone with you, she will become bold and dare to be open about her sexuality too. The passive kind may not necessarily be fit for the above trait.

You can trust a Sagittarian woman in matters of the heart. Her love is for keeps and once she has committed herself she is not a fool to waste a relationship for meaningless flings and one-night-stands. But her loyalty comes at a price…her want of freedom. If you are ready to keep her secure and happy in the knowledge of her freedom, she will be at your side in rain or shine…laughing at every weird idea and smiling at every adverse condition. This applies to both kinds of Sagittarius women.

Compatibility quotient:

Compatibility between two people depends on the seen as well as unseen aspects of their personality. While it is obvious that a Sagittarian girl is an adventure-seeking, pleasure-loving individual, it doesn't make her emotionally neutral. She has her own set of 'fairies to please and demons to fight'. To be compatible with her means much more than just sharing a good laugh. Let's find out more about the Sagittarian woman and her compatibility with men on the zodiac.

Sagittarian woman and…

Aries man: 7/10. The Arien has enough intelligence and passion to impress the Sagittarian. Moreover both share a common love for adventure and travel and have a good sense of humour too. Although their personality traits are attuned to each other, their blunt tongues might be a health hazard for their long-term relationship.

Taurus man: 5.5/10. These two may have a hard time adjusting with each other. The Sagittarian spirit will not accept the bossiness of the Taurean male unless he is the passive kind where she can boss him around. His possessiveness will also stop her from exercising free will. His stubborn and inflexible stand on most things can make her lose her patience and very likely her head too. If she meets the passive kind who lets her be for who she is, it might just work out well for both.

Gemini man: 8/10. Deference for each other can make a world of a difference to this relationship. Both are extroverts and social beings who love to party. While the Sagittarian also needs the security of a sound home, the Gemini needs the mature love of an understanding woman. If both are able to adjust with each other on these aspects, this relationship can go places.

Cancer man: 5/10. This relationship calls for a lot of compromises. The Sagittarian will be averse to the Cancerian hypersensitivity, while he will find her adventurous nature a bit too much to take. But if they are able to gauge each other's innate traits and make adjustments accordingly, a successful alliance can be formed.

Leo man: 7/10. Just like with the Arien, the Sagittarian shares a lot with the Leo man. But the bone of contention here would be the word 'attention'. While the Leo man wants absolute attention, the Sagittarian desires it in a covert way. If both are able to handle their love for attention, this relationship can work wonderfully.

Virgo man: 6/10. Although a love match between these two can work well, there are certain basic differences that might mar a long-term relationship. The conservative Virgo man would need to get used to the wild Sagittarian nature. And the outspoken Sagittarian girl would need to understand the Virgo's reserved personality.

Libra man: 8/10. He will love her spontaneity and outgoing nature. This relationship can be full of passion and romance. There is also likely to be great chemistry between these two. With a little bit of understanding they can iron out their differences and it would be smooth sailing for them thereon.

Scorpio man: 4/10. This match is too unstable to eke out in the long run. Her outgoing and free spirited nature is too much for the possessive Scorpio to handle. She in turn will find him too interfering and dominating.

Sagittarius man: 9/10. Both the archers have their arrows pointed in the right direction. The Sagittarian woman shares a lot in common with her male counterpart. Adventurous, fun-loving and optimistic, they'd get along like a house on fire. However, one of them must have his/her foot firmly grounded to avoid waywardness and frivolity.

Capricorn man: 4/10. It won't be easy once courtship is over. The Capricornian will be irked by the Sagittarian love for the outdoors and she will find his emotional needs difficult to fathom. For a successful relationship, both will need to accept the essential differences in their traits and learn to live with it.

Aquarius man: 9.5/10. This relationship rocks! Passion and romance it definitely has, but added to that is limited emotional dependence and possessiveness. Since each loves his/her own freedom, they would appreciate it in the other too.

Pisces man: 4/10. Again hypersensitivity can come in the way of their mutual understanding. The Piscean emotional needs will be thwarted by the Sagittarian and she will never understand his spiritual depth either. Over all...a difficult relationship!

Famous Sagittarius women personalities:

Britney Spears	Christina Aguilera
Diya Mirza	Monica Seles
Tina Turner	Tyra Banks